Policy and Politics in the
United States

Policy and Politics in Industrial States

A series edited by Douglas E. Ashford, Peter Katzenstein, and T. J. Pempel

E. W. Kelley

Policy and Politics in the
United States

The Limits of Localism

Temple University Press

Philadelphia

Temple University Press, Philadelphia 19122
Copyright © 1987 by Temple University. All rights reserved
Published 1987
Printed in the United States of America

Library of Congress Cataloging-in-Publication Data
Kelley, E. W.
    Policy and politics in the United States.

    (Policy and politics in industrial states)
    Bibliography: p. 307
    Includes index.
    1. United States—Politics and government—1945–
    2. United States—Economic policy.
    3. United States—Social policy.
    4. Policy sciences.
    I. Title. II. Series.
    JK271.K32   1987   320.973   87–5042
    ISBN 0-87722-267-3 (alk. paper)
    ISBN 0-87722-268-1 (pbk. : alk. paper)

The paper used in this publication meets the minimum
requirements of American National Standard for Information
Sciences—Permanence of Paper for Printed Library Materials,
ANSI Z39.48-1984.

To

Sherry

*without whose love and patience
this book could never have been
done*

Contents

Editors' Preface

All industrial states face a tension between bureaucracy and democracy. Modern governments have found it increasingly difficult to formulate policies adequate to the complex tasks they undertake. At the same time the growing specialization and widening scope of government have led many to question whether it can still be controlled democratically. Policy and Politics in Industrial States explores how some of the major democracies have dealt with this dilemma.

Policy is a pattern of purposive action by which political institutions shape society. It typically involves a wide variety of efforts to address certain societal problems. Politics is also a much broader concept, involving the conflict and choices linking individuals and social forces to the political institutions that make policy. Comparative analysis of the interaction between policy and politics is an essential beginning in understanding how and why industrial states differ or converge in their responses to common problems.

The fact that the advanced industrial states are pursuing many similar aims such as increasing social well-being, reducing social conflict, and achieving higher levels of employment and economic productivity means neither that they will all do so in the same way nor that the relevance of politics to such behavior will always be the same. In looking at an array of problems common to all industrial states, the books in this series argue that policies are shaped primarily by the manner in which power is organized within each country. Thus, Britain, Japan, the United States, West Germany, Sweden, and France set distinctive priorities and follow distinctive policies designed to achieve them. In this respect, the series dissents from the view that the nature of the problem faced is the most important feature in determining the politics surrounding efforts at its resolution. Taken to its logical extreme, this view supports the expectation that all states will pursue broadly similar goals in politically similar ways. Though this series will illustrate some important similarities among the policies of different countries, one of the key conclusions to which it points is the distinctive approach that each state takes in managing the problems it confronts.

A second important feature of the series is its sensitivity to the difficulties involved in evaluating policy success or failure. Goals are ambiguous and often contradictory from one area of policy to another; past precedents often shape present options. Conversely, adhering to choices made at an earlier time is often impossible or undesirable at a later period. Hence evaluation must transcend the application of simple economic or managerial criteria of rationality, efficiency, or effectiveness. What appears from such perspectives as irrational, inefficient, or ineffective is often, from a political standpoint, quite intelligible.

To facilitate comparison, the books in the series follow a common format. In each book, the first chapter introduces the reader to the country's political institutions and social forces, spells out how these are linked to form that country's distinctive configuration of power, and explores how that configuration can be expected to influence policy. A concluding chapter seeks to integrate the country argument developed in the first chapter with the subsequent policy analysis and provides more general observations about the ways in which the specific country findings fit into current debates about policy and politics.

The intervening six chapters provide policy cases designed to illustrate, extend, and refine the country argument. Each of the six policy analyses follows a common format. The first section analyzes the *context* of the policy problem: its historical roots, competing perceptions of the problem by major political and social groups, and its interdependence with other problems facing the country. The second section deals with the *agenda* set out for the problem: the pressures generating action and the explicit and implicit motives of important political actors, including the government's objectives. The third section deals with *process:* the formulation of the issue, its attempted resolution, and the instruments involved in policy implementation. The fourth and final section of analysis traces the *consequences* of policy for official objectives, for the power distribution in the issue area, for other policies, and for the country's capacity to make policy choices in the future. The element of arbitrariness such a schema introduces into the discussion of policy and politics is a price the series gladly pays in the interest of facilitating comparative analysis of policy and politics.

An important feature of these cases is the inclusion, for each policy problem, of selected readings drawn primarily from official policy documents, interpretations, or critiques of policy by different actors, and politically informed analysis. We have become persuaded that the actual language used in policy debates within each country provides an important clue to the relationship between that country's policy and its politics. Since appropriate readings are more widely available for Britain and the United States than for the non-English-speaking countries in the series, we have included somewhat more policy materials for these countries. In all instances, the readings are selected as illustration, rather than confirmation, of each book's argument.

Also distinctive of the series, and essential to its comparative approach, is the selection of common policy cases. Each volume analyzes at least one case involving intergovernmental problems: reform of the national bureaucracy or the interaction among national, regional, and local governments. Each also includes two cases dealing with economic problems: economic policy and labor-management relations. Lastly, each book includes at least two cases focusing on the relationship of individual citizens to the state, among them social welfare. Our choice is designed to provide a basis for cross-national and cross-issue comparison while being sufficiently flexible to make allowance for the idiosyncrasies of the countries (and the authors). By using such a framework, we hope that these books will convey the richness and diversity of each country's efforts to solve major problems, as well as the similarities of the interaction between policy and politics in industrial states.

D.E.A.

P.J.K.

T.J.P.

Preface

This book deals with public policy in the United States from the perspective of the national government. The perspective must be clear from the outset. In the United States, unlike some other advanced industrial democracies, policies that affect citizens are often determined, and almost always delivered, at the local level. Historically, policies in areas such as education, welfare, labor-management negotiations, workman's compensation, water management, and energy use and consumption have tended to be locally determined; that is, state governments or their delegated surrogates—city and county governments and school boards—tax and spend for services that are determined at that same level. By contrast, national policies are those that are decided upon and funded by the federal government. Of course, most federal services are also delivered by local providers in the public or private sector. Even federal interstate highways are built by contractors based near each particular area of construction.

Clearly, then, much of what would be called public policy in the United States must escape the attention of this book. Including it would require many volumes devoted to similarities and differences in state and local governments and state and local policy formation and funding. The task would not be simple. Not only do policies vary tremendously across the American states, but so do the ways in which policy is determined, even those areas in which the federal government is involved. Welfare payments in New York are almost three times as large as those in Mississippi. Even on a per capita basis, medicaid payments are much greater in New York and California than in Indiana. In the area of industrial relations, some states have "right to work" laws while others provide for a open union shop. States also have the power to tax businesses and other commercial activities, principally through the use of the property tax. States often vary property tax rates for businesses in order to attract new industry. A given company with factories or places of business around the country might face a different property tax rate in each state.

Our task in this book is to analyze the policies the national government has attempted to get a handle on or control over and the various methods by which that government creates and implements policy. This involves discussion of both the institutions of government and administration and the ways in which coordination and incentives have been and are used by the federal government. Finally, we will inquire as to the results: just what kind of control over public policy does the federal government have? Does this control vary by policy area?

Significant federal influence or control over many policies is a relatively recent phenomenon. The introduction of federal money results in cooperative coordination of policy across levels. By itself, this does not diminish the freedom of action of state governments, although federal programs involving matching funds may encourage modest redirections of state budgets. However, federal influence has not been exercised only through the traditional federal tools of fiscal incentives or coordination. It has in addition been achieved through threats that the federal government will cease to fund programs already in place. Through this kind of negative regulation, the federal government has recently been able to dramatically alter state and local policy and spending preferences.

Thus, state and local governments are responsive to the mandates of the federal government, even though in most cases the federal government has no direct power to compel acquiescence. While not always representing the major part of the funding for any social program or activity, federal funding represents a necessary part. Even the most conservative states find it hard to turn down or return federal monies, and the electorate in those states is as distressed as any when there is a threat that existing federal aid will be withdrawn. Homogenization of policy across states, then, is advanced at federal initiative through the threat of imposing federal sanctions. The use of this threat has evolved in all areas of public policy (Chapters 3–6).

Also consistent across areas of public policy are the efforts of interest groups to use the public sector to reduce their risks, displace their start-up costs, or prevent free-riding. These efforts follow a predictable sequence: Business and agricultural interests successfully displace costs and risks on the public sector first, followed by professional groups and labor, government employees (particularly professionals), and consumer groups and the poor.

The evolution of interest group penetration of government (historically one might say interest group creation of government) and the use of negative regulation (or threats) is shared by all advanced industrialized democracies. Yet the ways in which national policies are determined, and even the ways in which particular policies receive the detailed attention of national-level legislatures, vary considerably. These practices depend on the way a nation has historically organized its party and electoral system. The United States has a "weak party" system: party candidates are locally selected and to be and remain successful must reflect strictly local interests in a national body. As a consequence, the evolution of policies, the role of national-level regulation, and the monitoring role of the legislature are distinctly different in the United States from that of Britain, Sweden, and a number of the other democracies.

A number of people have provided assistance during the preparation of this book. The series editors and, especially, an anonymous reviewer selected by Temple University Press all gave thorough and constructive comments on earlier drafts of these chapters. Various research, typing and editing tasks were shared by Angela Antonelli, Nancy Dickson, Daryl Stevens, and Chris Weeks. The office and staff of the Government Department at Cornell University has generously assisted in the preparation and typing of this manuscript. Mike Ames has shown patience and persistence in urging this book to completion. Jane Barry did an unbelievably good job of editing the final manuscript. Any awkwardness remaining in the text is mine as are any errors of fact or interpretation.

Policy and Politics in the
United States

1 Political Institutions and Policymaking: The Evolving National Focus

For almost two hundred years, the United States has been called a nation of states, or, better, a nation of states and localities. Both Madison and Calhoun saw authority over most activities that affect the lives of individuals as properly belonging to individuals themselves or to states; the national government, in contrast, had restricted and well-defined duties. Tyranny, it was believed, usually emanated from the government rather than private groups. Even into the 1950s and 1960s, it was possible to maintain that for purposes of policy analysis, the United States is a collection of states (Elazar, 1964). Most activities that affect the day-to-day lives of citizens, whether they involve education, social services, welfare, labor relations, or transportation, were thought to be within the purview of state and local governments. This approach to politics and policy formation in the United States has an impressive lineage. After all, it was the states that had to ratify the original Constitution and must still ratify constitutional amendments.

Yet coexistent with the tradition of state and local policy determination is the undeniable increase in the scope and activities of the federal government. Until the early part of the twentieth century, American national policy was principally concerned with two constitutionally mandated areas: interstate commerce and war and peace. The role of the federal government in the national economy has increased with every war and depression. As wars have become more encompassing, the need to involve more of the American economy in the war effort has vastly extended the episodic domain of federal planning and resource allocation. Reactions to various depressions—and, in particular, the Great Depression of the late 1920s and 1930s—have similarly extended the scope of federal activity in the social security and welfare areas.

Wars and depressions prompted the reorientation of the electorate (Burnham 1970), as well as an increase in amount and type of federal-level involvement in the economy and in the lives of citizens. This expansion is not to be viewed as occurring at the expense of state and local public-sector activities. In fact, public-sector activities at all levels show a secular increase over the past one hundred years. Increases in state and local activity, as represented by budgetary increases, paralleled or outstripped federal increases at least until the late 1970s (ACIR, 1978). Nor does this increasing activity in the public sector imply a reduction in the domain of individual action. Rather, both public- and private-sector activities present an increasing number of choices to citizens in the modern world. Clearly, all elements of life in the modern state have become more complex. The role of national government has been to organize this complexity.

Legacy of Localism

State legislatures were well in place before the adoption of the American Constitution. In fact, some parts of the Constitution represent a reaction by commercial interests to excesses of state legislative activity, such as tariffs. Besides asserting federal control over interstate commerce, the Constitution limits the power of state governments and state banks to create coinage, in part to remove their capacity to print money, for state-madated inflationary efforts. The Virginia legislature had, for example, lowered the value of outstanding loans in this way (Beard and Beard, 1930). Bankruptcy was made a matter of federal jurisdiction to prevent repeated declarations that would have had the effect of nullifying debts.

A useful rule of thumb for the historical development of American public policy is that policy is in the hands of the states until such time as the federal government makes explicit fiscal or regulatory provision for it. Until the early part of the twentieth century, only business interests had expanded beyond state boundaries. National government in the early United States, then, reflected mercantile interests, while other interests were left in the hands of states and localities.

Federal involvement in business activities took many forms. Just before and after the Civil War, it provided large grants of land and, on occasion, loan guarantees to companies building transcontinental and other railroads. Although many business-labor clashes were handled by state militias, on several occasions, notably the Pullman strike in 1894, the army was called into service in a manner almost totally beneficial to business interests. This is not to suggest that states are not and have not been active in the commercial arena. The regulation of pensions, insurance companies, and state banks is a state responsibility. States certify professional groups, such as doctors and lawyers. In fact, the entry of professional groups onto the national policy scene is a relatively recent event. As we will see, doctors and lawyers concentrated their political activities on influencing state-level legislation until the 1960s (see Chapter 5). Federal entry into welfare policy and workman's compensation has been gradual and recent in the United States, as in other industrial countries. In all, the organization of trade groups, such as carpenters and silversmiths, occurred on a city-by-city basis: as McConnell (1966) points out, trade unions in the United States, unlike those in Europe, viewed government as a potential source of tyranny and hence attempted to invoke its powers to a lesser extent than their European counterparts. Also education and welfare were localized. As recently as the early 1950s, welfare programs in the United States often took the form of a transfer program like those found in French villages, maintained, in part, through historically high agricultural tariffs. Similarly, education in Britain was essentially locally supported and controlled until World War II.

A principal difference between the United States and other economically developed democracies is that in the former the powers of state-level government extend to all domains except those explicitly forbidden. Except for the federal government's exclusive powers over diplomacy and interstate commerce, powers are either concurrent or reserved for states and citizens. Local governments in many other countries lack this extensive constitutional base. In England local governments exist at the pleasure of Parliament. In France, local governments have had independent taxing powers for over a century; administratively, however, they are much more closely linked to the national government than are local governments in the United States (see Ashford, 1981). In Japan local elections for mayors and heads of prefectures are a post-World War II phenomenon (see Muramatsu, 1982; Pempel, 1982). Hence, although a certain degree of local autonomy exists in principle in France and Japan, it is not nearly as extensive as that which has historically and constitutionally existed in the United States. This situation, of course, must color and constrain the way in which the U.S. national government pursues policy objectives.

The Evolution of Policy Areas

In the United States, as in other economically developed democracies, the entry of organized groups into the policy arena has followed a regular and consistent sequence. Business, commercial, and large agricultural interests entered the policy arena first, at both national and state levels, and professional groups and unions second. Because groups did not usually look to national government as a source of authority or legitimacy, professional groups, organizing first at the state and local levels were often allowed to determine both policy itself and the mechanisms by which it would be implemented. This power occasioned considerable struggles in many states—for example, between doctors and osteopaths in the latter part of the nineteenth century, and between state legislators and lawyers in the early part of the twentieth, particularly in the West. A third phase, the extensive entry of public-sector administrators and professionals as service providers, has occurred only in the last fifty years. Although such groups organized as early as the 1930s in Britain and some other European countries, they had little impact before the late 1950s and 1960s in the United States. Dedicated to the promotion of more public-sector programs at all levels of government, these groups have been instrumental in organizing the most recent entrants onto the policy stage: recipient groups (i.e., those receiving public welfare benefits) and consumers.

These new policy demands have been added to those of the older groups, making the coordination of federal, state, and local policy activities much more difficult. Old groups and old demands do not go away; they are augmented by the demands of increasingly large numbers of people organized into increasingly large numbers of groups. The organization of national government reflects the tremendous variety of sectoral interests and geographically based policy demands while it preserves the critical centralizing, coordinating function that has allowed for the growth of federal policy initiatives.

Types of Federal Activity

Interest groups, as noted above, usually seek benefits at the state level first, and many use both state and federal levels of government. Therefore, increased federal activity does not necessarily erode state benefits to groups and citizens or state powers. Much federal activity in fact enhances the states' ability to provide benefits to their citizens. A clear example is the Elementary and Secondary Education Act (ESEA), Title I, which augmented with massive amounts of funding many similar state programs already in place.

In responding to imperatives from local governments and private groups, the national government has sometimes developed entitlement programs that establish a fiscal or service relationship between itself and the citizen: Social Security is an example. More typically however, such programs involve the private sector or local government in service delivery. The role of the federal government is principally fiscal and coordinating; whatever the intervening vehicle, national government has very little direct, positive authority over the policy. For example, the federal government cannot force states, localities, or the private sector to provide mental health care in communities. All it can do is provide monies for such community-based activities, which, it is hoped, might possibly effect the redirection of state monies to that area. The federal government likewise cannot monitor or direct the way states spend money on education. It can, however, monitor and regulate the way its money is spent by local school districts and in that way become involved in the issue of whether equitable education is being provided. States do not have to have unemployment insurance; yet to take advantage of federal matching monies and coordinating activities, they must develop their own programs in this area.

A principal activity of the federal government is the coordination of state and local government activities. The development of the interstate highway system is an example. The system is jointly planned but locally built. Yet 90 percent of the monies spent on the system are federally collected. Another instance of federal coordination, but one with a less direct fiscal incentive, is the development of common weights and standards for use in commercial activity. This federal responsibility had been recognized since the inception of American national government. Federal aid to higher education can be considered an attempt to coordinate scientific training in the post-Sputnik era. In this case, as in that of the highway system, grants of money are associated with coordinating activities.

The intermediary role of local governments, including local boards of education, in the policy implementation process is evident; the equally central intermediary role of the private sector is best illustrated by the National Recovery Act (NRA) of 1933. The national government attempted to respond to the Great Depression by coordinating commercial activity across all the states in a manner that would leave existing corporate and productive organizations intact. In other words, at a time when there was a deflationary spiral in the economy, the national government was used as a vehicle by organized business interests to reduce their long-term dependence on marketplace forces. Associated with this objective was another principle of national-level policy activity that the United States shares with a number of other developed countries: the delegation of authority over policy implementation. This delegation also occurs in less precipitous times, as McConnell (1966) demonstrates in the case of the farm bureau and government agricultural policy.

Under NRA the federal government coordinated entrepreneurial activities across interstate boundaries, using an administrative apparatus principally made up of the business and trade associations that were to be regulated. In almost every case it was these groups that developed and supervised production and pricing codes. We will encounter other instances of the delegation of policy implementation to private groups.

The United States remains, like other industrial democracies, in the historical stage at which groups may organize and use government for their private benefits. Yet the institutions in which U.S. national policies are formulated are quite different from those of other industrial democracies. In particular, the division of powers among institutions at the federal level and the very localized bases for elections to Congress lead to a process of policy formation very different from that which occurs in other industrialized democracies.

National Institutions of Policy Formation and Implementation

The powers of the federal government originate in the legislative powers of Congress. They are enumerated in Article I, Sections 7 and 8, of the U.S. Constitution. The power of Congress to legislate is restricted to those areas which the Constitution specifies. The President is to administer the laws of Congress and, in addition, is given emergency and war powers. The federal courts' very limited areas of original jurisdiction are stated in Article 3. Hence, federal initiative in policy areas had to take rather subtle forms. The federal government can promote equality of educational opportunity or the teaching of science, for example, only if it can get states and localities to accept federal monies with such strings attached.

These tools of fiscal incentives and cross-jurisdictional planning and coordination have gradually increased its involvement in public policies that directly affect groups and individuals.

The federal government and the national party system remain the normal focus for studies of policy formulation and execution at the national level in the United States. Directly or indirectly, almost all public policies that emanate from the federal level have their origin in some legislative act. Congress has the power to tax and the power to spend and does both for a variety of collective motives. Many expenditures, and many provisions of the tax code, benefit only particular groups, economic sections, or geographic areas. Much direct legislation, then, can be considered, in Lowi's (1969) term, distributive. Congress also delegates much legislation in at least two senses. In setting up the statutory regulatory agencies, it delegated to them the task of regulating certain scarce goods (e.g., airwaves for television stations) and externalities of economic activity (e.g., water pollution) in a manner consistent with the public interest. The "public interest" is not specified. Other legislation delegates to line administrative agencies such as the Department of Education or the Department of Health and Human Services (HHS) the task of detailing what a law means, as when the Department of Education must specify the requirements of federal education grants. In the case of Chapter 1 of the Consolidated Education Improvement Act, for example, Congress has merely provided general guidelines declaring that funds are principally intended for districts with certain economic characteristics and for students who are low achievers. The formula used to provide funds to the states is determined by the department.

Congress cannot specify in a vacuum what it means by the "public interest," "equal opportunity," and other terms as they would apply to many applications of a law in different parts of the country. Ideally application is both rule-governed and sensitive to variations in local need. If Congress, on the whole, does not know in detail what equal access to medical care means or what the interstate highway system should look like, it is unclear why they should legislate beyond their own capacities in terms of both time and expertise. As Congress devotes more time to oversight, it has less time to deal with technical or judgmental issues. Nor do members of Congress want to spend more time than necessary on issues that do not affect constituents. It is far more efficient for individual members and Congress as a whole to ask others to come up with particular rules and to provide for themselves an arena with the oversight committee hearings, to fine-tune the effects of these rules. Additionally, the use of such terms and the delegation of the task of determining their meaning often masks general legislative agreement that some law is necessarily accompanied by disagreement over the particular policies to be embodied there. As we will see, this is true of civil rights legislation as it affects education and mental health.

Criticisms of administrative rule-making are no more or less valid in the United States than in other industrial democracies. In all, administrators have proven to be remarkably homogeneous in their practical interpretation of ambiguous terms. Most of the time legislatures would assume that administrators would know what these words mean. Getting rid of inequality of health care, for example, means producing rules, regulations, funding, and access to care that make it possible for the child of a very poor parent to get an appendectomy when he or she needs one. The meaning of these terms is determined in most bureaucracies, by accumulated instances of application as reviewed by courts and through legislative oversight. In this sense, administrative decisions over a sequence of cases create the law or at least flesh out its applications.

The executive branch encompasses a number of distinct elements. Members of the independent statutory agencies are appointed by the President, are approved by the Senate, and serve a fixed term. These agencies are presumed to be somewhat free of presidential influence on policymaking. Certainly they are believed to be freer than the various departments in the federal bureaucracy. The heads of these departments, sometimes cabinet members, serve at the Presidents' pleasure, although they too must be initially approved by the Senate. Finally, there is the Office of the President and its environs. It is this last element of the federal bureaucracy that is most imprinted with the President's views concerning policy formation and execution.

Among leaders of industrial democracies, few have less formal power over policy formation and execution than the President of the United States. He can neither raise money nor implement a policy, except under conditions of national emergency, without the consent of Congress. Moreover, there is no way that one person or a few people can successfully oversee and control the implementation of tens of thousands of policies by the extensive federal bureaucracy. Yet the power of the President should not be underestimated. The President's powers, particularly the veto, allow him to bargain very effectively with congressional leaders for some of his own policies. The fact that Congress externalizes the considerable cost of budget preparation onto the executive branch forces Congress now to rely upon the expertise of that branch. Budgetary elements that a particular President regards as important are brought into the Office of the President or a near neighbor, such as the Office of Management and Budget (OMB), so that they can be closely overseen. The same is true of the regulatory review process. In addition, any domestic legislation that might bear upon foreign policy or the conduct of the military is considered to be in the domain of appropriate presidential influence, since the President is charged to conduct foreign affairs and is commander-in-chief of the armed forces.

Thus, the Social Security Administration operates without presidential interference. On the other hand, the attempts of the Justice Department to prosecute antitrust cases, the Office of Civil Rights to force greater spending on bilingual education, or the Department of Transportation to force the inclusion of passive restraints in automobiles pass through both the Office of Management and Budget (OMB) and the Office of the President. This is a matter not of law, but of presidential directive and is quite legal given the President's nominal authority over the implementation of all legislation in the federal bureaucracies. He cannot change the locus of policy implementation, but he can declare its terms and often delay or modify it. When this occurs, there is often conflict between branches of government; such conflict usually winds up in the federal courts if a negotiated settlement cannot be reached.

OMB is the focal point of another kind of federal policy control. Once money is authorized and appropriated for a program, it is not automatically delivered to citizens. Checks must be written at specified times, and cash flow at the federal level must be monitored. These and similar tasks are carried out by OMB. Sometimes the rate at which the money is disbursed is written into legislation; often it is not. It is particularly in the latter case that decisions made by OMB, usually with the approval of the President, determine whether policies are implemented rapidly or barely implemented at all. This function of OMB—the management of money and cash flow—is right at the juncture between public-sector management and politics.

The independent statutory agencies are creatures more of Congress than of the President. Agencies such as the Federal Communication Commission (FCC) and the Interstate Commerce Commission (ICC) are

usually formed in response to pressures on Congress from well-organized groups. Congress's response is not to legislate in detail, but to
provide what might be called bargaining arenas in which organized and
somewhat adversarial economic groups can bargain over markets and
prices, or the allocation of scarce goods like airwave frequencies for
radio stations. The tools needed for successful bargaining vary by agency. It should be noted, however, that the general standard of "the public
good" that is attached to the mission of all such statutory agencies is
never well defined in legislation or subsequent court decisions. What
Congress does, in effect, is legislate an area of concern, but avoid the
effects on incumbency that particular decisions would incur.

The third branch of the federal government is the federal judiciary.
Like the other branches, the judiciary has functions that overlap elements of state and local government. It is involved in policymaking in
three distinct ways. First, it interprets the Constitution and the intent of
Congress when challenges to administrative application and policy interpretation are brought to the courts. In such cases it is "presumed" to
hold executive administration or local-level implementation against
congressional intent. Given the extent to which the details of legislation
are delegated, this is a very delicate task—a matter of judgment at best,
of rulemaking at worst.

Second, the judiciary is directly involved in the redistribution of
rights, opportunities, and goods and services through judgments and
decisions involving equal access to education, wiretapping, gerryman-
dering, rights of patients, and other issues. The processes of the judicial
system are sufficiently intricate and costly that its use may slow down
redistribution. For example, complaints about unequal access to jobs or
unequal pay may go first to state-level equal employment commissions,
then to the federal-level Equal Employment Opportunity Commission,
and finally to the federal courts. A complaint may be in federal court for
several years, particularly if the federal appellate process is involved.
Often by the end of the process jobs have become available through
attrition.

Finally, the judiciary has a role in the federal coordination of the
delivery of social services and other goods and particularly in the application of sanctions. These, as we will see, are the most effective
federal-level tool for influencing the policy choices of states and
localities.

Policy Coordination and Implementation at the Local Level

With a few exceptions (e.g., social security), domestic policies funded at the federal level are implemented at the local level, often by school districts, states, local governments, private community mental health centers, or even profit-making companies. Federal bureaucrats do not educate a child, build a new highway, or improve mental health. In areas involving capital construction, the private sector is centrally involved in implementing policy; usually businesses as well as consumers or the poor benefit from the use of federal money to build or subsidize housing or sewage plants. Congress also attempts to provide help to state and local governments, in part because the federal government is the most efficient collector of taxes, but also because state and local governments fund and design the programs that actually deliver services to citizens. Hence, from a federal perspective intergovernmental relations involve not only coordinating activities through legislation, but also coordinating and supporting the activities of other governments.

The tenth amendment to the Constitution reserves for the states and the people those powers not explicitly delegated to the federal government. The Constitution also guarantees to the citizens of every state a state government that is democratic in form. State governments themselves reflect the federal division of powers, each having a judiciary, an executive, and a legislature. All the legislatures except one (that of Nebraska) have two bodies equivalent to the U.S. Senate and the House of Representatives. Beyond this, however, no necessary commonality exists in the way the states organize themselves to tax and spend in the public interest. No two states are organized in precisely the same way in terms of subunits of administration. This complicates the federal role in coordinating activities with the various states. It is almost impossible for a federal bureaucracy to use legislation passed by a locally elected Congress to force homogeneity or uniformity on state administrative units, even using the promise of money for programs as bait.

On the other hand, it would be prohibitively expensive for the federal government to organize itself in a manner that reflects the differences in state administration in order to achieve perfect federal-state coordination. Actual practices fall somewhere in between. For example, to receive Title I and federal education funds, every state must have a person in its state education authority (SEA) responsible for Title I programs, enforcement of equal protection under Title VI, and so on. However, the location of this person within the SEA may vary from state to state—he or she may report directly to the head of the SEA or be a minor functionary with little impact on policy. Either way, this individual's position within the state education bureaucracy will clearly have some effect on the monitoring of Title I or Title VI activities (Hill, 1981).

Over and above the confusion caused by different types of state organization, states divide themselves into subunits in a number of different ways. Every state is divided into counties, but then the variation begins. Geographically, the next unit down is a township, although not all states have townships. States give to cities a number of independent responsibilities, some of which are also given to towns (not to be confused with townships) and villages. In addition, every state has school districts, which may be coterminous with counties, townships, cities, and so on. For particular purposes, which again vary across states, the state legislature may give each of these entities power to tax and spend. In fact, that is what is meant by a subunit of government: a group of individuals elected directly or indirectly by registered voters.

Sometimes special districts carry out only a single function, and in these districts the principle of "fiscal equivalence" obtains. "Fiscal equivalence" means that for a particular function—for example, sewage—those people receiving the service are exactly those who pay for it. There is no subsidy; further, if the user does not pay, the service is withdrawn. Special districts often may not have elected rule-makers; rather, those individuals who set rates and level of service will be appointed by members of a more generally elected authority, such as a state legislature or a city council. Other special authorities cross city and/or state lines and, again, often do not have elected leaders. Such authorities handle activities that are often more efficiently planned or more economically performed without regard to already existing political subunits within or across states. An example is the New York Port Authority, which manages commerce and transportation in and around a port surrounded by three states: New York, Connecticut, and New Jersey.

Even individual subunits within one state are not organized internally in the same manner. Some cities have an elected mayor and city council; others an elected council and an appointed city manager. In New York State at least two types of township government and two types of county government exist. These differences in organization may affect access to policymaking in particular areas. The situation is simpler in Britain, where the principal variation is that some services (e.g., social services) provided by rural county authorities are provided in urban areas by the geographically smaller metropolitan districts.

The location of effective decision-makers and formulators of public policies varies considerably across states. To some degree effective decisionmaking follows financial responsibility. However, this is not always true. New York State, for example, provides only 43.7 percent of the combined state and local funding for education. Yet it has a highly professionalized bureaucracy and a board of regents that is continually increasing high school graduation requirements through a progressively more difficult minimum competency test. In California, on the other hand, 90.6 percent of combined state and local funding comes from the state. In this case, however, as in the case of the mental health money that goes to the counties, the state is merely a dollar-collector and fiscal pass-through agent. The state bureaucracy is considerably weaker in both areas than that of New York. Although California has minimum competency tests, the consequences of failing them varies by district, and local school districts can even have their own test forms. Services in California, then, are centrally funded but locally controlled, whereas in New York they are centrally controlled but locally funded.

New York is actually an intermediate state with respect to centralization and control. In Massachusetts education and mental health services are subject to even more centralized program control. Yet Massachusetts provides only 41.4 percent of the state and local total for education, although the state's share will increase because of recent constitutional limitations on local property-taxing authority. Arizona and Indiana have a very decentralized ideology across all policy areas. State-level education officials in Indiana almost invariably claim that education is a local responsibility, yet the state provides 62.6 percent of the combined state and local funding for education, a figure above the national average. Arizona provides state dollars for education and other services at about the national average, but it's statutes resist both federal and state influence over policy areas. Whenever federal program money is brought into Arizona, program funding requirements from other sources, including the state, must be listed for a ten-year period; otherwise the state legislature will refuse to appropriate funds for the same program then or later. Thus, the legislature, cannot be trapped by declining federal grants or other federal activities aimed at redirecting the package of state expenditures.

Arizona also has no Medicaid program, although a scaled-down state version of that program was certified in 1984 for matching federal funding. States are not obliged to accept Medicaid, a "carrot" offered by the federal government to which states must contribute half or more of the funds. The only way the federal government can mandate a program is to by-pass states entirely and establish the program under a contract between the federal government and individual citizens, as is the case with social security. The fact that monies for ESEA Title I and Aid to Families with Dependent Children (AFDC), go through the states reflects the varied character of even nationally based legislation.

The example of federal-state cooperation in highway funding provides evidence that policy variation exists not just across states, but also across policy areas. Because so many highways are funded primarily by the federal and state governments, almost all states view highway construction as a state, rather than an local, activity. In the area of education, as we have seen, there is much greater emphasis on localism in the determination of policy in Arizona than in New York. The difference is much less striking in highway construction. Indeed, Arizona contributes a much higher percentage of total state and local highway monies than New York.

States also vary greatly in the degree to which policies of universal application (such as education) are equally funded for all citizens of a state. The federal Constitution does not require equal funding for all students in an educational system. In Texas, equal educational funding on a per pupil basis is not mandated by the state constitution either. California, however, has moved toward equalization since a state court ruled that the state constitution guaranteed both equal protection under the law and education as a right of all citizens.

Many states place funding limits on local authorities. California and Massachusetts capped property taxes in the late 1970s. In New York State the largest cities (those of class 1) can only tax 2.5 percent of real property values to support all functions funded by the state government. This means that different local authorities—in particular city governments and school districts—must negotiate the relative levels of service (fire protection, education, etc.) to be provided. In other states educational funding at every level of government is strictly separated from funding for other programs.

The Policy Consequences of Elections

The fact that the United States has competitive elections for its national legislature has consequences for federal policies. In other industrialized democracies, party organization and candidate selection occur on a more national level. As a consequence, policymaking takes place within political parties or institutions; parties dominate rather than legislative committees, as in the United States. In Britain, for example, where public policies are established in the cabinet by the party in power, parliamentary ratification is often such a formality that laws are enforced before being formally passed.

In all these countries, however, similarities of policy evolution may be traced to the existence of competitive elections. Interest groups penetrate the policymaking process in the sequence described earlier. Moreover, there has been a consistent redistribution of income (not capital) into the middle and lower classes over the last 150 years. Occurring in different countries at different times, this process reflects the gradual enfranchisement of the population. In every Western system, there have been many more voters below the mean income than above it. Hence, successful candidates—or parties in strong party systems such as Britain's—must at times advocate programs that redistribute income to those below the mean. Disputes over income are relatively mild in the United States. Policy tends not to be defined in terms of its effect on income flows, in part because no labor or socialist party ever developed here. There are two critical reasons for this. The first is that the effective enfranchisement of non-property-holders in most states occurred before the Industrial Revolution reached that particular state. There was no need for workers to organize to secure political rights in addition to economic ones. The second reason concerns the effect of the expanding frontier on individual mobility (Hartz, 1955), the American view that government was the principal source of tyranny over the individual or the group, and the huge space that had to be conquered before unions or other nonbusiness interests could begin to organize in the early and middle parts of the nineteenth century.

Central to the representation of local and sectoral interests at the national level is the manner in which national-level representatives are selected in the United States. The United States has what is commonly termed a "weak" party system. Parties are organized nationally, principally to contest presidential elections. State parties vary from collections of local interests to hierarchically organized sets of professional politicians. For our purposes, the most important feature of this de-centralized party system is that candidates are selected from within states and congressional districts. Party officials and members outside a particular electoral district have very little impact on the selection of candidates. If candidates and eventual winners of elections to the House and Senate owe their selection and election to local officials and voters, one would expect congresspeople to be more responsive to these voters than to any other group of individuals. This is in fact the case. When congressional action bears upon some organized interest in a constituency, that constituency will usually determine a congressperson's vote. The notion that many congressional votes are bought through campaign contributions from outside the district may or may not be true. However, we do know that outside money almost never buys a vote against the interests of a well-organized group within the member's constituency (Green, 1983).

The responsiveness of individual congresspeople to the preferences of their constituencies has been subject to a variety of confused analyses. The confusion is almost inevitable, since it is extremely difficult to untangle the influence of the constituency's attitude on the congressperson's behavior and the influence of the congressperson's behavior (including the creation of salient issues) on the opinion of the constituency. We find, however. that congresspeople respond to changing constituent interests, or they do not stay in office very long. This maxim was illustrated in the aftermath of the Voter Rights Act of 1965 in a number of southern congressional districts. The new voters had distinctly different and definable interests. These interests were reflected in the voting patterns, committee assignments, and bill proposals of already sitting congresspeople, or, in most cases, they were soon defeated (Sanders, 1978). This result suggests that there are limits to representatives' ability to tell constituents what their interests are, and a definite limit to the electoral advantages of incumbency. Incumbency is valuable, but not as valuable as a pattern of representative behavior that is consistent with the expressed interests of constituents.

The Organizational Consequences of a Weak Party System

Like all legislatures, Congress is organized to deal efficiently with the needs of its members, central among which is the need to be reelected. Congress must therefore expeditiously pass legislation benefiting organized interests and deal with this legislation in such a way that is consistent with the electoral (incumbency) needs of each of its members. This concern cuts across party lines, since a member from one district does not compete electorally against other members.

Because the House of Representatives is larger than the Senate, effective organization is more difficult there. However, both bodies employ similar organizational strategies. The House is organized into a committee system. Membership on the many "subject matter" committees is voluntary. With political party and seniority as organizing principles, individuals are placed on committees that authorize programs or policies that affect organized constituents in their districts. In many cases this principle extends to subcommittee assignments. Members are few, and bargaining over policy and funding is possible (Bensel, 1979). When legislation comes out of a committee or subcommittee with unanimous or almost unanimous approval, approval by the larger body is assured. In fact, one hears congresspeople ask, as they walk toward the floor of the House, what the committee vote on a piece of legislation was. This principle of voting automatically for bills that are overwhelmingly approved in committees—"floor reciprocity"—is a low-cost method of ensuring that the business of Congress is completed efficiently while allowing each member to retain some control over legislation that affects his or her district.

Coordination between committees and interaction with the executive branch must occur to ensure consistency between the total amounts of money spent and total taxes collected. Two committees that perform this task are the Senate Economic Committee and the House Committee on Ways and Means. These committees, unlike the subject-matter committees, are representative of the many diverse interests in the various congressional districts and states. Through them Congress coordinates the distribution of particularized benefits to many congressional districts.

The entire process is somewhat divorced from the taxing process. Taxing and spending bills are passed in distinctly different ways and have distinct forms. Tax legislation is rule-governed. Just as a person is entitled to a certain amount of social security at a given age after so many years of work, people who make a certain amount of money and pay a certain amount of interest owe a certain tax. This is quite different from agricultural or highway bills, which send money and programs to particular areas and people.

This gap between the legislative mechanisms of taxing and spending, and the difference between the area over which taxes are collected (all people) and the areas to which benefits are targeted (small groups of people or interests), generates a large fiscal inequivalence. In all economically advanced democracies, when fiscal inequivalence increases in extent or involves more people, public-sector spending will typically increase more than it would have otherwise. This is what has happened in the United States. Undoubtedly, welfare benefits, highways spending, and even some educational expenditures are greater because money is collected nationally through rule-governed assessments and distributed to localities through committee-generated appropriations. Were the states to attempt the same distributions, we would expect a lower level of public-sector spending relative to the tax base. This actually occurs in almost all states that have programs comparable to federal programs in education, welfare, highways, and so on. Any large state-level spending in some of these areas—for example, education—is primarily due to the states' longer history of fiscal responsibility in those areas.

Many federal bureaucracies and agencies that are closely associated with congressional committees and subcommittees are also organized on a decentralized basis. In the Department of Agriculture, for example, policy initiatives often come from the local and state levels. These are amalgamated at the national level and included in the President's budget. When this legislation is sent to Congress, it already reflects the diverse interests of organized agriculture in different parts of the country. The legislation is fine-tuned in committee and subcommittee by those members who are most affected by the passage of such legislation. Notice that all participants in the process are beneficiaries. The bureaucracy—in this case the Department of Agriculture—avoids the risk of job terminations and program cutbacks by advancing programs that are of interest to locally organized groups. It is in the interest of congresspeople from agricultural areas to pass legislation that confers particular benefits on organized groups in their districts, which, of course, themselves benefit from this approach. In this instance and others, the cost of bureaucratic or legislative amalgamation—that is, the burden of putting the diverse benefits together into legislation or administrative rules—is often borne by the general taxpayer, since it is the bureaucracy, supported by general tax revenues, that actually coordinates and writes the legislation.

National Institutions and Policy Centralization

Tendencies toward policy decentralization are countered in at least two ways through presidential selection and leadership. First, the election of the President by an electoral college forces candidates to concentrate on states in which Democrats and Republicans are electorally competitive and which have a large number of electoral votes. In a presidential election, the winner of the state's popular vote usually obtains all its electoral votes. Since people are concentrated in cities, this system emphasizes the importance of states with large urban populations. In appealing to urban voters, presidential candidates sometimes define issues and policies that transcend those that have historically influenced reciprocity in Congress. Second, the executive can encourage the organization of recipient groups for electoral gain. Examples of such legislation are Title I of ESEA as amended (particularly the regulation requiring parent advisory councils) and the participation requirements of the Model Cities legislation of 1966. In both cases Democratic presidential incumbents made the organization of local beneficiaries a condition for receiving benefits. However, such groups may make policy demands that are not welcomed by the politicians who encouraged their organization.

The Congress and President taken together are well equipped to receive policy demands from diverse and geographically localized interests and constituencies and coordinate them into some kind of national policy. A stream of policies provide particularized benefits, and individual legislators have access to and some control over the policies that affect significant groups in their districts. Such programs as the Community Mental Health Centers Act, Medicaid, Social Security, and highways construction, though not exactly the outcome of national planning, are at least national in scope and operate everywhere under one set of rules.

Once programs are developed, program administrators become principal lobbyists for the continuation and expansion of benefits. In most Western countries this is a twentieth-century phenomenon. It represents the same sort of risk aversion and job protection that occurs when a businessman tries to get a loan guarantee or use government to soften the blows of competition in the marketplace. One way to keep a public-sector job and a predictable career pattern is to ensure that the scope and mission of the agency persist and expand. Governmental bureaucracies and politicians may also organize beneficiary groups to help in future legislative contests.

The federal budget cycle is a centralizing force in the development and implementation of public policies. The various federal agencies are all on the same budget cycle. The federal monies that go to states or local governments as well as to federal agencies and private-sector service providers are released and monitored on both a monthly and a quarterly basis by OMB. The legislative timetable for all appropriations is about the same. The appearance of all programs in one federal budget permits a comparison between taxing and spending and especially among spending items, by both OMB and, increasingly, the Joint Economic Committee of Congress. The monthly and quarterly cash-flow controls exercised by OMB are very similar for all federal programs. In addition, most federal programs, even when they are targeted to particular congressional constituencies and even when they maximize local discretion in the expenditure of funds, operate under nominally uniform rules.

The increasing capacity of the executive to provide information to Congress and to package legislation compatible with members' needs points up Congress's dependence on the executive for information if it is to legislate at all. Since executive bureaucrats and the President do not share the electoral needs and interests of individual congresspeople, this dependence is combined with a high degree of suspicion. Changing demographics, technological change, and need for rationalization and information prompt congressional reorganization once every several decades (see Chapter 2). These factors also enhance the role of what might be called service committees. These committees exist for the purpose of coordinating information and rationalizing the costs of congressional policies with revenues. A consequence is that a locally elected Congress has the capacity to play an even larger role in the national coordination of policies.

Although Congress can usually integrate the programs and activities of its diverse interest-specific committees, it is not able to coordinate all types of policies. Consider energy. Any tax on coal or oil is considered by congresspeople from natural-resource-producing districts as a redistribution away from their constituents, both taxpayers and businesspeople, to the rest of the country. Deregulation of natural gas prices is viewed in exactly the opposite manner. Members from areas producing natural gas see deregulation as a benefit; members from urban areas in the Northeast see it as an increased cost to constituents. Water management in the West has been a similar issue since the 1970s; any change in the legislated use of water resources appears to be a redistribution of this good away from the constituencies of former users to the constituencies of future users. The organization of Congress itself militates against the development of coherent policies in the areas of energy and water management. In general, then, Congress is not effectively organized to provide centralized planning and guidance in a policy area that involves tradeoffs across different constituencies, especially in the long term. Congress can not effectively deal with issues in which the same policy confers both benefits and costs to people already organized in different congressional districts.

Coordinating Public Policies Across Programs and Localities

A principal method of coordinating public policy nationally in any particular area is to attach conditions to the financial aid that Congress gives to states, localities, and private interests. Nationally planned, locally built highways must meet certain safety and other standards in order to receive federal contributions. Federal Housing Authority (FHA) home loan guarantees are another instance in which the federal government encourages a particular type of private activity through financial subsidy. FHA mortgages and agricultural price supports are voluntary. The government cannot compel a citizen to accept a FHA mortgage or a farmer to accept limitations on producing acreage in return for a price support guarantee, but the financial incentive is attractive enough that potential homeowners and farmers voluntarily comply. As a consequence, the availability of housing and the quantities of different agricultural products in the national market will be coordinated.

Not all federal efforts at policy coordination operate through the provision of financial "carrots," any more than all federal programs represent the centralized coordination and encouragement of centrifugal interests. Programs like Social Security and the National Defense Education Act represent national-level responses to clear and recognizable needs as justified by a possible national emergency. These programs have very particular ends in mind, and most of the costs of obtaining them are borne by the federal government. In these cases, the method of coordination is programmatic: a federal-level bureaucracy administers a rule-governed program. Once begun, these programs expand in scope and size, partly as a consequence of the lobbying activities of the more hierarchically organized bureaucrats who administer the program. The process is very subtle and involves the use of expertise, monopoly of information, and public agenda setting.

At the federal level, there are at least three other kinds of policy-coordinating activities. The first is coordination through the use of shared professional training and values. A classic example is the U.S. Forest Service (Kaufman, 1960). The organizational structure of the forest service is nonhierarchical. Chief foresters of U.S. forests and parks have a great deal of discretion with respect to decisions about land and forest management. Internal tensions rarely arise, principally because most foresters, both in the forest service and in industry, share presumptions, values, and a type of professional training that render their views reasonably homogeneous. One is much more likely to find an adversarial relationship between the forest service and a congressional committee or subcommittee than to find intense internal disagreement over the proper management of a particular national forest or park.

The classical regulatory activities, such as those performed by the ICC and the FCC, can be considered a second mode of coordination. The interests coordinated, ever since regulation began in the United States in the mid-nineteenth century, are usually of a commercial, financial, or agricultural character. Similar problems of coordination in Britain or France are frequently handled by statute or statutory instruments. In the United States, regulation represents delegated coordination. Although classical regulatory activities may once have represented reactions to abuses of market position in many industries, the long-term effect of these activities has often been to coordinate the pricing and marketing policies of a number of firms producing substitutable products or services. The ICC, for example, has acted to maintain the economic viability of both trucking and railroads, even in localities where one or the other would have an obvious competitive advantage. The consequence of this sectoral delegation of coordinating activities is typically to increase prices for the rest of society; the beneficiaries are clearly those who, in spite of marketplace forces to the contrary, stay in business.

The third type of policy coordination has the fiscal audit as its instrument. "Audit" here refers to a verification of the use of monies and allows bureaucrats and congressional committee staff to track the implementation of targeted programs. Funds for highways, community mental health centers, mass transit, education for the disadvantaged, and bilingual education (Titles I and VII of ESEA, respectively) are all subject to both program and fiscal audits. At least two features of such programs are checked. The first is whether the intended beneficiaries as defined by the program actually received services compatible with its intent. This involves checking recipients and programs. A second check, more fiscal in nature, is intended to monitor both the efficiency and the integrity of the program. Were needlessly expensive community-based facilities built for mental health patients? Were redundant materials purchased for Title I students? Was Title VII money used to pay off a building contractor?

When government programs, as well as transfer payments, are directed toward the poor, the non-English-speaking, the handicapped, and so on, it is difficult for Congress and the federal bureaucracy to tell whether those designated to receive services actually do so. Congress is much better able to appropriate money to be spent than to direct the spending process itself. The groups that historically have used the political system to obtain particularized benefits or avoid the risks of the marketplace were well organized enough to notify Congress or the bureaucracy if they fail to receive a designated benefit. This is not true of the unorganized poor, who often do not know that they are entitled to a benefit and certainly are not well-informed or organized enough to translate a complaint into political action. Hence, over the last twenty years, fiscal audits have served to track appropriated monies. Additionally, many programs benefiting the poor—for example, Model Cities—have required that they organize their recipients. The resultant organizations can signal Congress when funds and programs are not appropriately delivered.

The auditing of expenditures is itself sometimes controversial, in part because it is often done by individuals with little knowledge of the program. Claims about unwise or illegal expenditures by community mental health centers or school districts are sometimes without warrant. Aspects of expenditures and monitoring by an entire state have been brought into question, as when the Office of Education challenged some California Title I expenditures. The principal issue was California's refusal to allow federal fiscal and program audits to force its Title I programs into a format used elsewhere across the country. The state's own compensatory education program was already directing extensive, locally programmed efforts to help the underachieving and very poor. It used federal money to augment its own programs rather than the other way around (SEA interview, California, 1975). This result is desirable from the perspective of Congress. Usually, these disputes are settled through bureaucratic bargaining, in the courts, or both. Usually federal and state-level bureaucrats or professionals are also program beneficiaries. The dispute cited has little to do with the content of education or any other policy area.

The use of positive incentives and coordinating institutions to affect state and local implementation of public policies has not always promoted similar or successful results. Nationally funded highways are sometimes built poorly by local contractors; bridges that are part of the interstate highway system sometimes collapse. ESEA Title I funds 13,000 programs spread around the school districts of the country (see Chapter 3). Various state tax laws encourage businesses and capital formation in different and sometimes contradictory ways. Welfare benefits vary widely across states, even though the federal government is the principal payer (see Chapter 6). Some states do not even use available federal monies for health and mental health care (see Chapter 5). This is not to suggest that there has been no standardization of policy across states. In fact, states themselves desire some commonality of coded law at least. Among the tasks of the National Association of State Legislatures is to recommend to the various states common types of statutes involving many areas that fall within the domain of state policymaking—laws involving marriage and divorce, alimony, no-fault insurance, business tax codes, and so on. Federal incentives to coordinate and homogenize policies are most successful when such coordination is in the interest of the state or local governments themselves.

Such positive federal incentives increase the policy capacity and powers of state and local governments without decreasing federal prerogatives. As mentioned before, it is a hallmark of a complicated federal system that increases in the power or expenditures of one level of government need not be taken from the expenditures, tax base, or power of other levels. Indeed, the capacities of all levels of government can increase simultaneously; as long as economic activity and innovation within the economy also increase, no diminution of human freedom need follow. Positive federal fiscal incentives for policy coordination cannot by themselves explain the view, commonly held by politician and citizen alike, that the powers of the federal government have vastly expanded relative to the powers of other levels. As we will see, there are sound reasons for such an observation.

Policy Implementation from the Federal Perspective

At the federal level, program regulation and review occur less often than fiscal review, at least when the entire sweep of federal government activities is considered. One reason is that programs are sometimes intended to be quite different in different areas of the country. An extreme example is urban renewal. Aside from the use of federal monies, the only two elements common to urban renewal areas were a mandatory planning component and the urban nature of the area of renewal (see Chapter 4). The lack of standards made review difficult, although fiscal audits still occurred. One would expect, then, to find less program review at the federal level in the United States than at the center in Britain, where a much higher percentage of even locally administered programs must follow rules or formulas specified in great detail by the center. This does not mean that local flexibility is always greater in the United States; it does mean that the British do less center-local negotiation over rules and standards than does the United States, both before and after the passage of legislation.

A second factor affecting federal program review is the concentration of public-sector professionals at the federal level. For example, more professional educators and administrators are located at the state and local levels than within the federal bureaucracy. On the other hand, there are probably many more health professionals and administrators in the federal bureaucracy or directly employed by the federal level than within the public sector at the state level. This suggests that federal programs in the general area of health are more likely to be directly reviewed at the federal level or by professionals in the federal government than are federally funded educational programs.

In the areas of health and mental health, federal-level bureaucrats often have exact models of service delivery in mind when a program is funded. Local as well as state providers of services to citizens may be subject to detailed annual program review when the program is supported entirely or in part with federal funds. This is certainly true of federally funded mental health centers and inoculation programs. On the other hand, in the area of educating the disadvantaged and underachieving, as well as similar areas, a somewhat different model of program review has evolved. This model uses intermediate public sector units. In the case of ESEA Title I, the unit involved is, as noted above, the SEA. This form of delegated review or regulation is becoming more common in the United States and is used in the monitoring of several of the more recent area-specific federal block grants.

As we have seen, the relationship between the SEA and the federal and local levels differs from state to state, depending in part on where Title I coordinators situated within the educational authority and in part on the extent to which the SEA is insulated from the state legislature. In states where SEA officials are indirectly appointed and their actions are not subject to continuous legislative review, most of their contacts are with other educational professionals, including those from the federal level. Where SEAs have elected heads or close relations with legislative committees, on the other hand, local concerns can swamp federal input into Title One program monitoring.

The transfer of bargaining over Title I and similar programs to the state level saves congresspeople time and ensures that policy will be responsive to local needs. Congress does not engage in continuous legislative oversight of such programs. The parameters for bargaining are set; bargaining occurs at the state level before federal dollars are translated into program benefits for constituents. So long as the dollars get there and the programs exist, the resultant activities are regarded by members of Congress as beneficial and productive. Certainly, most of them are also electorally relevant to congresspeople. At the same time, the political climate of the state is reflected in the bargaining that goes on. In a state with a strong party system, the party, through the legislature, will likely have a significant impact on budgeting within the SEA just as it structures congressional nominations and reelection. The reflection of locally based political realities in the bargaining process relieves congresspeople of the tasks of making judgments as to the relative influence of potentially contending local parties or participants and casting laws to match the diverse policy structures of states other than their own.

Intergovernmental Relations

Intergovernmental relations revolve around money. In fact, it is through expenditures on state and local activities that the federal government obtains most of its capacity to influence program decisions as they affect citizens. Most federal-level technical assistance or standard setting occurs when state, local, or private entities use federal monies to provide services. One might contrast the British case, in which nationally determined standards for elementary education, mental health, or highways are established independently of the fiscal resources given to local governments by national government. Again, however, it is our federal system and the many powers reserved for states and localities that lead to the continual programmatic and fiscal interactions between the federal government and states and localities. In many cases the federal government would have no constitutional standing to set standards or provide assistance if it did not provide some of the money.

Federal fiscal assistance comes in a variety of forms. Proceeding from a broad to a narrow focus of activity, a list would include general revenue sharing; general-purpose shared revenue programs; shared revenue earmarked for specific programs; broad-based functional block grants; formula-based categorical grants; and grants for specific purposes on projects. The most common forms are general revenue sharing (since the late 1970s), block grants, categorical grants, and project grants. Examples of the last three, respectively, are the Comprehensive Employment and Training Act (CETA) of 1973 (see Chapter 6), the Elementary and Secondary Education Act (ESEA) of 1965 (see Chapter 3), and yearly appropriations that provide funds for building a post office, a federally insured grain elevator, or new housing (see Chapter 4).

The declared congressional rationale for such aid to states and localities also varies greatly. The most common reasons, however, all involve the stimulation of state, local, and private activities. As noted above, however, the distribution of general tax revenues to particular beneficiary groups is also important for electoral reasons.

The form of federal-level assistance has evolved since World War II. In the 1950s and 1960s, the most common forms of federal aid were the formula-based categorical grants and the specific project grants. The latter, as in the case of federal support for state and interstate highway construction, often required state matching funds. In the cases of ESEA Title I, highway construction (see Chapter 4), and even AFDC (see Chapter 6), Congress was not so much trying to redirect the pattern of state and local spending as to augment that spending in areas of perceived need. In doing this it required strict matching state monies for highway construction and variable state matching funds for AFDC and Medicaid. The latter variation takes into account the capacity of states (and localities) to fund programs, since this varies with their effective tax base and state income levels. In all these programs, planning occurs at the state and local level. States receive special funds to administer ESEA Title I; local contractors build interstate highways.

In the early 1960s a second form of federal aid, categorical grants, was introduced. This aid was often provided directly to localities and nonprofit service providers. In some cases the expressed intent of federal bureaucrats was to support a new, worthwhile activity and, additionally, to encourage a redirection of state and local funding. Two examples are the Community Mental Health Centers Act of 1963 and the Model Cities Program of 1965.

Two key questions are whether federal monies introduced at the local level can force a redirection of state monies for programs in the same area, and whether this redirection will be maintained if federal monies are reduced. The designers of the Community Mental Health Centers and Model Cities programs initially intended that federal monies would be gradually withdrawn. In both cases states do appear to have spent new monies that they would have spent without the federal impetus. Moreover, as federal monies have been withdrawn in the last several years, both the local programs and their costs have been absorbed into the state system, largely on terms dictated by the state, not the local providers. Yet the federal government has found it impossible to withdraw its funds and still maintain the same emphasis on federal service priorities. For example, the federal emphasis on prevention in community mental health centers simply disappeared whenever federal money was unavailable.

Beginning in 1966 Congress passed five block grant programs. These programs provided funds for a number of different areas, each of which had formerly been the subject of a categorical program. CETA, for example, consolidated seventeen programs, while the Housing and Community Development Act of 1974 consolidated six. All programs, with the exception of CETA, used population as the principal basis for distributing money. All the programs except Housing and Community Development provided funds to states as the primary recipient. (Local units of government received the Housing and Community Development funds and some CETA funds.)

Paralleling the development of these block grants was the development of general revenue sharing after 1972. General revenue sharing was devised with the equalization of state fiscal capacity in mind: when significant monies were involved in revenue sharing, allocations did tend to equalize the fiscal capacities of rich and poor states. Although revenue sharing to both state and local governments peaked at around $9 billion a year in the mid-1970s, it has since trickled away to almost nothing.

More recently, interest in area-specific block grants has grown. Nine new block grants have been created since 1980. However, it remains unclear whether the motivation behind them is the same as that which prompted the passage of CETA, the Partnership for Health, the Omnibus Crime and Safe Streets bill, Housing and Community Development, and Title XX training and internships for social services between 1966 and 1974. Earlier block grants were funded on an increasingly generous basis in subsequent years. The goal appeared to be to increase both state and local flexibility with regard to how monies should be spent while boosting expenditures in broad areas that Congress felt needed assistance. The principal motive behind the more recent block grants (in mental health, maternal and child care, education, etc.) appears to be a desire to restrict the amount of federal aid while placing the responsibility for deciding who will bear the cost of these cuts on other levels of government (Kelley, 1983; Rich and Kelley, 1983). One consequence of such block grants, and of the categorical programs administered through the states, is an increase in state programmatic authority at the expense of local-level planners, bureaucrats, and service providers. This has certainly been a consequence of such diverse programs as Title I of ESEA, the mental health block grant, and Title VI of the Civil Rights Act.

Although federal contributions to services provided through state or local government can be trimmed and modified, they cannot be eliminated. Federal influence over state and local programs through the power of the dollar is here to stay. This is no different from the relationship between the federal government and organized groups in the private sector, where federal loan guarantees, federal provision of bargaining arenas for business and labor, and federal expenditures for research and development all carry weight. Moreover, none of the federal level's coordinating techniques or incentives can direct or redirect state and local monies unless state legislatures agree to such shifts. Historically states have been able to twist the program intentions of federal funding as easily as the states themselves could be maneuvered to shift their own priorities through matching provisions in federal programs. Indeed, states and localities have an advantage in the sense that their officials are on the scene when services are actually delivered and can better determine their character and quality.

Congress, however, has developed another method not only to ensure compliance with the intent of federal legislation, but also to drastically shift state and local funding priorities in some policy areas. This tool can be termed negative regulation. Although it has vast coordinating capacities, it also has the potential to cause vast conflicts between levels of government. In enforcing some constitutional mandate or federal legislation, Congress may provide insufficient monies, or none at all, but still attempt to compel states and localities to organize their own activities, programs, and funding levels in a particular way. Examples vary from a prohibition against using violence to prevent blacks from voting in local elections to a prohibition of mother-daughter banquets after high school athletic events—in other words, from the significant to the ridiculous.

In its most pronounced attempts at negative regulation, Congress uses the prior provision of federal money as a lever. A similar effect is achieved in Britain through the penalties associated with rate supports or block grants from the central government to local authorities: local government must obey the law, or centrally provided monies are lost. In the United States, however, there can be a slight twist. Congress will legislate, for example, that the provisions of Title VI of the Civil Rights Act of 1964 must be satisfied by state and local governments, or federal funding for a variety of programs will be lost. These provisions will often require the redirection of billions of dollars of state and locally collected tax monies to different sets of recipients. Yet little or no federal money will be provided to this same end. These substantive conditions are similar to those contained in regulations or circulars issued by the Department of Education and Science or the Department of Health and Social Security in Britain. To ignore such circulars, particularly in the case of education and science, is to be derelict in the provision of services that are deemed necessary by professional consensus. In the extreme case in Britain, the central government might take over the provision of a particular service in a local authority. In the extreme case in the United States, federal troops might be sent to implement the law, as in the case of the desegregation of Little Rock schools in 1954, or federal monies might be withdrawn.

Congress explicitly uses negative regulation to force states to legislate (sometimes uniformly) in areas in which the federal government has no power. Examples include the establishment of a fifty-five-mile-per-hour (MPH) speed limit, a twenty-one-year-old drinking age (see Chapter 4), and Medicaid fraud control (see Chapter 5). Although these areas are subject to state control, the threat of withdrawing previously existing federal grants is sufficient to produce almost uniform policy outcomes across state legislatures. This is true even when the federal funds "at risk" constitute only a small part of a state or local budget: any part of the budget is hard to replace, since doing so involves either cutting beneficiaries, increasing taxes, or both.

Federal monies are, of course, almost never withdrawn. However, the time, energy, and money spent negotiating with an extensive federal regulatory bureaucracy has the effect of bringing the behavior of state and local governments into compliance with federal legislation. To a county health authority or a state-level educational bureaucrat, loss of time, administrative efficacy, and reputation is a more serious sanction than the particular costs that the federal government could impose. This is a lesson that has yet to be learned in the regulation of U.S. business activities.

The application of civil rights legislation to state and local activities in education, voting, transportation, and so on is a typical example of federal regulation that results in the homogenization or coordination of services provided by these levels of government. The federal government does not provide significant funds for bilingual education, busing, or school desegregation. However, it does assert that the states and localities must provide such services in a manner consistent with the interpretation of the thirteenth, fourteenth, and fifteenth amendments as given and augmented in the Civil Rights Act of 1964. The Education of All Handicapped Children Act, for example, does not attempt to augment or interpret basic freedoms; rather, it asserts a congressional policy. If states receive federal money, localities and school districts must educate all handicapped children, in mainstream programs if possible and, if not, in a manner appropriate to their well-being. This mandate redirects billions of dollars in education, health, and other services to beneficiaries whom state and local legislatures might not have chosen. If the services are not provided, the federal bureaucracy is empowered directly or through the courts to withdraw many forms of federal aid for education, mental health, highways, or other programs.

The federal government is not alone in forcing state and local governments to shift their policy priorities. The many groups organized for purposes of receiving federal funds—Title I parent advisory councils, neighborhood housing corporations, Model Cities advisory boards, and so on—also act to shift the state priorities. These groups are very sensitive to the presence or absence of state and local responses to federal policy mandates, and most have the capacity to use the federal courts to compel state and local compliance with constitutional and legal mandates. These groups inform Congress when state and local governments are not providing the specified shifts in funding and programs. In fact, they sometimes sue the federal government to compel it to enforce federal laws or the Constitution. One example, affecting the redirection of about $2 billion of state and local educational funding, is *Alaska* v. *Califano*. In this case the Office of Civil Rights was sued to force it to provide clear standards for bilingual education for the 13,000 school districts across the country. The court ruled that OCR must do so even though it and the administration as a whole were reluctant to become involved in the issue. Hence, we find that not only government, but government-created groups of private citizens as well, can use both the threat of withholding funding and the federal courts to compel shifts in state and local policy priorities.

Ironically, the federal government appears to have the most power when it uses a stick rather than a carrot. The 13,000 ESEA Title I programs are subject to a federal fiscal audit, but program audits are negotiated at the state level. The federal government's control over what goes on in a Title I classroom does not begin to approach its control over whether children receive transitional bilingual education, instruction in English as a second language, or other modes of educational enrichment mandated by Title VI of the Civil Rights Act of 1964. Failure to provide such programs threatens federal transfers. It is difficult for elected politicians to suggest that federal funds should be sent back to Washington so that state and local government can pursue their own activities as they see fit, since these funds provide benefits for some set of voters. As a consequence, Congress more frequently uses negative regulation to force state and local governments to pursue policies that are of electoral benefit to its members. An additional consequence of negative regulation is an increased homogenization and uniformity of state and federal policies. It is only since the late 1960s that Congress, using such legislation, has successfully taken control of American public policy.

Conclusion

One way to obtain an overview of the ways in which the American national government influences policies that affect citizens is to look briefly at the activities that fall under the rubric of "regulation." Each form parallels the entry of a new group into the legislative arena. What might be termed classical regulation is really very similar in its effects to the passage of legislation that directly reduces marketplace risks for business and agriculture. The ICC, for example, allows various substitutable modes of transportation to fix prices in such a manner that they can stay in business. National funding of internal improvements such as railroads and canals and classical regulation are different responses of the national legislature to the demands or needs of particular groups. These needs are still present, and Congress still responds. In doing so, Congress does not set policy so much as it reacts to the policy needs of others, particularly in business and agriculture (see Chapter 7).

A second type of regulation is that of professional groups. In the United States this is done principally at the state level. Such regulation usually delegates to professional guilds control over entry to a profession, training, distribution of services, and rate of remuneration. State governments have been very active in this area, while national government has principally used these professional groups to provide goods and services with the money voted at the national level in areas such as education, health, and other social services. Delegated state-level regulation of professional groups and federal funding of their services continue (see Chapter 5).

The loose regulation of entitlements and benefits constitutes a third category. An instance is the use of fiscal audits to enforce ESEA Title I. Almost all fiscal audits of federal programs fall into this category. Such audits, along with program auditing and the monitoring of federally funded activities by states and by local groups created with federal monies, are intended to ensure that the dollars Congress provides get to the designated beneficiary groups through designated service providers. There is, of course, a lot of slippage in this process, as there must be if spending at the local level is to be responsive to the local needs of both beneficiaries and service providers. This activity does not enhance the policy powers of the federal government except in those cases where the programs funded require matching money from the states. In such cases states can be gradually teased into shifting their funding priorities. Fiscal audits, while helping to ensure that money goes to areas that will provide incumbency benefits for congresspeople, may introduce administrative inefficiency at the state level (see Chapter 3).

A fourth type of regulation deals with market asymmetries. This regulation is quite recent. Examples are the Clean Air Act and, to a lesser degree, the work of the Environmental Protection Agency (EPA). It is only in the last fifteen or twenty years that consumer groups and similar organizations have overcome the high cost of organization to make demands on Congress. The groups that benefit from this kind of legislation and regulation are usually widely dispersed (less so in the case of EPA) and often middle class by income. As a general rule, such regulation represents the transfer of some of the externalities of manufacturing or service provision from consumer groups back to the producing organization or business. The bargaining among all these groups over relevant pollution levels, safe work conditions, and so on, is closely akin to the bargaining among participants involved in classical regulation. As new groups have organized in the economy, their collective needs have been brought into the various negotiating arenas provided by national government. This does not necessarily enhance the policy powers of national government; rather, it brings the interests of more groups into the process by which policy is formed.

None of the preceding forms of regulation force state and local governments to change their policy priorities in a dramatic fashion. However, the introduction of negative regulation, the use of the federal courts by private groups, and the establishment of policy regulations without full funding by the federal government have forced states and localities to shift their funding priorities to a considerable degree. Principally it is through the use of these processes over the last fifteen years that the federal government has obtained some control over the policy priorities of states. On a policy by policy basis, redirect state and local spending priorities even without the infusion of federal funds.

The evolution of congressional influence on both national and state policy formation is the same across most policy areas (see Chapters 3–6). Both grants and negative regulation are used in almost all areas of domestic concern, and the beneficiaries can be any of the groups in the policymaking arena. These groups benefit from public policies in the same sequential order in every policy area, an order reflected in the evolution of regulatory legislation at the national and state levels. In the next chapter we will look at how the federal government changes its own institutional arrangements to accomodate interests as they evolve around the country. In subsequent chapters see the application of these principles to the evolution of a number of policy areas.

2 Government Reorganization

The internal structures of federal governmental institutions and their interactions are shaped and called into play by the articulation of interests and subsequent policy formulation and implementation. In the last chapter we saw how Congress organized itself to facilitate the efficient passage of legislation; the timely provision of real and symbolic benefits to constituents, district by district, is important to the incumbency of each congressperson, regardless of party. In response to a sequence of crises (e.g., the Depression, World War II) and the increased demands made on government by more groups, Congress must sometimes fine-tune its internal structure to maintain incumbency advantage.

At the same time congresspeople are continuously asked to increase the efficiency and effectiveness with which the executive departments carry out policy. This can occur through reorganization of executive branch activities and through increased delegation of decision-making powers to bureaucracies. Agencies may sometimes make decisions and develop regulations inconsistent with the needs of congresspeople involved in the original legislation (see particularly the discussion of Title IX of the Higher Education Act in Chapter 3). In these cases, congressional committee and subcommittee oversight hearings often communicate necessary changes to bureaucrats without the need for subsequent legislation. However, the formal capacity of congressional committees or Congress itself to nullify regulations is a source of constant controversy.

This controversy emanates in large part from the conflicting needs of the executive and Congress. Congress needs to conserve time, yet it must be sure that bureaus deliver money and services to intended beneficiaries. Hence, congresspeople prefer to deal formally only with those cases of program administration that are inimical to legislative incumbency. The federal executive, however, uses delegated legislation and regulations across a number of policy areas to increase the efficiency of governance and to communicate a somewhat different set of policy preferences to the bureaucracy. Since the President has nominal line authority over most federal executive employees, such integration and substitution is possible. This administrative power and the capacity to produce integrated budgets are two of very few powers that the President has to balance the legislative edge constitutionally given Congress.

As a consequence Congress and the President battle over legislated regulations, the power of Congress to oversee and "veto" such regulations, and formal executive-branch reorganization. Presidents want to reorganize bureaus to increase White House control over program implementation, integration, and information. Congress will often accede to executive requests for reorganization, but will never alter the close budgetary association between its committees federal bureaus or programs. In this way members can modify and keep track of programs relevant to their chances for reelection.

The institutional arrangements through which the federal government implements federal policy affect who gets money and services. Control over the rules and regulations attached to programs is valuable to presidents, congresspeople, and even lower-level governments. Even the way in which the federal government funds programs that affect citizens at the state and local level can alter the pattern of programs in state government. We will see examples of this in the consequences of negative regulation in the areas of transportation and education. Later, we will see in the case of community-based mental health services that total federal funding is not sufficient to alter state and local program priorities and budgeting. The introduction of fiscal federalism, through the use of general revenue sharing and block grants to state and local governments, can alter the way in which those governments organize themselves to pursue their own programmatic agenda. In this latter case, the reorganization of state and local administrative apparatuses is a response not to the legislated needs of congresspeople and their constituencies, but to the necessities of administration per se. Cities cannot spend federal revenue-sharing monies unless they develop an administrative or legislative apparatus for deciding how those monies are to be spent. States cannot administer community development or alcohol and drug abuse block grant monies unless they have set up the relevant and required administrative apparatus.

Although changes in the way Congress appropriates money or the executive administers policies will be considered in this chapter, the focus is on the reorganization of federal branches themselves. The internal structure of Congress (the House of Representatives in particular) underwent major reorganizations in 1946 and 1970. In both cases, reorganization was prompted by the need to deal with the increased capacity of the federal executive to establish an agenda for congressional action and with new patterns of interest's legislative districts after a time of rapid economic change or a geographic redistribution of population and industry.

However, most visible reorganization in the federal government involves the executive branch. Since 1953 five cabinet departments have been created: Health, Education and Welfare (HEW) in 1953; Housing and Urban Development (HUD) in 1965; Transportation in 1966; Energy in 1978 and Education in 1979. The Office of the President was created in 1939 and vastly reorganized in 1970. Many independent regulatory agencies have been established since the Acts to Regulate Commerce created the ICC in 1887. Special authorities have been created to enhance economic development or provide power or transportation (e.g., the Tennessee Valley Authority, Conrail, and Amtrak). These developments may be traced to a number of causes. Often Congress intends to promote more efficient policy implementation, to lower expenditures (without cutting off funding), or to facilitate constituency-oriented services. Some of Richard Nixon's attempts at reorganization represented an attempt to thwart the independent policymaking activity of professional groups in the government bureaucracy. Both Franklin Roosevelt and Lyndon Johnson used reorganization as a symbolic reward to organized professional groups or voters and as a guideline for the kinds of policymaking initiatives that were expected during their administrations.

In the creation of new departments, as in reorganizations in general, one should not expect the relations between federal agencies and the congressional committee system to change, for the reasons noted above. The president is allowed by statute to suggest potential reorganization's to Congress and make adjustments in the internal organization of the executive department to increase its effectiveness so long as such reorganization does not change the congressional venue of any program or budget. In other words, any reorganization with fiscal or programmatic consequences must be passed by both houses of Congress. This will only happen when all those interests that might be affected by such bureaucratic change have agreed that their own relationships with their constituencies will not be harmed as a result.

Context

Since Grover Cleveland, presidents have urged the reorganization of one aspect or another of the executive branch. In 1885 and 1888 Cleveland stated that before the nation restored its Navy, it must reorganize the Naval Department. With the exception of Woodrow Wilson and Calvin Coolidge, every President since 1912 has presented actual reorganization plans to Congress (Graves, 1949). Even Wilson was the beneficiary of the Overman Act of 1918, which authorized him to redistribute functions among executive agencies until six months after the close of World War I.

Presidents usually justified reorganization on grounds of increasing efficiency or lowering the cost of government. This was true of the creation of the independent regulatory commissions. The FCC, for example, was designed to divide the airwaves fairly and effectively so that communication could occur without interference. The original ICC was intended to provide an effective bargaining arena for meat-packers and railroads so that neither would attempt to drive the other out of business while pursuing its own profits. We can extend this rationale to the National Recovery Administration under Roosevelt. The NRA was organized to prevent the individually rational actions of small businessmen in some sectors of the economy from bankrupting their industries. As smaller businesses lowered prices because of declining sales, everyone had to follow suit until profits disappeared. If one multiplies these losses by the 497 industrial areas that produced codes under the NRA, one can see that without collective intervention a downward wage-price cycle could endure for a long time. The NRA forced the setting of wages, prices, and market shares in each industrial sector. Although the NRA was declared unconstitutional (*U.S.* v. *Schechter*), by 1937 most of its features were preserved through piecemeal legislation. Roosevelt also encouraged the creation of other independent regulatory commissions, like the Federal Deposit Insurance Corporation, which basically pooled the risks of bad judgment and bank failures.

The regulatory commissions established to deal with the consequences of the Depression represent a governmental response to a new situation in which the forces of the marketplace could not themselves ensure perpetuation of the marketplace. Roosevelt recommended the creation of organizations to increase demand in the economy or provide infrastructure for economic expansion. The Tennessee Valley Authority was probably the first U.S. government corporation run by an independent board of governors, a practice that is much more common in France and Britain. The TVA was established because the government had invested in a dam and several plants in Tennessee River Valley and wanted also to promote labor-intensive activities to help generate demand for products produced elsewhere in the economy.

Partial reorganization of the executive occurred before and during World War II. Roosevelt was loath to delegate to the private sector or to the military the degree of responsibility for production that had been given them in World War I. In preparation for possible war, a number of federal labor-management coordinating agencies were created within the federal government in 1939 and 1940. Roosevelt's Executive Order 248 stated that in the event of a national emergency, an office for emergency management would be set up in the executive office at the President's order. This became the effective coordinating body for the prewar effort until the first War Powers Act of 1941 was approved on December 18. This bill, similar to the Overman Act of 1918, authorized the President to make the administrative changes necessary for promoting the war effort. Changes were to last no more than six months after the war was over, and they were limited to those necessary for the actual conduct of war. The Reorganization Act of 1945 made permanent whatever changes appeared to increase the efficiency of the war effort without removing congresspeople from direct contact with their constituencies.

The cumulative impact of two wars and one major depression had produced a federal bureaucracy in which line authority was not clear. This meant that congresspeople and congressional committee staff did not know exactly which bureaus could implement various laws affecting particular constituencies. In 1947 Congress established the first Hoover Commission to suggest changes that would simplify and clarify line authority in the executive agencies (Emmerich, 1971, chap. 5). The Reorganization Act of 1949 authorizes the President to examine and continually reexamine the organization of agencies to promote a more effective management, reduce expenditures, and promote economy (see Reading 2-1). While placing the burden of compiling, examining, and making suggestions on the President, Congress reserved a single-house veto over any such suggestions. In other words, the President's suggestions must be passed as normal legislation. Five months after the passage of this act, Truman proposed seven reorganization plans with the common objective of lowering the costs of government (see Reading 2–1). A second Hoover Commission was authorized in 1953 with the more limited mission of ferreting out duplication and waste within agencies.

The two biggest instances of reorganization between World War II and 1960 were the amalgamation of the Department of Defense from the separate foreign service departments and the creation of the Department of Health, Education and Welfare (HEW). The original Department of Defense can be considered a federation, and it is unclear whether its secretary had as much power as the secretaries of the individual services or any of the joint chiefs of staff. It was the genius of Robert McNamara that brought about some degree of coordination in the department through the secretary's office, not so much by statute as by the rerouting of information, which is itself an informal way of reorganizing almost anything.

HEW was created in the first year of the Eisenhower administration. Dwight David Eisenhower opposed an enlarged executive; congresspeople, however, liked the idea of grouping and emphasizing a number of already existing programs that did not fall easily into the other cabinet departments. Congressional committees and subcommittees involved with the authorization and appropriation of funds for each of the agencies falling under the rubric of health, education, and welfare did not change and relations between agencies and congressional subcommittees persisted without change. (Some opponents of the department doubted that it could effectively be administered by a nonprofessional— that is, someone who was not a doctor or an educator. Ironically, less than twenty years later, Nixon would try to reorganize government with the express purpose of limiting the influence of HEW professionals who "disrupted" his programs.) In view of the sequence of beneficiaries of government action noted earlier it is of some interest that the executive branch reorganizations described above facilitated policies benefiting first commerce, then the military, and finally professional groups.

Even many small changes in executive organization cannot be undertaken without congressional approval. For example, the creation of most oceanic or atmospheric surveys involves reorganization. The reorganization of locomotive inspection procedures involves congressional approval after consultation with the Bureau of the Budget, the ICC, and the Brotherhood of Locomotive, Firemen and Engineers. Not all such reorganization proposals, whether small or large in scope, are approved. Even though, a conservative when it came to reorganization of governmental activities, Eisenhower sometimes received congressional veto of charges (see Reading 2–2).

Possibly the most important legislative reorganization between World War II and 1960 occur in the 1946 Legislative Reorganization Act. The details of this act, as well as the mechanics by which congresspeople reduced number of committees creating disharmony and conflict, are quite complex (see Bensel, 1978). Like the executive reorganization that began in 1949, congressional reorganization was necessary to deal with the new role of the government in the economy, developments in world affairs, and the changing demographic characteristics of many congressional constituencies. Adding more single-issue subcommittees and dividing each member's time in more ways did not adequately serve the members incumbency requirements. Hence, new committees were created, and members were assigned to them in a manner that reflected new geographical combinations of economic interests. Congress still continually contracts or expands the membership of particular committees or subcommittees to accommodate the needs of members who face changing economies and constituencies in their districts.

Congress has also attempted to improve its effectiveness by delegating power to the executive, subject to congressional review, particularly in areas normally associated with executive power, such as defense and foreign trade. In 1932 Congress gave Herbert Hoover power to reorganize the executive branch, but maintained a single-house veto over all developments. After his defeat, Hoover's extensive use of this power was swiftly vetoed by the House of Representatives. Congress allowed Roosevelt extensive power of executive branch reorganization subject only to the veto of both houses of Congress. After Roosevelt's extensive use of this power, Congress never again allowed so much reorganization initiative to lie with the executive. Yet the single-house veto remains a convenient way to accommodate the policy flexibility and concern for efficiency the executive desires with the need of congresspeople to oversee the rules affecting benefits for their constituents.

Agenda

Increased efficiency is only one of several reasons for executive branch reorganization. The executive branch and the President also offer reorganization plans to reward new constituencies, either symbolically or actually. This has been true since Johnson's creation of HUD; a recent example is Jimmy Carter's 1979 creation of the Department of Education. In neither case did Congress approve changes in the organization of the federal bureaucracy which altered the relationship between federal agencies and the congressional committee system.

Congress often resists reorganizations when the politically sensitive relations between bureaus and congressional subcommittees are ignored. This occurred when the 1964 report of the President's Task Force on Government Reorganization (the Price Report) suggested the creation of a Department of Transportation, a transportation and regulatory commission, a Department of Education, a Department of Housing and Community Development, a Department of Economic Development, and, contingently, a Department of Natural Resources (see Reading 2–3). Initially, Congress also resisted Johnson's proposed Department of Housing and Urban Development. The principal lobbyists against it were the National Mortgage Bankers' Association, the Association of Real Estate Boards, the National Association of Bankers, the American Farm Bureau Association, and the U.S. Chamber of Commerce (Redford and Blisset, 1981: chap. 2). The latter two groups were concerned with the increased emphasis on urban problems and housing at the expense of government support for business and farm activities. Yet business and agricultural activities, as well as middle-class housing development, were well represented in existing federal expenditures. In 1965 the executive wished to make at least a gesture toward providing benefits outside the marketplace to urban low-income and poorly housed people. Such agencies as the Federal Housing Administration would be included in the new department as entities with their own undersecretaries. The administration emphasized that HUD would concern itself with physical assistance for urban areas. It would exclude purely social and economic factors, and it would not be in charge of the overall urban policy of the federal government, according to a memorandum from Robert C. Weaver to Bill Moyers, dated December 3, 1964 (now in the files at the Bill Moyers LBJ Library). Sen. Robert Kennedy's amendment adding mass transit to the physical aspects of urban areas to be considered by HUD, facilitated its passage by providing benefits for more congressional districts and states.

HUD's internal organization paralleled that of many other federal departments; in emphasizing lines of authority and maintaining a program area across levels of government. Although this form organization thwarts the integration of programs and efficiency at the local level, line authority allows agencies to provide program information to those congressional committees that authorize their budgets. Congress can keep track of what kinds of benefits in each program are going to which constituents in which districts.

That HUD would never become the focal point for federal activities in urban areas was evidenced by the creation and organization of the Office of Economic Opportunity (OEO) and the Model Cities program. The department's powers extended only over the distribution of its own funds and the encouragement of local level collaborative programs funded through other departments. HUD funds were administered in a deliberately decentralized manner, and it was less than totally successful in its attempts to coordinate the categorical-aid programs of other federal-level departments (see Chapter 3). Model Cities, nominally coordinated through HUD, was an example of the department's ineffective structure.

OEO was created under the Economic Opportunity Act of 1966. Although its director was a special assistant to the President and the agency was located in the Executive Office of the President, OEO was an operating agency. The programs funded during the first year included the Job Corps (rural and urban residential centers), work-training programs for unemployed youth, and work-study programs in institutions of higher education (all under Title I); general community action programs, adult basic education programs, and a voluntary assistance program for needy children; (Title II); special programs to combat poverty in rural areas, assistance for migrant and other seasonally employed agricultural workers and their families (Title III); employment and investment incentives for small businesses (Title IV); work-experience programs for unemployed fathers and other needy persons (Title V); and VISTA and Administration (Title VI). The total amount authorized for the first year was slightly under $1 billion. Congress understood that the actual administration of these programs, as opposed to their coordination in OEO would be delegated to the executive departments. The programs delegated in the first year were Title I-B: a work-training program (Neighborhood Youth Corps) delegated to the Department of Labor; Title I-C: the college work-study program, to HEW; Title II-B: adult basic education, to HEW; Title III-A: rural loans, to the Department of Agriculture; Title IV: small business loans, to the Small Business Administration; Title V: work experience, to HEW (Redford and Blisset, 1981, pp. 85–87). OEO was clearly not a superagency. It placed within the Office of the President the capacity to design and coordinate programs affecting urban property. By having OEO involved in the legislative design stage, the coordination necessary for successful program integration across the cabinet departments could be achieved through the planning process. This was an improvement on the planning situation of HUD, which found itself with only the power to cajole other federal departments. Note, additionally, that none of the operation responsibilities for OEO programs went to HUD. We can see that the short-term price for the creation of HUD was its narrow focus on the financial and capital-intensive aspects of housing and its avoidance of distributive and welfare programs. Agencies within HEW, in contrast, already had links with various congressional committees dealing with programs and distributions affecting welfare, education, and work.

Not all of the attempts to gain control over programs and budgeting were successful. President Johnson attempted to merge the Departments of Commerce and Labor into a new Department of Business and Labor. This recommendation had the support of the Price Commission on governmental reorganization (see Reading 2–3), but it was rejected because it threatened long-established working relationships between agencies in the federal departments and parallel appropriation committees. Much of the reorganization activity in this period also involved what must have appeared to the outside observer as rather picayune issues. For example, the creation of a new position and a slight reorganization within the ICC required passage of a reorganization act, Reorganization Plan No. 3 of 1965. Finally, the 1960s also saw an attempt to change the manner of program planning and budgeting so as to obtain greater executive control over the actions of federal departments. The Johnson administration attempted to force agencies as well as cabinet-level officers to make concrete decisions about the goals of the programs they administered and to choose means of achieving them that minimized the cost and other consequences of such changes. This system never worked well because many programs serve a variety of goals whose relative importance varies with the location of the observer. Food stamps benefit farmers, the poor, and, to a lesser degree, food retailers. Just what is the "real" goal of the program? Many programs revolve around the benefits that accrue to those who actually deliver the goods or services. Organized professional service providers are among the best lobbyists for government programs. To them it makes little difference whether the objects of a program are simple, complex, or confused.

Reorganization for the purposes of emphasizing and promoting programs favored by the executive continued through the 1970s. The Department of Energy was created in 1977 in an attempt to coordinate the diverse activities of bureaus scattered through the government and ill-equipped to develop national plans for either energy or water production and utilization. President Carter sought to influence the activities of a number of congressional committees by having energy activities planned in one place in the executive. This worked as long as the plans that went to the committees were consistent with the electoral needs of the congresspeople on them. Early in his administration, however Carter attempted to slow down or halt the construction of several dozen water and hydroelectric projects, principally in the western states, because these expenditures did not fit into the administration's energy plans. The executive's powerlessness to force planned development in any area on an elected Congress is illustrated by the fact that all of these projects were well under way before Carter left office and have since been completed.

The creation of the Department of Education in 1979 highlights the responsiveness of both the Democrats and the Carter administration to the needs of educational professionals in the United States. The National Education Association, one of the two largest unions in the United States, supported Carter in both of his presidential campaigns. Educational professionals, whether administrators or providers of services, overwhelmingly supported Democratic candidates at almost all levels of government. The creation of the Department of Education institutionalized the federal concern for the planning of educational activities that were supported by federal funding (see Reading 2–4). Yet relationships between existing agencies and the congressional committees that authorized their budgets were unchanged.

Two other tendencies in government reorganization during the 1970s are worth noting. Congressional oversight activities increased as many more complex programs came to be administered through the executive branch. It became impossible for Congress to legislate all the details of organization and program. More often we find that congressional intent and the rudiments of organization are specified in legislation, and the apparatus is fine-tuned in congressional oversight and reauthorization hearings. The proportion of congressional time spent on such hearings increased by about 50 percent from the late 1950s to the early and mid-1970s.

The Office of the President usually has difficulty controlling the activities of federal agencies because those agencies are so responsive to the congressional committees that authorize and appropriate their funds. Additionally, federal agencies often recruit professionals who do not necessarily have the goals of the President and his advisors. Presidential efforts at program control may involve the coordination of federal regulations—a strategy used by Richard Nixon and Ronald Reagan. For example, Reagan required all department regulation to be reviewed by OMB, which could stall or attempt to modify them. Often the President's obligation to provide Congress with a cohesive budget (see Chapter 7) is used by the White House to control the flow of information from the executive branch to Congress. Whereas Johnson used a more incremental program planning and budgeting system to clarify choices to be made by political decision-makers, Carter attempted to use zero-based budgeting for these purposes. Every program was required to start from zero and justify every expense. No program could actually operate when so much of its manpower had to be devoted to developing budgets from nothing, as opposed to simply noting changes in already existing budgets. The attempt to control the federal bureaucracy through planning and budgeting was not a notorious success.

Process

An administration or Congress will reorganize not only to increase efficiency, but also to emphasize that it will be active in certain program areas and will institutionally protect various interests against the possible absence of goodwill from the President or OMB (see Reading 2–4). Reorganization is not only a process of expanding the number and types of interests that have access to the federal bureaucracy; it is also an attempt to control the activities of those interests, and of the federal bureaucracy itself, so that they are not totally inconsistent with the political objectives of the President. One can see this in the Price Reports statement (Reading 2–3) that reorganization should be designed not only to increase efficiency in government, but also to bring about the policy ends of the executive branch.

Both Johnson and Nixon attempted this, although in somewhat different directions. Johnson suggested HUD and the Department of Transportation to forward his policy goals in those areas. Nixon attempted to reorganize the Office of President and created OMB in order to get a better handle on the professional groups that dominated policy formation in the various cabinet departments. He and his principal aides succeeded in keeping staff appointments to the domestic council outside the civil service and providing that the staff director of the council would not be available for questioning by Congress, on the grounds that the domestic council is advisory to the President only (see Reading 2–5). The domestic council and OMB obviously represent attempts to centralize the planning and evaluation of programs across executive departments. What gets put into the budget and evaluated as successful is that which serves the administration's policy ends.

Nixon tried to interrupt the flow of finances and communications between organized constituency groups and elements of the federal bureaucracy in order to lessen the power of interest group professionals and federal bureaucrats over the implementation and interpretation of policy. He also attempted to eliminate the professional dominance over program planning and budgeting within the departments, particularly those that were somewhat "expert-controlled," such as HEW. He wanted budgeting and program evaluation to be consistent with the political objectives of his administration and, thus, the will of the electorate. The creation of OMB in particular facilitated central management of budgets and evaluations. It did not, however, prevent Congress from overwhelmingly passing constituency-oriented legislation that funded programs inconsistent with budgets proposed by OMB. Up until 1972, when he had to run for reelection, Nixon signed much of this legislation. Federal spending on middle-class-oriented domestic programs rose more rapidly between 1968 and 1972 than during any other four-year period in recent American history.

Nixon also attempted to redesign the departments of Agriculture, Commerce, Labor, and Transportation by distributing their functions around more goal-oriented departments: Community Development, Economic Affairs, Human Resources and Natural Resources. The efficiency arguments in favor of such a reorganization were well presented; however, congresspeople and their constituencies were unenthusiastic about it because they would have to alter their pattern of interactions with bureaus of the executive branch. None of the changes were enacted (Seidman, 1976, pp. 111–15).

Decentralization was another way the executive attempted to control the connections among interests and federal bureaus and the organized expertise of professionals. Under Nixon this strategy was labeled the "new federalism" (see Reading 2–6). It consisted of a number of fiscal measures, including the use of a negative income tax in lieu of the federal component of the welfare system (see Chapter 6); the use of federal revenue sharing; and the initiation of some of the earliest of the federal block grants: the Comprehensive Employment and Training Act of 1973 and the Community Development Block Act portion of the Housing and Community Development Act of 1974 (see Chapter 4). The purpose of revenue sharing is not only to break the control of the federal bureaucracy over the implementation of federally funded programs, but also to keep Congress from targeting monies to constituencies on the basis of electoral need. Taken together, these moves were to strengthen the Office of the President by lessening the roles of professionals in the federal bureaucracy and the ties among interest groups, federal agencies, and congressional committees. From 1971 to 1974 Nixon also attempted to impound federal funds committed to a number of programs, including highways (see Chapter 4). Under court review these attempts eventually failed. At the same time, they created serious ill-will in Congress, which may have had some bearing on its willingness to consider impeachment after the Watergate revelations. Congresspeople do not like the executive tampering with its mechanisms for ensuring incumbency.

The Nixon reorganization initiatives failed in part because Congress resisted them, in part because revenue sharing depended upon an uncertain congressional willingness to maintain a long-term flow of funds to lower levels of government, and in part because Nixon's presidency came to an abrupt end. In retrospect, the limits of revenue sharing are clear. Although Congress may enact it and local legislatures may enthusiastically support it, revenue sharing does not provide continually new electorally relevant benefits to targeted congressional constituencies.

To expedite legislative action and yet provide some congressional control over the consequent regulations and administrative procedures, Congress often used the one- and two-house veto in the 1970s. It adopted a one-house veto over the General Services Administration's regulations on Nixon's papers in 1974, a one-house veto over regulations issued by the Federal Energy Commission in 1976, and a two-house veto over Federal Trade Commission rules in 1980 and many others. Congress never passed a general statute giving it a veto over all regulations made pursuant to legislation. Some of these vetoes were incorporated into legislation in response to excessively independent rule making within the Nixon White House; others accompanied legislation giving powers to federal administrators that were unimaginable without the veto.

Two apparently significant pieces of legislation in the 1970s represented congressional or public interest responses to the reorganization activities of the federal government: the Legislative Reorganization Act of 1970 and the Sunset Act of 1976. The latter, as one congressional staffer describes it, merely means that every two years he has to go through several thousand pieces of legislated authorizations, which may have no appropriations attached to them, to see where they stand. He can say, when a piece of legislation needs reauthorization, whether there is money involved in the program or not. To gauge the real congressional sentiment concerning sunset laws, one need only look at the proposed 1979 Sunset Act, which would have included a periodic review of all the exemptions in the federal tax code. Although the bill received considerable attention, it never passed. Tax benefits and exemptions are a primary conduit through which Congress provides attributable benefits, particularly to districts.

The Legislative Reauthorization Act of 1970 was not a dramatic innovation in legislative democracy; it codified what had always been the case. Committee chairs in positions of leadership have never been chosen only on the basis of seniority. When seniority produced conflict or interfered with legislative needs, it was in the selection process that parties used to organize their committee structure. Although it caused some inconvenience to Democratic party organization, the bill did not change the fact that competent senior incumbents took leadership roles in the House.

Consequences

During the 1970s Congress gave greater rule-making power to the bureaucracy, but concurrently devised a tool to withdraw that power selectively: the legislative veto. In addition to the one- and two-house vetoes mentioned above, Congress instituted the committee veto. Since the major work of Congress occurred in committees and subcommittees (see Chapter 1), why take everyone's time overseeing administrative regulations? Let those most concerned with the regulation—the members of the committee that originated the legislation—exercise the oversight and veto function. In doing this, Congress was acting in the interests of both the executive and its own members. It continued to track and control funds that went to states and localities by increasing its own support staff. However, when cutting benefits became necessary, Congress was willing to legislate block grants that devolved onto the states decisions as to who should not receive benefits. Organized voters often support those who provide them with benefits; they always oppose those who take benefits away.

The creation of support staff for Congress helped rectify the executive branch's near monopoly of program information. In order to deal with continued executive initiatives Congress increased its capacity to deal with the federal agencies and the federal budget, principally through the Congressional Budget and Impoundment Control Act of 1974. Concurrent with the Nixon resignation, this act attempted to deal with executive control of funds and to force upon Congress a budgetary regimen that would provide information about, if not control over, how monies were spent (see Reading 2–7). The control aspect of the law provided for an initial congressional budgetary statement in March and April for the fiscal year that began the following October 1. The act provided for a second budget statement in June and for authorizations and appropriations to be completed before September 30. Congress has almost never met this deadline. Contrary to the intent of the bill, nothing more specific than a continuing resolution is passed until after the budgetary year begins on October 1. It is not uncommon for the new budget to be detailed only after the first three or four months of the budgetary year have passed. These first few months are usually covered by a continuing resolution. This means that domestic programs are funded on a quarterly or month-by-month basis to the extent that they were funded in the preceding fiscal year. This process tends to frustrate attempts to contract total budgetary outlays on domestic programs. Congress will not pass legislation to recapture money that has been allocated even if it passes legislation that will for the remainder of the fiscal year reduce the quarterly allocations.

The reason for seeking control of presidential impoundment is clear. After several Presidents who either hesitated or simply refused to spend money for programs they did not approve of, Congress authorized legislation that limited presidential impoundment for the purpose of fiscal control to six months.

Congress also authorized the establishment of the Congressional Budget Office in 1974 and the General Accounting Office in 1977. Both agencies were politically neutral bodies intended to audit and project federal budget expenditures in a reasonably nonpartisan manner and offer Congress independent expertise on budgetary considerations. These two offices have probably been most successful in counteracting the excessively optimistic or pessimistic budgetary projections of the federal agencies and the Office of the President. As leveling agents they have certainly provided warrant for members of Congress who share party membership with the President to express doubt about, and in some cases vote against, presidential budget initiatives. During the Johnson and Nixon administrations, the period of both the Vietnam War and the expansion of domestic spending, this capacity simply did not exist. Congresspeople were without information about the effects of defense and domestic spending.

In each year of the Ford, Carter, and Reagan administrations, the amounts appropriated for general revenue sharing increased less than the rate of inflation or even decreased sharply. Simply throwing money to localities—for example, through the passage in 1981–82 of nine block grants to state governments—offers no incumbency advantages. The nine grants in areas ranging from maternal and child care and health to education (see Chapters 3 and 5), were area-specific, making it somewhat easier for Congress to track what happened to former beneficiaries of programs financed by the block grants. Additionally, as one congressional staffer put it, "Under the sunset legislation of 1976 I had to investigate the activities of 7,000 grants; when some of these are block-granted, my task is a lot easier."

In addition to their decentralizing function, the block grants were a device for cutting the budget when federal revenues failed to up with projections. The average amounts allocated in the first year of the block grants were 24 percent less than the total funds spent for the consolidated programs in the preceding year. As might be expected, the block grants had some strings (see Reading 2–8). State legislatures and executives quickly discovered that although passing out new funds was exciting, passing out lower funds was a political liability. According to one survey, twenty-one state legislatures initially attempted to assume responsibility for the allocation of block grants so far as was allowed by law. Within a year, none wanted such explicit control. Rather, allocations were determined by formulas or negotiation by bureaucrats at the state level in a process several stages removed from electoral politics. The obvious reason was that the block grants represented lesser money or a lower level of services for beneficiaries. No member of Congress suffered the consequences of decreased funds to a particular constituency.

The block grants thus accommodate the needs of both the President and Congress, very much as the legislative veto did. The latter, however, has been upset by the aggressive use of the courts by the Reagan administration. In 1982 the District of Columbia Court of Appeals struck down a one-house veto of Federal Energy Regulatory Commission regulations, a two-house veto of Federal Trade Commission regulations, and a committee veto of HUD reorganization plans. In 1983 the Supreme Court declared the one-house legislative veto unconstitutional for reasons that would be sufficient to make the two-house and committee vetoes unconstitutional as well.

These court decisions can be viewed as an attempt by the executive to gain back the control over federal program spending lost, in the aftermath of Nixon's resignation, with the passage of the Congressional Budget and Impoundment Control Act (see Reading 2–7). Nixon had ignored the accommodations involving impoundments and legislative vetoes that had evolved over the three previous decades. In attempting to reassert control over how much federal monies would be spent and what groups would benefit, the Reagan administration moved to a more defensible variant of the same kind of presidential policymaking.

Court cases do not determine the outcome of legislative-executive bargaining over policy; they only set the framework within which bargaining is possible. The effect of any one court case involving the constitutionality of legislation or administration may be to strengthen the capacity of either branch to determine policy. Yet almost all policies are decided, not by courts, but by bargaining among Congress, the President, the bureaucracy, and organized interests (see Chapter 1). Even the constitutional context for such bargaining involves some degree of balance between the advantages of the executive and of Congress: a federal district court ruled in May, 1966 that presidential impoundment of program funds under the Congressional Budget and Impoundment Control Act is unconstitutional, since Congress would never have given the President impoundment powers if its members had thought that they would not have a legislative veto over the use of such powers (see Reading 2–8).

Presidents and Congress use federal reorganization to respond or symbolically respond to the needs of newly emerging pressure groups. In some cases the Executive, President Nixon in particular, attempted to use federal reorganization to limit the influence of organized professional bureaucrats in the budgetary process. After requiring the executive to produce a budget, Congress has provided itself with an independent institutional input into the federal budgeting process. Like the Tax

Code, institutional reorganization is one of the less known tools for benefitting constituency interests or introducing control over the impact of constituency interests in federal legislative and bureaucratic processes. However the effects of reorganization should not be overestimated. Congress has almost never allowed reorganization of the Executive branch to the extent that it uncoupled the congressional committees and subcommittees from the agencies that provide services to constituents located in the congressional districts of members of those same committees. Congress has acted independently, particularly in 1946 and a lesser extent in 1970 and 1974 to reorganize itself and to increase institutional capacity to handle information. This is done so that Congress can continue to provide constituency benefits, so as to maximize the probability of incumbency for all members.

Even in the details of block grant legislation, we can see that Congress is somewhat unwilling to let go of all strings. Almost all of the nine block grants passed in 1981–82 contained some conditions that ensured continued funding of favored local-level service providers. As time went on the block grants assumed even more strings (see Reading 2-9). An endless cycle of reform and revision dominates the way Congress apprpriates funds. When program-specific legislation has been reauthorized a number of times, it becomes sufficiently broad in scope that to shift to a qualified block grant with strings is a conceptually difficult move for Congress. This is particularly true when one needs to mask funding reduction in times of fiscal austerity. Yet the block grants over time assume the characteristics of normal, targeted, programmatic legislation as conditions are added with each yearly cyle of appropriations.

We have seen the forces that drive the evolution of federal policies and the institutions within which these policies are made. As technology and the economy change, the interests that try to use the public sector to displace the costs or risks involved in their own activities change also. None leave the political area, but others are added. Paralleling the evolution of interests is the evolution of the institutions that formulate and carry out policies. This change makes the incorporation of new interests easier and provides the context within which the different branches of the federal government attempt to respond to these interests. Yet a few basic features of political institutions remain constant. The close tie between the congressional committee or subcommittee and the implementing federal agency, in particular seems to survive institutional and electoral changes. Subsequent chapters will lay out the distinctive features of federal policy formation, evolution, and current practice in a number of dissimilar policy areas. Although the details will vary, the constancy of policy evolution and form will be apparent throughout.

Readings

2-1. LIMITS ON THE REORGANIZATION POWERS
OF THE PRESIDENCY

The Reorganization Act of 1949 (P.L. 81–109) as reauthorized is still in effect. Literally dozens of reorganization proposals have been sent to Congress under this act and its successors. The work attendant to reorganization is done by the executive; Congress merely looks at the proposals to see whether they affect the relationships among congressional committees, federal bureaus, and interest groups organized at the level of the congressional district. The heart of the Reorganization Act is Section 5, which has the effect of limiting presidentially ordered spending incentives and executive department consolidations. Under Section 5, for example, a president cannot abolish the Department of Education by consolidating its functions with those of another department. Later amendments to the Act guarded even more closely the tie between congressional committees and agencies.

Need for Reorganizations

Sec. 2 (a) The President shall examine and from time to time reexamine the organization of all agencies of the Government and shall determine what changes therein are necessary to accomplish the following purposes:

(1) to promote the better execution of the laws, the more effective management of the executive branch of the Government and of its agencies and function, and the expeditious administration of the public business;

(2) to reduce expenditures and promote economy, to the fullest extent consistent with the efficient operation of the Government;

(3) to increase the efficiency of the operations of the Government to the fullest extent practicable;

(4) to group, coordinate and consolidate agencies and functions of the Government, as nearly as may be, according to major purposes;

(5) to reduce the number of agencies by consolidating those having similar functions under a single head, and to abolish such agencies or functions thereof as may not be necessary for the efficient conduct of the Government; and

(6) to eliminate overlapping and duplication of effort.

(b) The Congress declares that the public interest demands the carrying out of the purposes specified in subsection (a) and that such purposes may be accomplished in great measure by proceeding under the provisions of this Act, and can be accomplished more speedily thereby than by the enactment of specific legislation. . . .

Limitations on Powers with Respect to Reorganizations

Sec. 5 No reorganization plan shall provide for, and no reorganization under this Act shall have the effect of—

(1) abolishing or transferring an executive department or all the functions thereof or consolidating any two or more executive departments or all the functions thereof; or

(2) continuing any agency beyond the period authorized by law for its existence or beyond the time when it would have terminated if the reorganization had not been made; or

(3) continuing any function beyond the period authorized by law for its exercise, or beyond the time when it would have terminated if the reorganization had not been made; or

(4) authorizing any agency to exercise any function which is not expressly authorized by law at the time the plan is transmitted to the Congress; or

(5) increasing the term of any office beyond that provided by law for such office; or

(6) transferring to or consolidating with any other agency the municipal government of the District of Columbia or all those functions

thereof which are subject to this Act, or abolishing said government or all said functions.

Taking Effect of Reorganizations

Sec. 6 (1) Except as may be otherwise provided pursuant to subsection (c) of this section, the provisions of the reorganization plan shall take effect upon the expiration of the first period of sixty calendar days, of continuous session of Congress, following the date on which the plan is transmitted to it; but only if, between the date of transmittal and the expiration of such sixty-day period there has not been passed by the two Houses a concurrent resolution stating in substance that the Congress does not favor the reorganization plan. (63 Stat. 203)

2-2. CONGRESSIONAL DISAPPROVAL OF A REORGANIZATION PLAN*

This is the format that Congress uses to disapprove of executive reorganizations proposed by the President. In effect, Congress refuses the consolidation of the Office of Defense Mobilization and the Federal Civil Defense Administration. Following the disapproval are excerpts from the Eisenhower reorganization message and from Senator Herbert Humphrey's comments on the reorganization.

S. Res. 297, 85th Congress, 2nd Session.

RESOLVED That the Senate does not favor the Reorganization Plan No. 1 of 1958 transmitted to Congress on April 24, 1958.

H. Doc. No. 375, 85th Congress, 2nd session. Reorganization Plan No. 1 of 1958

Message from the President of the United States Transmitting Reorganization Plan No. 1 of 1958, Providing New Arrangements for the Conduct of Federal Defense Mobilization and Civil Defense Functions

To the Congress of the United States:

I transmit herewith Reorganization Plan No. 1 of 1958, prepared in accordance with the Reorganization Act of 1949, as amended. The re-

*From hearings before a subcommittee of the committee on Governmental Operations in the United States Senate. Washington D.C., U.S. Government Printing Office 1958.

organization plan provides new arrangements for the conduct of the Federal defense mobilization and civil defense functions.

In formulating Reorganization Plan No. 1, I have had the benefit of several studies made by the executive branch as well as those conducted by the Congress. The reorganization plan will overcome the major difficulties revealed by those studies mentioned in my 1959 budget message where I made the following statement:

"The structure of the Federal organization for planning, coordination, and conduct of our nonmilitary defense programs has been reviewed, and I have concluded that the existing statutes assigning responsibilities for central coordination and direction of these programs are out of date. The rapid technical advances of military science have led to a serious overlap among agencies carrying on these leadership and planning functions. Because the situation will continue to change and because these functions transcend the responsibility of any one department or agency, I have concluded that they should be vested in no one short of the President. I will make recommendations to the Congress on this subject."

. . . . .

Senator Humphrey: Now whether each Member agrees about the depth of concern, the majority of the Congress wants to restrict the Office of Education; that is, we are not looking for a Federal education program per se. The majority of the Congress wants to make sure that the United States Public Health Service performs to the letter of the law the duties that are there and does not venture off into unchartered areas of highly controversial social practice.

Now the same thing is true for at least one Member of the Congress in reference to this reorganization plan.

I say that if in the Reorganization Plan No. 1 of 1953, you could provide for the Office of Education, United States Public Health Service and the Commissioner of Social Security, that you can have something in Reorganization Plan No. 1 of 1958 that provides to see to it that the Office of Civil Defense, for example, does not lose its identity.

I know my State. I am also close to my people. Senator Thurmond knows his State. Senator Martin knows his state. I was mayor of my city of Minneapolis and I know how long it takes to build up a civil defense organization, then all at once you just behead the king, you say, "Well, we've got sort of a regency appointed here. We have a new kind of leadership."

People ask, "Who really runs this show?" The Government is getting so big anyway, it is hard for people to keep track of it. I think there needs to be in this reorganization plan some assurance that you are not going to lose the identity of what we have known as civil defense activity, we need to have Mr. Big, whatever his name is, so when Mr. Herbert Schoen, director of civil defense in the state of Minnesota, appointed by the Governor, confirmed by the legislature, comes to Washington, he doesn't have to go to the Bureau of the Budget. I want him to go to somebody, I say that most respectfully, I want him to go to somebody who runs something.

2-3. JUSTIFICATION FOR EXECUTIVE REORGANIZATION*

The following excerpt from the Price Report speaks for itself. Reorganization is justified on grounds of efficiency rather than political considerations. Notice that the report recommends a Department of Education. By 1980 three of the new government departments recommended—Housing and Urban Development, Transportation, and Education—had been created.

The primary issue of organization, as we see it during your next term, is how to focus the efforts of the Government, and the attention of the country on the purpose of building the Great Society. This must be done in a way which also assures that the public will receive full value for its tax dollars.

During the past two decades, we concentrated our national attention on problems of defense and international affairs. And we did so, we learned four big lessons in Government administration, which we may now apply to the domestic problems of this Nation:

(1) Government need no longer maintain a distant relationship with private institutions and corporations; it may enlist them in full cooperation, while taking care to maintain responsible control of policy and programs. (2) Research and education are likely to be the key to new

*Report of the President's task force on Governmental Reorganization, Public Paper available in the Lyndon B. Johnson Papers at the University of Texas.

policy developments and new domestic policy opportunities. (3) Most important programs require the cooperation of two or more departments and agencies and such teamwork requires, among other things, (a) the use of Presidential staff agencies, and (b) a system for higher personnel that assures responsiveness to new policy and program objectives. (4) Effective, economical, and responsible Executive organization depends on the full cooperation of the Congress; internal Congressional organization and procedures can support or frustrate Presidential responsibility.

In order to apply these lessons to the organization of domestic programs, it is not necessary to set up another so-called Hoover Commission. In fact, that would be a mistake. The unhappy experience of the Eisenhower Administration with the second Hoover Commission shows that the planning of organizations should be done within the circle of your responsible advisers—especially in the Bureau of the Budget and the rest of the Executive Office.

We recommend the creation of five new Executive Departments, each of which would make a significant contribution to the attainment of our national goals.

1. Department of Transportation; and a Transportation Regulatory Commission

A healthy economy in a private enterprise system requires an effective system of transportation, in which all elements develop in balance, each taking full advantage of technological progress. We have not developed such a system in part because the Federal Government, by dealing with various forms of transportation through separate agencies, has made it difficult to develop a coherent policy or rational balance. To achieve a measure of "decontrol" with less regulation and less subsidy, we need unity of policy and more consistency in our various methods of regulation. We therefore recommend

(a) *a new department of Transportation,* to administer all functions (other than economic regulation) relating to the major forms of land, sea, and air transportation:

(1) the agencies or functions concerned with promotion, subsicy, service and safety regulation; i.e., the Bureau of Public Roads, the Maritime Administration, the Coast Guard, and the Federal Aviation Agency, the safety and car service activities of the ICC, and

the subsidy functions of the CAB: and whatever may be needed in the way of policy or planning staff to deal with problems relating to the railroads.

(2) Other agencies and functions, e.g., the Alaska Railroad, the Panama Canal Company (and the Canal Zone Government), the St. Lawrence Seaway Development Corporation, and the Great Lakes Pilotage Administration.

(b) a new Transportation Regulatory Commission, to include the economic regulation functions of

(1) the Interstate Commerce Commission,
(2) the Federal Maritime Commission, and
(3) the Civil Aeronautics Board. . . .

2. Department of Education

. . . Because the schools have been afraid of the Federal domination, the Government has never had a comprehensive policy for the advancement of education and research. But it is unrealistic to think that we can protect the freedom of education by pretending to ignore it. We need to organize in a manner that will simultaneously

—facilitate our understanding of the effect of Federal actions on the education and research institutions of the Nation;
—help distinguish between broad policy decisions regarding financial support, which must be controlled by responsible Federal officials and by law, and subordinate decisions regarding the educational or scientific merit of projects, institutions, or individuals. (The latter decisions can and should be made with the participation of educational and research leaders in such a way that everyone will know that the Federal Government is not intruding politically on academic freedom.)

Our present excessive dispersion of organization has helped to bring about an *unsound balance* between

(a) *higher education and elementary and secondary education* . . . ;
(b) *the sciences and other areas of learning:* our emphasis on research project grants for military and space purposes has led to disproportionate emphasis on technology by comparison with the humanities and the social sciences;

(c) *research and teaching:* we are flooding the university laboratories with money, while neglecting, by comparison, the teaching side of education at all levels.

We therefore recommend the creation of the Department of Education. We do not believe that it should be the only channel by which aid is given to educational and research institutions. Every major agency will need to have its own programs of research and education, and many will need the support for basic research. But a Department is warranted in order to help deal with the fundamental policies of aid to the State and private institutions and to the general advancement of knowledge as the basis of national progress.

3. Department of Housing and Community Development

The Nation is now too heavily urbanized to put all Federal programs affecting cities in a single department. A Department of Housing and Community Development should be constituted under which would be administered major programs relating to the physical development of our towns and cities, especially in metropolitan areas, and other programs for raising the quality and quantity of our housing. . . .

The proposed department would include the following programs and functions:

(a) All those now in HHFA (including housing, urban renewal, and other community development functions). (b) The functions of the Federal Home Loan Bank board (including direction of the Federal Savings and Loan Insurance Corporation, but *only* if it is feasible to replace the present Board with a single administrator appointed by the Secretary or to make the Secretary Chairman of the Board. (c) The housing loan and guarantee functions of the Veterans' Administration. Home loans, loans for housing the elderly, and loans for the construction of community water supply systems from the Farmers' Home Administration. Grants for the construction of waste treatment facilities from the Department of Health, Education and Welfare.

4. Department of Economic Development

. . . A program [to develop the economy] will require extensive collaboration among various Departments and agencies, but it should be led by the principal Executive Department that is concerned with the general economic development of the Nation.

For this reason, we recommend the creation of a Department of Economic Development.

5. Department of Natural Resources

The unique American system of agricultural education and research, plus the conservation and development of our land and water resources, have helped to make the Nation highly productive. But this productivity has been accompanied by the wasteful use of resources, by continuing rural poverty, by pollution of our water and atmosphere, and by the destruction of natural beauty. . . .

We therefore recommend the creation of a Department of Natural Resources, which would be a merger of parts of Agriculture and Interior, together with the aspects of civil functions of the Army Engineers that pertain to resource development.

2-4. THE POLITICAL PURPOSES
BEHIND BUREAUCRATIC CHANGE*

In the following excerpts from hearings before the Senate Committee on Government Affairs, the list of witnesses commenting on the proposed Department of Education indicates the beneficiary groups: educators. The testimony of Ernest Boyer, commissioner of education, and the excerpt from the bill itself reveal that the purpose of the department is to institutionalize the federal concern for education independent of the goodwill of the President or the Office of the President. At the same time it is carefully stated that the states' power over education will not be intruded upon.

Witnesses

Tuesday, February 6, 1979

Rev. Jesse Jackson, president, Operation PUSH, accompanied by Dr. Thurmond Evans, bureau chief in Washington, and James Demus, head of the Education Department, from Chicago; Dr. Craig A. Phillips, North Carolina State Superintendent of Public Instruction, and president, Council of Chief State School Officers; Lucille Maurer, delegate,

*Hearings Before the Committee on Government Affairs, U.S. Senate, 96th Congress, Sess., Feb. 6, 8, 1979.

State of Maryland Assembly, representing the National Conference of State Legislatures; Linda Albert, president, New Jersey School Boards Association, representing National School Boards Association; Henrik N. Dullea, assistant secretary to Governor Hugh Carey for education and the arts, representing the National Governors Association and education commission of the States; Joanne Goldsmith, member, Maryland State Board of Education, representing National Association of State Boards of Education; Richard Fulton, mayor, Nashville, Tennessee; Frank Lewis, chairman, executive board, Nebraska State Legislature; Dr. Ralph Steffek, treasurer, National Association of Administrators of State and Federal Education Programs, accompanied by Betty A. Colden, president, Michigan Association of State and Federal Program Specialists; and Rex C. Fortune, Jr., chairperson, National Alliance of Black School Educators. . . .

Thursday, February 8, 1979

James T. McIntyre, Jr., Director, Office of Management and Budget, accompanied by Harrison Wellford, Executive Associate Director for Reorganization and Management; Patricia Gwaltney, Deputy Associate Director for Human Resource Organization Studies; Dr. Mary F. Berry, Assistant Secretary for Education, Department of Health, Education and Welfare; Dr. Ernest Boyer, U.S. Commissioner of Education; and Dr. Patricia Albjerg Graham, Director, National Institute of Education.

Testimony of Ernest Boyer

Chairman Ribicoff: Dr. Boyer, you are an outstanding educator. You serve with distinction as Commissioner of Education. It is my understanding you will be leaving soon, too?

Dr. Boyer: Senator, I will assume the presidency of the Carnegie Foundation for the Advancement of Teaching in January 1980.

Chairman Ribicoff: I am pleased, too, with your cooperation with the President and Secretary Califano in their commitment. But yet I have read your statement that you are concerned with the structure of the Commissioner of Education, Education in HEW, like most of us are. I wonder if you could share with us some of your thinking about the problem of the structure of education in HEW, and how it would be better for education to have a separate department.

Dr. Boyer: Senator, I have come to the conviction that a separate department is in the interest of education and it is not a conviction that I felt strongly when I assumed the commissionership in January 1977. My reasons are as follows:

First, education is profoundly important as a central function in this country. It needs to be given the status and recognition it merits. One in every four persons in this country is involved in education. It has a budget over $127 billion. This democracy is driven by education, and not to have it participate in the councils of government and in formulation of our priorities seems to me to be a dramatic oversight in recognizing such an essential function of our society.

I should point out that we create Cabinet level offices, not because their programs are controlled from Washington, but because they represent the priorities in our society. Labor, Commerce, Transportation, all of these are carried out in a variety of ways, both public and private. They have participated in the Cabinet level because they are of such importance in our democracy.

Coming to the organizational question, I am convinced that a separate Department would add greater administrative effectiveness to the management of the educational programs that now exist. It has already been stated that within HEW we have four or five separate units that have central education purposes. Even with the splendid leadership of secretary Califano and the great ability of Secretary Berry, it is very clear that the coordination within HEW is difficult. Lines of authority are not clear. HEW has line and staff relationships that are not obscure. That leaves out the issue of education activities beyond HEW. It is my judgment that the current organizational arrangement is not efficient, and that greater administrative clarity would in fact lead to efficiency and effectiveness in management. . . .

I should add one final point. I have personally been extremely well supported in my work as Commissioner. I have not had during my tenure as Commissioner the kinds of frustrations that other Commissioners have testified to. Secretary Califano has given full support to education, as has the President.

On the other hand, I have come to the conclusion that my satisfactory experience in the job has been the result of the attitudes of the Secretary and the President. I do not believe that education should be the result of the friendliness or the unfriendliness of the supervisor in that given Department. I believe that it merits its own stature and should be given that recognition. For these reasons, Mr. Chairman, I endorse the proposal of President Carter to form a new Department of Education.

A Bill to Establish a Department of Education

Be it enacted by the Senate and the House of Representatives of the United States of America in Congress assembled, That this Act may be cited as the "Department of Education Organization Act of 1979."

Sec. 101. The Congress declares that—

(1) education is fundamental to the growth and achievement of the Nation;

(2) there is a continual need to provide equal access to education for all Americans;

(3) the primary responsibility for education has in the past, and must continue in the future, to reside with State, local and tribunal governments, public and nonpublic educational institutions, communities, and families;

(4) in our Federal system, the primary responsibility for education is reserved respectively to the States and to their diverse instrumentalities;

(5) the dispersion of education programs across a large number of Federal agencies has led to the fragmented, duplicative, and often inconsistent Federal policies relating to education;

(6) there is a lack of coordination of Federal resources for State, local and tribunal governments and public and nonprofit educational institutions;

(7) Presidential and public consideration of issues relating to education is hindered by the present organizational position of education programs in the executive branch of the Government;

(8) the importance of education is increasing as new technologies and alternative approaches to traditional education are considered, as society becomes more complex, and as equal opportunities in education and employment are promoted; and

(9) therefore, it is in the public interest and general welfare of the United States to establish a Department of Education.

State and Local Responsibilities for Education

Sec. 103. It is the intention of the Congress in the creation of the Department of Education to protect the rights of State, local and tribunal governments and public and nonpublic education institutions in the areas of educational policies, administration of programs, competency testing, and selection of curricula and program content, and to strengthen and improve the direction of such governments and institutions over their educational programs and policies.

2-5. MAKING THE BUREAUCRACY RESPONSIVE TO THE PRESIDENT*

Reorganization Plan No. 2 of 1970 created the Domestic Advisory Council and changed the Bureau of the Budget into the Office of Management and Budget. As the following excerpts indicate, both agencies—and especially OMB—were intended to coordinate and evaluate all executive department programs. OMB is no longer merely a budget preparatory body, but a means by which the executive attempts to obtain control over programs voted by Congress.

To the Congress of the United States [from the President]:

We in government often are quick to call for reform in other institutions, but slow to reform ourselves. Yet nowhere today is modern management more needed than in government itself.

In 1939, President Franklin D. Roosevelt proposed and the Congress accepted a reorganization plan that laid the groundwork for providing managerial assistance for a modern Presidency.

The plan placed the Bureau of the Budget within the Executive Office of the President. It made available to the President direct access to important new management instruments. The purpose of the plan was to improve the administration of the Government—to ensure that the Government could perform "promptly, effectively, without waste or lost motion."

Over the three decades, the Executive Office of the President has mushroomed but not by conscious design. In many areas it does not provide the kind of staff assistance and support the President needs in order to deal with the problems of government in the 1970s. We confront the 1970s with a staff organization geared in large measure to the tasks of the 1940s and 1950s.

One result, over the years, has been a tendency to enlarge the immediate White House staff, that is, the President's personal staff, as distinct from the institutional structure—to assist with management functions for which the President is responsible. This has blurred the distinction between personal staff and management institutions; it has left key management functions to be performed only intermittently and some not at all. It has perpetuated outdated structures.

*Reorganization Plan No 2 of 1970, 84 Stat 2085 5U56, Appendix

Another result has been, paradoxically, to inhibit the delegation of authority to Departments and agencies.

A President whose programs are carefully coordinated, whose information system keeps him adequately informed, and whose organizational assignments are plainly set out, can delegate authority with security and confidence. A President whose office is deficient in these respects will be inclined, instead, to retain close control of operating responsibilities which he cannot and should not handle. . . .

Essentially, the plan recognizes that two closely connected but basically separate functions both center in the President's office: policy determination and executive management. This involves (1) what government should do, and (2) how it goes about doing it.

My proposed reorganization creates a new entity to deal with each of these functions:

—it establishes a Domestic Council to coordinate policy formulation in the domestic area. This Cabinet group would be provided with an institutional staff, and to a considerable degree would be the domestic part of the National Security Council.

—it establishes an Office of Management and Budget, which would be the President's principal arm for the exercise of his managerial functions.

The Domestic Council will be primarily concerned with what we do; the Office of Management and Budget will be primarily concerned with how we do it, and how well we do it. . . .

Office of Management and Budget

Under the reorganization plan, the technical and formal means by which the Office of Management and Budget is created is by re-designing the Bureau of the Budget as the Office of Management and Budget. The functions currently vested by law in the Bureau, or in its director, are transferred to the President with the provision that he can then re-delegate them.

As soon as the reorganization plan takes effect, I intend to delegate those statutory functions to the Director of the new Office of Management and Budget, including those under section 212 of the Budget and Accounting Act, 1921.

However, the creation of the Office of Management and Budget represents far more than a mere change of name for the Bureau of the

Budget. It represents a basic change in concept and emphasis, reflecting the broader management needs of the Office of the President.

The new Office will still perform the key function of assisting the President in the preparation of the annual Federal Budget and overseeing its execution. It will draw upon the skills and experience of an extraordinarily able and dedicated career staff developed by the Bureau of the Budget. But preparation of the budget as such will no longer be its dominant, overriding concern.

While the budget function remains a vital tool of management, it will be strengthened by the greater emphasis the new office will place on fiscal analysis. The budget function is only one of several important management tools that the President must now have. He must also have a substantially enhanced institutional staff capability in other areas of executive management—particularly in program evaluation and coordination, improvement of Executive Branch organization, information and management systems, and development of executive talent. Under this plan, strengthened capability in these areas will be provided partly through internal reorganization, and it will also require additional staff resources.

The new Office of Management and Budget will place much greater emphasis on the evaluation of program performance: on assessing the extent to which programs are actually achieving their intended results, and delivering the intended services to the intended recipients. This is needed on a continuing basis, not as a one time effort. Program evaluation will remain a function of the individual agencies as it is today. However, a single agency cannot fairly be expected to judge overall effectiveness in programs that cross agency lines—and the difference between agency and Presidential perspectives requires a capacity in the Executive Office to evaluate program performance whenever appropriate.

Significance of the Changes

The people deserve a more responsive and more effective Government. The times require it. The changes will help provide it.

Each reorganization included in the plan which accompanies this message is necessary to accomplish one or more of the purposes set forth in Section 901 (a) of Title 5 of the United States Code. In particular, the plan is responsive to Section 901 (a) (1), "to promote the better execution of laws, the more effective management of the Executive

Branch and of its agencies and functions, and the expeditious administration of the public business;" and Section 901 (a) (3), "to increase
the efficiency of the operation of the Government to the fullest extent
practicable."

2-6. ELIMINATING THE POWERS OF SPECIAL INTERESTS*

*These excerpts from Nixon's address on the New Federalism in 1969
are intended implement the themes expressed in the 1969 speech. The
initiative represent one yet another attempt to remove control of the
people's monies and federal programs from the hands of special interests and professionals, who are often found in the cabinet departments themselves.*

The New Federalism

Target: Reforms

Since taking office, one of my first priorities has been to repair the
machinery of government, to put it in shape for the 1970s. I have made
many changes designed to improve the functioning of the executive
branch. And I have asked Congress for a number of important structural
reforms; among others, a wide-ranging postal reform, a comprehensive
reform of the draft, a reform of unemployment insurance, a reform of
our hunger programs, a reform of the present confusing hodge-podge of
Federal grant-in-aid.

Last April 21, I sent Congress a message asking for a package of
major tax reforms, including both the closing of loopholes and the removal of more than 2 million low-income families from the tax rolls
altogether [negative income tax]. I am glad that Congress is now acting
on tax reform, and I hope the Congress will begin to act on the other
reforms that I have requested. . . .

During last year's election campaign, I often made a point that touch-
ed a responsive chord wherever I traveled.

I said that this Nation became great not because of what government
did for people, but because of what people did for themselves.

This new approach aims at helping the American people do more for

*From the Public Papers of the President of the United States, Richard Nixon, 1971,
Book 1, Washington D.C., Government Printing Office. 1971 pp. 637–644.

themselves. It aims at getting everyone able to work off welfare rolls and onto payrolls.

It aims at ending the unfairness in a system that has become unfair to the welfare recipient, unfair to the working poor, and unfair to the taxpayer.

This new approach aims to make it possible for people—wherever in America they live—to receive their fair share of opportunity. It aims to ensure that people receiving aid, and who are able to work, contribute their fair share of productivity.

This new approach is embodied in a package of four measures: First, a complete replacement of the present welfare system; second, a comprehensive new job training and placement program; third, a revamping of the Office of Economic Opportunity; and fourth, a start on the sharing of Federal Tax revenues with the States. . . .

Revenue Sharing

. . . For a third of a century, power and responsibility have flowed toward Washington, and Washington has taken for its own the best sources of revenue.

We intend to reverse this tide, and to turn back to the States a greater measure of responsibility—not as a way of avoiding problems, but as a better way of solving problems.

Along with this would go a share of Federal revenues. I shall propose to the Congress next week that a set portion of the revenues from Federal income taxes be remitted directly to the States, with a minimum of Federal restrictions on how those dollars are to be used, and with a requirement that a percentage of them be channeled through for the use of local governments.

The funds provided under this program will not be great in the first year. But the principle will have been established, and the amounts will increase as our budgetary situation improves.

This start on revenue sharing is a step toward what I call the New Federalism. It is a gesture of faith in America's State and local governments and in the principle of democratic self-government. . . .

Now these proposals will be controversial, just as any new program is controversial. They are also expensive. Let us face that fact frankly and directly.

The first-year costs of the new family assistance program, including the child care center and job training, would be $4 billion. I deliberated long and hard over whether we could afford such an outlay. I decided in favor of it for two reasons: First, because the costs will not begin until fiscal year 1971, when I expect the funds to be available within the budget; and second, because I concluded that this reform we cannot afford not to undertake. The cost of continuing the present system, in financial as well as human terms, is staggering if projected into the 1970s.

Revenue sharing would begin in the middle of fiscal 1971, at a half-year cost of a half billion dollars. This cuts into the Federal budget, but it represents relief for the equally hard-pressed States. It would help curb the rise in State and local taxes which are such a burden to millions of American families.

Overall, we would be spending more—in the short run—to help people who now are poor and who now are unready for work or unable to find work.

But I see it this way: Every businessman, every workingman knows what "start-up costs" are. They are a heavy investment made in early years in the expectation that they will more than pay for themselves in future years.

The investment in these proposals is a human investment; it also is a "start-up cost" in turning around our dangerous decline into welfarism in America. We cannot produce productive people with antiquated, wheezing, overloaded machine we now call the welfare system. . . .

[The new system] removes the present incentive for families to break apart and substitutes an incentive for families to stay together.

It removes the blatant inequities and injustices and indignities of the welfare system.

It establishes a basic Federal floor so that children in any State can have at least the minimum essentials of life.

Together, these measures cushion the impact of welfare costs on States and localities, many of which have found themselves in fiscal crises as costs have escalated.

They bring reason, order, and purpose into a tangle of overlapping prgrams, and show that Government can be made to work.

Poverty will not be defeated by a stroke of a pen signing a check, and it will not be reduced to nothing overnight with slogans or ringing exhortations.

Poverty is not only a state of income. It is also a state of mind, a state of health. Poverty must be conquered without sacrificing the will to work, for if we take the route of the permanent handout, the American character will itself be impoverished.

In my recent trip around the world, I visited countries in all stages of economic development; countries with different social systems, different economic systems, different political systems.

In all of them, however, I found that one event had caught the imagination of the people and lifted their spirits almost beyond measure: the trip of Apollo II to the moon and back. On that historic day, when the astronauts set foot on the moon, the spirit of Apollo truly swept through this world. It was a spirit of peace and brotherhood and adventure, a spirit that thrilled to the knowledge that man had dreamed the impossible, dared the impossible, and done the impossible.

Abolishing poverty, putting an end to dependency—like reaching the moon a generation ago—may seem to be impossible. But in the spirit of Apollo, we can lift our sights and marshal our best efforts. We can resolve to make this the year not that we reached the goal, but that we turned the corner—turned the corner from a dismal cycle of dependency toward a new birth of independence; from despair toward hope; from an ominously mounting impotence of government toward a new effectiveness of government, and toward a full opportunity for every American to share the bounty of this rich land.

Thank you and goodnight.

2-7. INCREASING EXECUTIVE AND LEGISLATIVE EFFICIENCY THROUGH IMPOUNDMENT

The Congressional Budget and Impoundment Control Act of 1974 (P.L. 93–344) limits the power of the President to impound funds for purposes of fiscal control. It is an attempt on the part of Congress to organize itself to deal expeditiously with the executive in determining the federal budget.

An Act

To establish a new congressional budget process; to establish a Committee on the Budget in each House; to establish a Congressional Budget Office; to establish a procedure providing congressional control over the impoundment of funds by the executive branch; and for other purposes.

Title 1 Short Titles

Sec 1. (a) Short titles—This Act may be cited as the "Congressional Budget and Impoundment Control Act of 1974." Titles I through IX may be cited as the "Impoundment Control Act of 1974."

Declaration of Purposes

Sec. 2. The Congress declares that it is essential—

(1) to assure effective congressional control over the budgetary process;
(2) to provide for the congressional determination each year of the appropriate level of Federal revenues and expenditures;
(3) to provide a system of impoundment control;
(4) to establish national budget priorities; and
(5) to provide for the furnishing of information by the executive branch in a manner that will assist the Congress in discharging its duties.

Title II—Congressional Budget Office

Establishment of Office

Sec. 201. (a) In General—

(1) There is established an office of the Congress to be known as the Congressional Budget Office (hereinafter in this title referred to as the "Office"). The Office shall be headed by a Director; and there shall be a Deputy Director who shall perform such duties as may be assigned to him by the Director and, during the absence or incapacity of the Director or during a vacancy in that office, shall act as Director. . . .

(d) Relationship to Executive Branch—The Director is authorized to secure information, data, estimates, and statistics directly from the various departments, agencies, and establishments of the executive branch of Government and the regulatory agencies and commissions of the Government. All such departments, agencies, establishments, and regulatory agencies and commissions shall furnish the Director any available material which he determines to be necessary in the performance of his duties and functions (other than material the disclosure of which would be a violation of law). The Director is also authorized, upon agreement with the head of any such department, agency, or establishment, or regulatory agency or commission to utilize its services, facilities, and personnel with or without reimbursement; and the head of each such department, agency, establishment, or regulatory agency or commission is authorized to provide the Office of such services, facilities, and personnel.

(e) Relationship to Other Agencies in Congress—In carrying out the duties and functions of the Office, and for the purposes of coordinating the operations of the Office with those of other congressional agencies with a view to utilizing most effectively the information, services, and capabilities of all such agencies in carrying out the various responsibilities assigned to each, the Director is authorized to obtain information, data, estimates, and statistics developed by the General Accounting Office, the Library of Congress, and the Office of Technology Assessment, and (upon agreement with them) to utilize their services, facilities, and personnel with or without reimbursement. The Comptroller General, the Librarian of Congress, and the Technology Assessment Board are authorized to provide the Office with the information, data, estimates, and statistics, and the services, facilities, and personnel referred to in the preceding sentence. (88 Stat. 297)

2-8. RECTIFYING THE BALANCE IN THE SEPARATION OF POWERS*

Ever anxious to advance the powers of the executive, the Reagan administration pursued the abolition of the single-house veto of administrative regulations in both the courts and the press. It was eventually successful: in 1983 the Supreme Court decided that the single-house veto was unconstitutional because it violated the principles of bicameralism and the constitutionally stipulated manner in which Congress must pass a bill and present it to the President. However, there is no reason to believe that Congress would delegate a large measure of power to the executive without a veto over the uses of that power. A federal judge recently agreed:

A federal district judge threw out a provision in a 1974 law that lets the president defer spending of funds appropriated by Congress.

*Stephen Wermiel and David Rogers, "Federal Judge Throws Out Provision Allowing President to Defer Spending," *Wall Street Journal,* May 19, 1986.

But Judge Thomas Jackson, who held the provision is unconstitutional, stayed his ruling indefinitely to permit the Reagan administration to appeal.

The provision lets the president defer budget expenditures, and in effect kill them, but permits either the House or the Senate to insist by a simple majority vote that the money be spent.

This procedure, known as a one-house legislative veto, was declared unconstitutional by the Supreme Court in 1983 in an unrelated case. The Supreme Court said the legislative veto turns the lawmaking process around. The Constitution says Congress may legislate by a simple majority but may override the president's veto only by a two-thirds majority.

The issue in the lawsuit was whether to simply strike the unconstitutional one-house veto from the law or to throw out the whole provision allowing the deferral. To decide that, the court had to answer the question of whether Congress would have given the president the authority to defer spending without retaining the control of the legislative veto.

Judge Jackson, who was appointed to the federal court by President Reagan in 1982, wrote, "It can be said with conviction that Congress would have preferred no statute to one without the one-house veto."

While the administration officials were still studying the ruling, a White House spokesman said, "We've long affirmed the president's authority to defer spending, and we continue to believe he can. We'll work to make sure our opinion is upheld."

The decision strengthens Congress's position in future budget negotiations with the administration and comes at a time when both houses already have approved fiscal 1982 spending plans that dramatically alter the priorities set by the president.

The deferral issue has been foremost a question for the House and Senate Appropriations Committees. At the urging of its appropriations panel, the House approved an amendment to a spending bill this month seeking to strip the president of his deferral authority under the 1974 law. The Senate version of the same bill doesn't include the House language, but the Senate Appropriations Committee last week chastised the administration and expressed sympathy for the House action.

A total of $24.7 billion in deferrals have been ordered by Mr. Reagan so far this fiscal year, but the fight with Congress centers on an estimated $4.9 billion that the administration acknowledges were made on policy, not efficiency, grounds. These include funds for the Economic

Development Administration, the Strategic Petroleum Reserve, and subsidized housing and community development programs. Mr. Reagan's broad use of the deferral power is unmatched except for one year under the Ford administration.

The lawsuit was filed by Democratic Reps. Bruce Morrison of Connecticut, Charles Schumer of New York, Barbara Boxer of California and Mike Lowry of Washington, by the National League of Cities and U.S. Conference of Mayors, and by the cities of New Haven, Conn., Seattle and Chicago. The suit was handled by the consumer-oriented Public Citizen Litigation Group.

Rep. Morrison said the decision is "a first step toward making clear that there is no back-door, line-item veto in the budget law. Congress didn't intend in 1974 to permit the president to sign appropriations law and then to pick and choose what he spends."

While the suit challenged the entire deferral process, it focused specifically on deferrals of housing aid for poor, handicapped and elderly people and on urban and community development funds that were deferred by President Reagan earlier this year.

"I think what happened . . . was a grab for power," Rep. Sidney Yates, a senior Democrat on the Appropriations Committee, said of the sweeping deferrals this year. The Illinois liberal said the House must pursue legislation limiting the president's power and not wait on a final resolution in the courts.

The ruling by Judge Jackson left intact other portions of the law that give the president the power to rescind budget authority for particular programs. The rescission authority requires the approval of both the House and Senate, and doesn't give the president the unilateral power that the deferral provisions created.

2-9. CONGRESS CANNOT RESIST TEMPTATION*

This reading describes the continued erosion of the block grant aspect of Chapter 2 of the Education Consolidation and Improvement Act (ECIA) of 1981. This block grant, like others, has become progressively more like targeted legislation, especially in its restrictions on the spending of funds.

*Anne Henderson, 'Strings Are Tied to Chapter 2," *Network*, Oct. 1984, p. 7.

The House Appropriations Committee approved a $200 million increase in Chapter 2, the Education Block Grant, requested by the Reagan Administration, but required that the additional funds be used only for identifiable projects to increase school effectiveness.

The measure was sponsored by Rep. Dave Obey (D-Wisc.), who said that if the limited funds available for education in the federal budget are to have any real impact in improving educational quality, the amount that states and local districts can use for administrative purposes must be capped.

Obey also sponsored an amendment approved by the Committee to prohibit states from using more than 10 percent of their total Chapter 2 grant for administration. "We know that a number of states are, by their own accounting, using nearly 20 percent of these funds to support state education bureaucracies. We know that in some states, the salaries of state employees have been transferred directly from state payrolls to this federal program simply because Congress and the Education Department have not demanded that more of the money go directly to the classroom where it is most needed."

One of the information sources on which the Committee relied was NCCE's [National Committee for Citizens in Education] interim report on Chapter 2, *No Strings Attached*. NCCE asked state Chapter 2 directors how state education agencies (SEAs) spent their funds (SEAs may keep up to 20 percent of the state's Chapter 2 grant), and published their response in our report. Of its share, the average SEA used 51.9 percent to strengthen its management capacity and 12.1 percent to administer the program. Most states kept the maximum of 20 percent allowed and spent less than 20 percent of that for services or grants to local districts. Obey commented that "we should not be in the business of expanding state payrolls beyond the levels their own state legislatures are willing to support."

The Obey amendment, if accepted by the Senate and not vetoed by the President, would mean that SEAs may not use more than 50 percent of their 20 percent share for administrative expenses, including "strengthening" activities.

Obey cited several abuses of state funds in making the case for his amendment. For example, he complained that Massachusetts used the block grant funds to install a computer system for the state, and that Missouri used its money to purchase home computers for members of the State Board of Education. New York transferred state education staff to the Chapter 2 payroll.

Although the amendment is opposed by the Council of Chief State School Officers and the National Association of State Boards of Education, congressional observers predict that it will become law later this fall.

3   Federal Involvement in Education

Traditionally and constitutionally, the provision of educational services has been a power reserved for the states and localities. Even within states, public education evolved first in very localized areas. Because of the primitive state of communication and transportation, it would probably be a misnomer even to refer to state educational systems until the middle or late nineteenth century. States had the right to organize public education—after all, local governments and legislatures, including school boards, are creations of and exist at the sufferance of state legislatures—but they had no reason to interfere with local schooling. The complex school districts in Boston and New York City represent the culmination of more than a century of efforts to establish free, public, and reasonably uniform education for all children in these urban areas (Katz, 1971).

The preeminently local character of public schools in the nineteenth century is probably responsible for the initial and continued dependence on the property tax for funding education. However, as the state became more involved in education, the funding base broadened to include statewide taxes. At present there is considerable variation in the extent to which schools across states are supported by property tax or such statewide taxes as income and sales tax. The states' share of nonfederal funds for public education has exceeded 50 percent only since 1979. If one excludes extreme cases like Hawaii, which has one school district, state (as opposed to locally derived) support for public education now ranges from about 20 percent to 85 percent of total costs.

Recently, many states have moved quickly to gain control over the curriculum and financing of schools. In this they have been aided by the evolution of state educational bureaucracies, sometimes supported by federal funding, and by the responsibility for both administering federal programs and responding to court challenges in the wake of the civil rights legislation of the 1960s. The real impetus for increased state activity came from federal activity rather than the other way around. Without legislative and judicial activity at the federal level from the late 1950s on, most states might still be satisfied with much more localized control of public education.

The federal government has always been involved in education to some extent. The provision of funds for education in the territories was a federal responsibility in 1791 as it is today. This does not mean that Congress must appropriate funds for education in areas of the Union that are not within states, but rather that it must provide for the raising of funds for public education, often through a mixture of locally derived taxes and congressional grants. The latter have been especially prevalent in territories that contain concentrations of minority groups. Although this is not a constitutional obligation, it is one that Congress has always assumed.

Now the federal role has expanded to the point that education has a separate Cabinet department for purposes of administering federal funding. As described in the last chapter, the consequences of this status are more symbolic than programmatic or fiscal. A recent budget for the Department of Education was over $22 billion. Programs represented in the budget ranged from direct aid to states and school districts for educating disadvantaged, displaced, handicapped, or underachieving children to special funding for Indian education and school districts that must expend large amounts of money pursuant to court orders to integrate their educational facilities. Even today, however, the federal government and the Department of Education are extremely sensitive to the often articulated belief that education is best organized and delivered at the state and local levels. Many pieces of legislation contain phraseology that prohibits federal control of curricula, programs of instruction, administration, or selection and retention of personnel in any educational institution or school system (see Reading 3-1, esp. National Defense Education Act, Title I, Sec. 102). In a memorandum distributed to all employees of the Department of Education in 1986, Secretary of Education William Bennett repeated this position. No action by any member of the department—including the administration of funding—was to intrude into the curriculum or organization of classrooms anywhere in the United States. The consistency of this memorandum with the obligation of the Department of Education and, particularly, the Office of Civil Rights to ensure equal protection under the laws and other constitutional guarantees in the area of education is problematic.

Federal education policy mixes strong nationalizing tendencies with a strong legacy of localism. Locally elected congresspeople carefully guard local and state control of curriculum and evaluation. Professional groups involved in delivering educational services are better organized at the state and local level, reinforcing state and local control. At the same time, locally elected congresspeople have encouraged a profusion of federal programs that bring federal monies for educational services into every congressional district. As a consequence, Congress can hold these monies hostage to force school districts and states to redirect their own budgeting priorities and program goals. Recently, Congress has often used this negative regulation to respond to the needs of geographically concentrated and electorally reluctant groups (e.g., the non-English-speaking, blacks, the physically and mentally handicapped).

The sequence of groups to which a locally elected Congress responds is the same for education as for other services (see Chapter 1). Until recently programs in education and other policy areas were directed toward the poor or disadvantaged primarily as a consequence of pressure on Congress by professional service providers in and out of government. But in contrast to a number of other policy areas (notably housing and medicine), federal funding of educational services passes through public rather than private sector service providers.

Context

Even though the provision of education is not a power granted to Congress under Article I, Section 7 or 8, the evolution of federal involvement in education closely parallels its involvement in other areas in which it can more directly legislate. As a corollary to the organization of the Northwest Territories under the Land Ordinance of 1785, Congress stipulated that the proceeds from the sale of one section of land out of every thirty-six were to be devoted to the maintenance of public schools. Since most of the land in the new territories belonged to the federal government, there was a large resource base that could be used to support public education. As states entered the Union, the federal government gave over to the states proceeds from the sale of up to 10 or 12 percent of federal lands in the state to further public education.

The next major piece of federal legislation in this area was the Morrill Act of 1863, which dedicated land and revenues from land to establishing one land-grant institution in every state to teach agricultural skills and military science. The act as amended in 1890 provided cash grants to states that maintained these land-grant colleges and provided education in agriculture, military science, and the mechanical arts. In 1917 the Smith-Hughes Act established a parallel program at the secondary level giving cash grants to high schools that taught agricultural science, industrial arts, and home economics. This was the first instance of federal support for vocational education. Both acts can be seen as externalizing the cost of training from the sectors of the economy that would employ these young people—the agricultural and industrial sectors—to the public at large. In 1946 state administration of these programs was funded; in 1956 practical nursing and fisheries management were added to the programs to which there would be training support. In the 1941 Lanham Act and its 1950 amendments, Congress provided federal aid to school districts that suffered income loss because of their inability to tax federal properties. The rationale was that large military bases would increase the demand for educational services but remove land from the property tax rolls; federal aid would "make whole" the financial bases from which public services were provided.

All of the federal funding for education introduced to this point represented either the byproduct of federal activity in other, constitutionally mandated areas or a congressional response to organized agricultural and business interests. The early timing of federal aid to education in agriculture and commerce reflects the organization of these groups at both the congressional district and the state levels since the early days of the Republic. Educational benefits in other areas would have to wait for the effective organization of other interest groups.

Legislation providing nutritional benefits for schoolchildren illustrates the interests to which Congress was responsive in that period. To advocate the health of the young is good, and such advocacy translates into programs where there is an agricultural surplus, as there was in 1933. Otherwise unsalable farm goods were purchased by the federal government and distributed to states and schools under the National School Lunch Act. Later, in 1954, the dairy lobby promoted the public interest by disposing of surplus milk under the School Milk Program Act. Both acts benefited schoolchildren; both acts were effectively subsidies to sectors of agriculture, paid for out of general tax revenues. The major initiators and supporters of both pieces of legislation were agricultural lobbies concentrated in several northern and midwestern congressional districts.

Other forms of federal aid to education have been proposed since at least the time of the Civil War. Some of these involved the creation of a national fund from further sales of federal lands. Proposed congressional legislation earmarked these funds for particular educational use in elementary and secondary education or by the land grant colleges, for buildings, or for teacher salaries; other proposals emphasized general aid to the states and localities. Attempts to launch programs for the educationally disadvantaged were common in the latter part of the nineteenth century. The precipitating factor behind such such proposals was the massive rate of illiteracy, particularly among blacks, in the South after the Civil War, and the goal was usually a system of cash grants to states based upon illiteracy rates. However, no such proposal ever became law (Advisory Commission on Intergovernmental Relations, 1981, pp. 13–16).

The Catholic hierarchy opposed federal aid to public education, since in some urban areas such aid would increase the attractiveness of public schools to the detriment of parochial ones. Additionally, many congresspeople feared that direct federal aid to education would result in eventual federal control or predominant influence over the organization and curriculum of individual schools. Once *Brown* v. *Board of Education* (1954) and *Brown* v. *Board of Education II* (1955) declared segregated schools to be illegal and ordered integration of educational facilities with all deliberate speed, many congresspeople supported (or opposed) federal aid to education as a means of promoting local school integration.

By the late 1950s, even many conservative northern legislators saw the need for federal funding for some types of aid to education, particularly for capital construction and the purchase of expensive scientific or medical equipment. If one had taken a straw vote in both bodies of Congress in, say, 1957 or 1958, one would have found a majority in both favoring the abstract principle of federal aid to elementary and secondary education so long as the federal government did not intrude into school organization or curriculum. At various times aid bills had passed both houses of Congress, but never in the same session. However, the terms of such aid divided its supporters. The intrusion of religious and racial dimensions into aid legislation invariably resulted in its defeat. In fact, these divisions were skillfully exploited by southerners opposing federal aid in both the 1959–60 and the 1961–62 sessions of Congress. After supporting the inclusion of aid to parochial schools, southerners joined civil libertarians in defeating the final legislation (Advisory Commission on Intergovernmental Relations, 1981, pp. 25–28.)

As is usually the case in such stalemates, it takes some kind of exogenous event—a war, a depression, an arms race—to change the terms of political discourse so that legislative changes can occur. In the case at hand, the stimulating event was the Soviet orbiting of the Sputnik in 1957.

Agenda

In 1958 congresspeople were looking for the juxtaposition of clear need, attributability, and a justification of aid as in the national interest before distributing funds to congressional districts to support education. For the preceding decade divisions over criteria for inclusion or exclusion and the uses to which the funds would be put had thwarted the congressional effort to spend more money on education. Before the enactment of the National Defense Education Act of 1958 (NDEA), the federal government spent only about $150 million annually on direct aid for education. The act increased that amount by 50 percent, citing the national interest in increasing the pool of skilled manpower in the sciences and improving language competency (see Reading 3-1). Since the funds were earmarked for particular defense-related programs in schools, the inclusion of an antisegregation stipulation late in the legislative process aroused less opposition than usual: representatives who would oppose the antisegregation provisions were usually committed to a strong national defense. While public schools got matching grants to build science and other facilities, parochial schools could obtain ten-year loans at an interest rate that was almost a giveaway. The divisive issues of race and religion were sufficiently defused to allow the legislation to pass, although the vote in the House was quite close.

NDEA provided funds for teacher training, particularly in the sciences and foreign languages, for the purchase of scientific equipment and other expenses; and for loans and scholarships for college students studying science and languages. Like aid to universities under the Morrill Act, NDEA aid to students was based not on economic need, but on what institutions and individuals would do with it. The justification in this case was national defense.

In some universities NDEA money may have replaced monies they would otherwise have had to raise in order to attract the students they wanted and was thus a cost-controlling measure. However, public schools dependent on property taxes would not have been able to raise large amounts of money for science labs and teacher training in the short run. To this extent, then, the money provided by NDEA brought about a change of emphasis in the curriculum of secondary schools. Despite the declared intentions of Congress, secondary school curriculum modification can occur simply because the taxpayers will not let school districts turn down federal funds, particularly when there is little chance of local funding for the same programs. It is pragmatically impossible for local school administrators and school boards to turn down federal money that can be used to train teachers, build science labs, and send students to college. As in almost all federal categorical grants, the purposes for which the money could be spent expanded with each reauthorization— simple reauthorization provides very little constituency credit for individual congresspeople. By 1976 the majority of students pursuing four-year college curricula were eligible for NDEA loans.

The only other federal aid-to-education bill passed before 1965 was the 1963 Vocational Education Act. This act actually reauthorized the 1958 NDEA, reauthorized federal aid to help with school desegregation (impact aid) and dramatically expanded the vocational educational programs that had been slowly evolving since the Smith-Hughes Act of 1917. For the first time, vocational educational expenditures were not tied to particular forms of subsequent employment. The criteria for distribution within states were made more flexible. A $200 million increase in funding, along with increased flexibility of expenditure, went almost unnoticed when accompanying the reauthorization of NDEA and impact aid. Yet these monies represented an almost 50 percent increase in total federal funding for education. Congress could easily contemplate this increase because historic patterns of distribution of such funds to districts had already been established. Interrogatories at subcommittee oversight hearings could always guide federal administrators as to what administrative or fiscal changes congresspeople needed to better meet the needs of local constituents or enhance the prospects of incumbency, which, in this case, are the same thing.

New groups become beneficiaries of congressional action when the economy is expanding sufficiently to produce federal revenues uncommitted to already existing programs. This is certainly true of the beginnings of categorical aid to the poor and underachieving in elementary and secondary education. Only with the expanding economy of the mid-1960s and the need of many Democrats to secure an additional electoral base could general educational aid to deprived groups pass. To improve their chances in presidential elections and to protect the incumbency of urban and some southern congresspeople once the Voting Rights Act had passed, the Democratic conservative vote had to be replaced by the votes of the underprivileged and minorities (Saunders, 1978; Piven and Cloward, 1971).

The lobbying impetus behind the expansion of aid came from professionals in education and educational administration across the country, but particularly in urban areas. These groups were overwhelmed by the educational needs of the poor and disadvantaged. Local property taxes did not provide sufficient funding to deal with all of the educational problems at hand. Hence, one found a federal executive, a number of congresspeople, elements of the federal bureaucracy, and organized professional interests all in accord in legislating additional educational benefits for new groups. The result was the Elementary and Secondary Education Act of 1965 (ESEA). The original act concentrated on providing programs and services for underachieving children in poor areas. As the program has been reauthorized in, for example, 1966, 1968, 1974, and 1978, its functions have expanded, and this expansion continued with the change to a block grant format in 1981. For example, in 1968 Title VII—authorizing programs to support bilingual education and bicultural maintenance—was included. ESEA and its reauthorizations were clearly instances of classical congressional distributions through already organized professional constituencies—the service providers—to potential voters. The organization of this part of the electorate was a requirement of the legislation. One of the conditions for receiving an ESEA Title I grant was that the local school district and the state organize parent advisory councils. Few professionals in education actually wanted advice from parents, particularly those who have historically been uninvolved in the education of their children. Rather, these councils initially provided a way for professional educators and politicians to convey information downward. Subsequently, of course, the councils began to find common interests and to pursue them. At present a national organization of Title I parents serves as a lobbying association in Washington and is housed in the Offices of the National Education Association.

Further evidence that the program is a literal distribution to definable groups located in geographically concentrated areas is evident from the fact that ESEA Title VII, originally passed in 1968 and as reauthorized in 1974, placed heavy emphasis on cultural maintenance of Spanish-speaking populations. It was not until 1978 that there was even a statutory or administrative requirement that teachers in bilingual classrooms be able to speak English.

At the time that ESEA was first passed, Congress directed aid for postsecondary education to the poor through the Higher Education Act of 1968. This act initiated guaranteed student loans and Pell grants for students from very low-income families. With progressive reauthorization and amendment, the income requirements became less and less stringent, and beneficiary groups expanded in the expected manner. Finally, in 1978, the symbols of legislation followed the substance. Appealing to the middle-class, often professionally employed, voter, Congress amended the 1968 act with the Middle Income Assistance Act of 1978.

While federal aid for the underachieving poor was increasing, other lobbies were making successful demands on the state legislatures. Lobbies representing the parents of the physically and mentally handicapped had been active at the state level since the Second World War. These groups were more easily organized than others that represented disadvantaged groups because the parents were often themselves middle-class professionals—professionals as well as the poor have physically or mentally disabled children. In eras when there was only one income provider per family, a considerable amount of free skilled and professional labor was available to organize these lobbies. By the late 1960s many states were already spending large amounts of money on educational opportunities for the handicapped. Just as ESEA Title I created a whole new category of teachers within the teaching profession, state-level activity promoting the education of the handicapped created other subfields such as that of the special education teacher.

By the late 1960s and early 1970s, Congress had created a number of small federal programs involving education of the handicapped. These programs usually involved individuals who became handicapped as a consequence of activities that were federally directed. For example, the Rehabilitation Act of 1973, perhaps the most comprehensive federal enactment up to that point, funded rehabilitation programs that were run by the states but must be made available to disabled federal employees and to public safety officers injured in the line of duty. The funding of education for the handicapped up through the 1973 act also concentrated heavily on vocational rehabilitation services. Again, the direct link with employability in the private sector is clear. However, a little-noted section of the 1973 act, Section 504, stated, "No otherwise qualified handicapped individual in the United States as defined in Section 7(b)(6), shall solely by reason of his handicap be excluded from participation in, be denied the benefits of, or be subjected to discrimination under any program or activity receiving federal financial assistance." This almost casual espousal of consideration for the handicapped was to cause considerable litigation in the late 1970s and early 1980s. Since Section 504 occurs in the enactment part of the statute and not as part of the intent or findings that precede the operative law, it is actionable in court. As we will see in the next section, it is one of a number of legislative enactments that have effectively increased federal control over education and other social services, even when these services are funded and delivered by the states.

Two years later, in 1975, Congress passed the Education for All Handicapped Children Act. This act codified the principle of equal access to educational opportunities that was implied by Section 504 of the 1973 act. Rather than refer to Section 504, the later act details some of the elements that are to be involved in the education of handicapped children. These include mainstreaming in regular classrooms as far as possible and the provision of individual instructional plans. A scale of increased federal funding was legislated: the funding was presumed to be the carrot that would induce state cooperation. The fact that the federal government promised eventually to fund 40 percent of the cost of educating the handicapped and in practice has funded only 12 percent was not critical, since many states already had extensive programs in place as a consequence of the activities of the handicapped lobby at that level. The stick was potential litigation under Section 504 of the 1973 act. The combination of the two acts resulted in largely state-level distributions for the purpose of educating the handicapped, but with organization and requirements dictated by federal legislation.

These acts were not designed to overcome the failure of most states to act in the area of educating the handicapped, since most states had in fact begun to do so. Although Congress appeared to be legislating a distribution to handicapped children, only a small portion of the funds spent for this purpose comes from Congress. This is the reverse of what happens, for example, in the construction of federal highways. Congress appropriates almost all the funds to be spent on the highways, allows the state to contract for building them, but insists that plans, safety features, and location meet federal approval.

In part, the Education for All Handicapped Children Act of 1975 represents a congressional response to the organized professionals who deliver services to the handicapped. The act therefore specifies many aspects of service delivery that are left to federal administrative bodies or local service providers in the case of other legislation (e.g., Title I of ESEA). Moreover, at the time it was passed there was not a lot of extra money in the federal budget. The problem Congress has faced, at least since the 1960s, is that it must continue to legislate distributions or apparent distributions even when there is little money to pay for them. Aid for the handicapped represents an ideal solution: program legislation that necessitates the continued employment and development of professions involved in educating the handicapped, record-keeping requirements that provide ready access to interest groups when they wish to challenge or alter the education of the handicapped in any state or school district, and an almost token amount of federal money.

Process

From the early 1970s on, both the federal executive and Congress attempted to control the level of federal domestic spending. The costs of federally funded services were increasing at a per unit rate greater than the then high rate of inflation. Yet congresspeople must provide distributive and symbolic benefits to geographically organized constituencies whether the economy is growing or not.

When tax monies are limited, Congress engages in the negative regulation described in Chapter 1. Such regulation is not uncommon in Europe. For example, German national legislation passed since 1975 forces the use of monies raised by urban taxes to fund some housing and other services. This control increases the homogeneity of some public policies funded and administered by urban areas across the country. The same is true of Congress's negative regulation of educational policies across states and localities.

Three congressional activities constitute negative regulation. First, Congress assures organized constituents of benefits it could not otherwise afford by forcing other sources of funds to alter their budgets in congressionally mandated ways or risk the withdrawal of already existing federal support. Second, instead of providing an actual distribution,

Congress provides a symbolic or apparent right. Title VI of the 1964 Civil Rights Act, for example, forbids discrimination on the basis of ethnicity or language spoken in the home but appropriates no money to ensure that such discrimination does not occur (see Pending 3-2). As we will see, later acts in the 1960s and the creation of the Office of Civil Rights put some dollars behind the educational rights granted to non-English-speakers. Section 504 of the Rehabilitation Act of 1973 asserts a right to participate in educational and other programs and requires the withdrawal of federal support from all programs that deny full access to the handicapped. Finally, since Congress is most concerned with distributions to geographically specific locations, it requires close physical accounting from the federal bureaucracies that administer program monies, usually to states or localities. Congress asks whether these monies were spent for the types of goods or services intended and, more particularly, whether they were spent on the right people located in the intended places. From these three types of congressional activity emanate most "negative" federal controls over educational services.

The first two activities often occur through the normal legislative processes involving committee hearings and floor reciprocity. An exception is civil rights legislation, which must usually command greater overall majorities before it can successfully pass the legislative process. The third type of negative regulation is a consequence of the information needs of Congress. Incumbency is better ensured if intended benefits, whether federally or state-funded, actually reach recipients in congressional districts. The only way Congress can be sure of this is to place a very high priority on the collection of information that describes either the dollars or the services delivered. Data collection may become almost as important to congresspeople as the delivery of the programs themselves.

As part of every piece of legislation, Congress directs the federal bureaucracy or the responsible cabinet official to issue such rules and regulations and to adopt such procedures as would be necessary to carry out the intent of Congress (see Reading 3-3, especially Sec. 602). In the case of ESEA Title I, HEW extracted from congressional testimony and the language of the law ten requirements that were to be met by all local-level programs funded by Title I. These requirements did not deal with program content per se, but with such concerns as establishing parent advisory councils and program evaluation or ensuring that federal money did not replace state or local money in programs (Hill et al.,

1976). Each of these requirements in turn was translated into a set of bureaucratic procedures and requirements for record keeping. While states provided assurance as to program adequacy, school districts passed through states to the Office of Education documents that provided evidence that the financial and administrative requirements of Title I were met. Program specialists did not look at these reports; auditors in HEW did, some of whom were ignorant of the intent of Title I. This resulted in many claims against local school districts and demands that they return misspent money to the federal government.

Millions of dollars in legal fees have been spent arguing over Title I audit exceptions in the federal courts, and this controversy continues. In 1983 the Sixth U.S. Circuit Court of Appeals ruled that Kentucky had reasonably interpreted federal rules when some of its school districts set up self-contained Title I classes exclusively for Spanish-speaking first and second graders. Historically, such classes had been suspect in the South and the border states because of the possibility of their use to resegregate classrooms. This was not the problem in Kentucky, however. There the difficulty was that the Department of Education auditors claimed that the use of these classrooms implied that state and local services for students were being replaced by Title I services, thus violating the non-supplanting clause of the ESEA regulations. Kentucky claimed that a substantive standard of fairness for the use of the monies was necessary in order to prevent inefficient restriction on the use of all funds for the purpose of educating Title I students. At first glance, the adequacy of educational programming and state compliance with federal law are the issues in this case. Behind the case, and behind the literal-minded position of the federal bureaucracy, is the bureaucracy's need to assure congresspeople that federal funds are being used to provide new, attributable benefits for constituents.

The federal emphasis, then, is on the accountability of funds as much as the adequacy of their use. This is consistent with what Congress can best do, which is to appropriate funds and ask the federal bureaucracies involved to trace the uses of such funds. The physical organization of local programs as well as the way in which locally spent funds are accounted for are continually pushed into a homogeneous format for bookkeeping purposes. There is continued bureaucratic confusion when federally mandated records are not kept. Failure to produce records appears to imply substantive noncompliance with program requirements in the minds of those bureaucrats who must process information on the chance that congresspeople might ask for it. Although this attitude is only tangentially related to the substantive adequacy of federally funded programs, it is immediately responsive to the potential needs of the educational bureaucrats' ultimate boss: the Senate and House committees that deal with education legislation.

The requirements of federal bookkeeping may produce inefficiency at the local level when any student is the recipient of services from more than one federally funded program. Most students who receive the benefits of ESEA Title I, ESEA Title VII (bilingual education), and the Education for All Handicapped Children Act must receive each of these services separately, often from separate teachers, for accounting purposes. When one teacher provides a number of these services, he or she must often physically walk out of the classroom and then walk back in order to allocate time among worksheets so that the different programs can be charged. Often different and redundant textual and other educational materials must be ordered under the different programs (Hill and Master, 1982).

The organizational and auditing regulations under the Education for All Handicapped Children Act vividly demonstrate what happens when the accountability needs of Congress conflict with the efficient organization and delivery of a service at the state or local level. Educational programs for the handicapped were already in place in most states by 1975, yet the act required states to employ a uniform reporting procedure and categorization of expenses, even though the federal government was initially putting in only 5 percent of the money for educating the handicapped. At oversight hearings on the act, state legislators complained to the House Select Committee on Education about the cost of program reorganization, which the federal government was not helping to offset. When asked during the same hearings whether greater administrative flexibility would be desirable, the commissioner of Education said no: if the federal bureaucracy were to be responsive to fifty different programs and their organizational variations, the overall thrust of the program would be lost in negotiations over details. Notice that the overall thrust of the program is identified with the minimal federal effort, not the already existing state programs. This push for administrative homogeneity required states to organize in a manner that was inconsistent with several sections of the Florida state constitution (see Reading 3-4). Moreover administrative homogeneity is crucial if congress is to get information about which groups in each school and congressional district receive federal funding and state funding when negative regulation is used. Congress cannot use the threat to withdraw federal funding in one or more areas when state and local governments do not redirect their laws and spending to match federal priorities if congressional committees do not know who receives money and services (see Reading 3-5).

In general, when Congress distributes the right to a good or service without full congressional funding, it either provides for the administration of such an act by the federal bureaucracy (Education for All Handicapped Children Act) or leaves it to people who feel they have been denied a proper distribution under the law to find remedy in federal court. (Section 504 of the Rehabilitation Act of 1973). Clearly, the latter strategy displaces a greater financial burden onto plaintive groups. Even in the former case, however, the federal bureaucracy (in the person of the secretary of education for example) may be sued by interest groups to force action consistent with the law. As a rule, where there is federal funding, the same legislation also creates the mechanism of administrative enforcement for cases of noncompliance. Where no federal funding is involved, as in the case of Section 504, concerned interest groups must use the federal courts directly.

The only sanction interest groups and Congress have is the withdrawal of federal funding. Sometimes this sanction is so generally interpreted that the distribution of a new benefit becomes almost a right, as was the case with the enforcement of Title IX of the Educational Amendments Act of 1972. Title IX prohibits discrimination on the basis of sex in any educational program that receives federal funding. Two points to be noted about the impact of Title IX are first, that "program" under the title refers to the specific organization or activity that spends the federal money, not to the entire university system, college, or school district, and, second, that the federal aid that triggers the application of Title IX can be indirect as well as direct. Hence, scholarship money or guaranteed loans given to students to spend at a university bring that university's loan program within the purview of Title IX (*Grove City College et al.* v. *Bell, Secretary of Education, et al.*, decided February 28, 1984). This interpretation of the application of Title IX is fairly straightforward (see Reading 3-6, Sec. 902). Title IX represents a redistribution of nonfederal monies based upon the requirements of federal legislation. Enforcement powers have been granted, since the law requires that funding be withheld where sex discrimination occurs. The distribution is not merely symbolic. The Office of Civil Rights can be sued to require school districts or universities to comply with the law or face withdrawal of federal funding.

The distinction between a congressional distribution without full funding and symbolic legislation is somewhat blurred. A piece of legislation like Title IX can be considered a case of both. With symbolic distribution, Congress is not passing out monies but is responding to the needs or demands of organized groups for new rights or standing in the courts so that their interests can be further pursued. Title IX, without enforcement, creates a symbolic right for women not to be discriminated against in educational programs. With enforcement, it creates pressure for redistribution of state and local public-sector funding to remedy previous discrimination. As noted above, symbolic legislation represents an important form of negative control over state- and locally provided services. Such regulation is paralleled in Britain by the Thatcher government's increased attempts at program and fiscal control at the local level and in Germany by national-level attempts to control the beneficiaries of urban programs. All these efforts at control and redirection are effective to the extent that an extensive national bureaucracy with powers of fiscal control is put in place to monitor the effects of legislation at the local level.

Consequences

The two immediate consequences of federal policies involving education were regulatory confusion and pressures for controlling federal expenditures. Introducing block grants is one method of doing the latter. One education block grant (ECIA; see Chapter 2) consolidated a number of small categorical programs that were of little significance to congresspeople. During a period of budgetary constraint, block grants (in education and healthcare alike; see Chapter 5) cut the total funding package for the consolidated programs, but left it to individual states and school districts to decide who would feel the cut in federal funding. The major categorical efforts, such as ESEA Titles I (now called ECIA, Chapter 1), and ESEA Title VII, NDEA, and the Vocational Education Act have been left in place with somewhat modified reporting requirements. The local-level burden of administering federal programs has been lessened. At the same time, attempts to dismantle the recently created Department of Education have not been strongly pursued, because the existence of the department has no serious budgetary consequences (see Chapter 2).

Regulatory confusion first resulted from congressional ambiguity.

The Office of Civil Rights in HEW was given initial jurisdiction over the implementation of Titles IV (racial segregation) and VI (protection for non-English-speaking minorities) of the Civil Rights Act and, subsequently, Title IX (discrimination based on sex) of the Educational Amendments Act of 1972. Only the legislative history of Title IV was clear (Rabkin, 1980): the Office of Civil Rights was to ferret out cases in which public schools resisted desegregation and pursue such cases in the courts. Congress intended to use negative sanctions to end segregation in public schools. The federal courts have been consistently active in supporting the intent of Congress when cases under Title IV have been brought by either the Office of Civil Rights or private parties (see Reading 3-7).

Congressional debates and the enactments themselves give the Office of Civil Rights no guidelines for the administration of Title VI and Title IX. In order not to thwart the intent of Congress, the Office of Civil Rights borrowed as its enforcement model for the latter acts the one stipulated for the enforcement of Title IV. In the case of Title VI, the response was rather slow to evolve. A 1970 directive to school districts with more than 5 percent minority-language students asserted that these school districts might have a Title VI compliance problem, that they should assess whether or not they have such a problem, that if they have such a problem they should do something about it, and that they should report on all of the preceding matters to the Office of Civil Rights. Amazingly, the memorandum as published in the *Federal Register* was referred to as the basis for the *Lau* decision (see Readings 3-2 and 3-8). Following the *Lau* decision, which used a clear results or effects standard to identify discrimination against linguistic minorities, the Office of Civil Rights produced what came to be called the "*Lau* remedies." These were not published in the *Federal Register* for comment, but were used to negotiate voluntary plans in over five hundred school districts.

The leverage wielded by the Office of Civil Rights in dealing with school districts depends on the loss of time, money, and professional status by local school districts and officials if they are continually harassed by to provide adequate bilingual education. Adequate bilingual education was defined in terms of a particular method of delivery: transitional bilingual education. Unlike the interpretation of the 1970 memorandum, that of Title VI was means-oriented. A school district must produce systematic information about the means it has worked out with the Office of Civil Rights in order to prevent further investigation, clearly another instance of bureaucratic response or overresponse to a congressional mandate.

At the same time, bureaucratic interpretation of Title VI did not fully satisfy advocates of more funding for bilingual education, who in 1978 forced the Office of Civil Rights to comply with a consent decree (*Northwest Arctic School District* v. *Califano*). The result was a notice of proposed rule making issued in 1980. The educational bureaucracy was caught in a conflict between the reporting and program needs of congresspeople and legal pressures brought under earlier acts of Congress.

The Reagan administration rescinded the notice of proposed rule making in 1981 in an attempt to decrease national control over local political authorities and acknowledge the lack of sufficient, local-level tax revenues to implement bilingual education to the extent required. Depending on their constituencies, congresspeople applauded or condemned this move. The new administration also shifted to ends- rather than means-oriented regulation. This proved difficult, since the Office of Civil Rights was still operating under a court consent decree involving the use of transitional bilingual education in its notice of proposed rule making. The consequence of this collision of legislative needs, bureaucratic procedures, and legal and other pressures from newly organized interests has been a stalemate. Enforcement of the Education For All Handicapped Children Act, and Title VI of the Civil Rights Act, and Title IX of the Educational Amendments Act of 1972 is effectively unchanged, although the style is different in that the Office of Civil Rights is required to litigate more and negotiate less.

This stalemate also applies to recent attempts to involve the private sector more in elementary and secondary education. In 1981 the Reagan administration proposed both more federal aid for private schools and a tuition tax credit to parents who send their children to such schools. Both were justified as increasing parent choice and, hence, using marketlike competition to increase the efficiency and accountability of all schools. No such legislation has come close to passing Congress; increased competition has nothing to do with the targeted benefits that are the staple of congressional incumbency. As a consequence of the stalemate, there has been almost no shift in the groups of people who are beneficiaries of federal programs involving education, in spite of protest to the contrary.

From 1787 onward, Congress has directly or indirectly appropriated monies for education. Most of the time, these benefits were directed toward those involved in the national defense effort, in agriculture, in commerce and in the practical arts. In delivering these benefits, a number of professionalized groups such as agricultural extension workers, some vocational education teachers, and professionals teaching industrial arts were benefitted as well. Federal funds paid for salary and, particularly, for equipment.

With the extension of the Vocational Education Act under drastically increased funding in 1963 and the passage of the Elementary and Secondary Education Act in 1965, many more professional groups as well as organized beneficiaries were brought into the orbit of Congressional targeting. In fact, in the 1960s legislation in education and social services often required not just the organization of professional groups for purposes of service delivery, but the organization of recipient groups as a condition of obtaining the benefits. All these organized groups had votes and it became very difficult for Congress not to continue to provide benefits to these groups even when the economic base for the growth of federal-level benefits dried up in the late 1960s.

Congress became and is now more concerned with accountability for funds spent to make sure they went to targeted groups in areas, and the use of distributions funded by other levels of government. The threat of withdrawal of already targeted federal funds served as the lever Congress used to move around funds derived from state and local taxation. Congress also passed symbolic legislation distributing new benefits to minorities and other groups. The latter was and is implemented both through bureaucratic oversight, as in the case of the use of the Office of Civil Rights, and the use of federal courts directly, as is customary when complaints are brought under Section 504 of the Rehabilitation Act of 1973.

Ironically, the less money Congress provides for programs, the less flexibility federal law gives states and localities in spending money in program areas. If we array EDEA Title I, the Education for All Handicapped Children Act, Civil Rights Title VI, and Section 504 of the Rehabilitation Act from left to right, we are also moving from more federal funding to less and from less overt federal control over programs (more local flexibility) to more federal control (less local flexibility). As this trend was established in the late 1960s and early 1970s, the autonomy of state and local educational programming declined. One might assume that classroom control and curriculum remain outside federal jurisdiction. This, however, is not quite the case. Section 103(b) of the Department of Education Organization Act of 1980 forbids the department to involve itself with curriculum or organization of individual classrooms in schools *except* when authorized by statute. Such statutes would include Title VI of the Civil Rights Act. In other words, the Department of Education cannot get involved in curriculum, pedagogy, and the organization of individual classrooms in schools unless Congress says it can. Almost all federal legislation of significance since the 1960s has supported curricula of some sort. Gone is the era when Congress really did nothing to affect classroom content. This also reflects the compelling tendency of the federal bureaucracy to require school districts to be responsive to bureaucratic needs for information and to the bureaucracy's prismed view of congressional intent. This compulsion is not easily undone (see Reading 3-9).

Readings

3-1. FEDERAL AID TO EDUCATION JUSTIFIED AS AN ASPECT OF NATIONAL DEFENSE

The National Defense Education Act of 1958 (P.L. 85-864) represented the largest increase in federal aid to education associated with one bill. It also provided aid to more areas—teaching, laboratories, student loans, and so on—than any previous legislation. Its justification was the "national need" for science and language education in response to the Soviet Union's orbiting of the earth satellite Sputnik. The legislation passed Congress only because of its national defense justification. In Section 102 Congress was careful to specify that this aid could not be used to justify intrusion into state and local prerogatives. However, Section 584 of the 1976 reauthorization of NDEA clearly illustrates the power of the Commissioner of Education, sub-cabinet position in HEW, to require states to develop and provide such information as the commissioner may need. This in turn can have clear implications for program organization even at the local level.

P.L. 85-864: Title I—General Provisions

Findings and Declaration of Policy

Sec. 101 the Congress hereby finds and declares that the security of the Nation requires the fullest development of the mental resources and technical skills of its young men and women. The present emergency demands that additional and more adequate educational opportunities be made available. The defense of this Nation depends upon the mastery of modern techniques developed from complex scientific principles, new techniques, and new knowledge.

We must increase our efforts to identify and educate more of the talent of our Nation. This requires programs that will give assurance that no student of ability will be denied an opportunity for higher education because of financial need; will correct as rapidly as possible the existing imbalances in our educational programs which have led to an insufficient proportion of our population educated in science, mathematics, and modern foreign languages and trained in technology.

The Congress reaffirms the principle and declares that the States and local communities have and must retain control over and primary responsibility for public education. The national interest requires, however, that the Federal Government give assistance to education for programs which are important to our defense.

To meet the present educational emergency requires additional effort at all levels of government. It is therefore the purpose of this Act to provide substantial assistance in various forms to individuals, and to States and their subdivisions, in order to insure trained manpower of sufficient quality and quantity to meet the national defense needs of the United States.

Federal Control of Education Prohibited

Sec. 102. Nothing contained in the Act shall be construed to authorize any department, agency, officer, or employee of the United States to exercise any direction, supervision, or control over the curriculum, program of instruction, administration, or personnel of any educational institution or school system. (72 Stat. 1581–82)

1976 Reauthorization: Title 20 (Education)

Sec 584. Administration of State Plans

(a) State plan approval; requirements No State plan submitted under one of the titles of this Act shall be approved by the Commissioner which does not—

(1) provide, in the case of a plan submitted under subchapter III or under subchapter V of this chapter or section 589 of this title, that the State educational agency will be the sole agency for administering the plan;

(2) provide that such commission or agency will make such reports to the Commissioner, in such form and containing such information, as may be reasonably necessary to enable the Commissioner to perform his duties under such subchapter or section and will keep such records and afford such access thereto as the Commissioner may find necessary to assure the correctness and verification of such reports; and

(3) provide for such fiscal control and fund accounting procedures as may be necessary to assure proper disbursement of and accounting for Federal funds paid to the State under such subchapter or section (including such funds paid by the State to the local educational agencies).

3-2. EQUAL EDUCATIONAL OPPORTUNITY FOR LANGUAGE MINORITIES

The San Francisco school system failed to provide English-language instruction to approximately 1,800 students of Chinese ancestry who did not speak English. Alternative instruction in the basic curriculum in a language other than English was not provided either. No relief was granted to the students until Lau et al.v. Nichols et al. *reached the Supreme Court. The Court interpreted Title VI (Sec. 601) of the Civil Rights Act as forbidding any discrimination in any educational program receiving federal funds if that discrimination has the effect of denying equal participation. In arriving at this conclusion, it depended on two Office of Civil Rights regulations issued in 1968 and 1970. These detailed the obligations of school districts to language-speaking minorities under Title VI. In a concurring opinion Mr. Justice Stewart pointed out that departmental regulations and consistent administrative construction pursuant to federal law are entitled to great weight. In the present case, that weight was sufficient basis for the court's decision. (See also Reading 3-8, the 1970 memorandum.)*

Lau et al. *v* Nichols et al.

Certiorari to the United States Court of Appeals for the Ninth Circuit No. 72-6250. Argued December 10, 1973—Decided January 21, 1974

Mr. Justice Douglas delivered the opinion of the Court.

. . . The San Francisco, California, school system was integrated in 1971 as a result of a federal court decree, 399 F. Supp. 1315. See *Lee* v.

Johnson, 404 U.S. 1215. The District Court found that there are 2,856 students of Chinese ancestry in the school system who do not speak English. Of those who have that language deficiency, about 1,000 are given supplemental courses in the English language. About 1,800, however, do not receive that instruction . . . .

We do not reach the Equal Protection Clause argument which has been advanced but rely solely on Sec. 601 of the Civil Rights Act of 1964, 42 U.S.C. Sec. 2000d, to reverse the Court of Appeals.

That section bans discrimination based "on the ground of race, color, or national origin," in "any program or activity receiving Federal financial assistance." The school district involved in this litigation receives large amounts of federal financial assistance. The Department of Health, Education, and Welfare (HEW), which has authority to promulgate regulations prohibiting discrimination in federally assisted school systems, 42 U.S.C. Sec. 2000d-1, in 1968 issued one guideline that "(s)chool systems are responsible for assuring that students of a particular race, color, or national origin are not denied the opportunity to obtain the education generally obtained by other students in the system." 33 Fed. Reg. 4956. In 1970 HEW made the guidelines more specific, requiring school districts that were federally funded "to rectify the language deficiency in order to open" the instruction to students who had "linguistic deficiencies," 35 Fed. Reg. 11595.

Discrimination is barred which has that *effect* even though no purposeful design is present: a recipient "may not . . . utilize criteria or methods of administration which have the effect of subjecting individuals to discrimination" or have "the effect of defeating or substantially impairing accomplishment of the objectives of the program as respect individuals of a particular race, color, or national origin." Id., Sec. 80.3(b)(2)

It seems obvious that the Chinese-speaking minority receive fewer benefits than the English-speaking majority from respondents' school system which denies them a meaningful opportunity to participate in the educational program—all earmarks of the discrimination banned by the regulations.

Respondent school district contractually agreed to "comply with title VI of the Civil Rights Act of 1964 . . . and all requirements imposed by or pursuant to the Regulation" of HEW (45 CFR pt. 80) which are "issued pursuant to that title . . ." and also immediately to "take any measures necessary to effectuate this agreement." The Federal Government has power to fix the terms on which its money allotments to the States shall be disbursed.

Senator Humphrey, during the floor debates on the Civil Rights Act of 1964, said: "Simple justice requires that public funds, to which all taxpayers of all races contribute, not be spent in any fashion which encourages, entrenches, subsidizes, or results in racial discrimination."

We accordingly reverse the judgment of the Court of Appeals and remand the case for the fashioning of appropriate relief. Reversed and remanded. (414 U.S. 563, 564, 566–567, 568–69)

3-3. EQUAL RIGHTS FOR LANGUAGE, RACIAL, AND ETHNIC MINORITIES

The Civil Rights Act of 1964 (P.L. 88-352) included provisions forbidding discrimination in employment and the use of federal funds in segregated schools and Title VI, which mandated equal access to all programs supported in any part by federal funds regardless of race, ethnicity, or language habitually spoken. In effect, it is a declaration of equal rights for various minority groups, much as Section 504 provides for equal access and opportunity for the handicapped. In both cases federal funds can be withdrawn from any program that does not comply with the act. Billions of state and local tax dollars have been redirected in order to comply with the mandates of Title VI.

The Act

To enforce the constitutional right to vote, to confer jurisdiction upon the district courts of the United States to provide injunctive relief against discrimination in public accommodations, to authorize the Attorney General to institute suits to protect constitutional rights in public facilities and public education, to extend the Commission on Civil Rights, to prevent discrimination in federally assisted programs, to establish a Commission on Equal Employment Opportunity, and for other purposes.

Be it enacted by the Senate and House of Representatives of the United States of America in Congress assembled, That this Act may be cited as the "Civil Rights Act of 1964." . . .

Title VI—Nondiscrimination in Federally Assisted Programs

Sec. 601. No person in the United States shall, on the ground of race, color, or national origin, be excluded from participation in, be denied the benefits of, or be subjected to discrimination under any program or activity receiving Federal financial assistance.

Sec. 602. Each Federal department and agency which is empowered to extend Federal financial assistance to any program or activity, by way of grant, loan, or contract other than a contract of insurance or guaranty, is authorized and directed to effectuate the provisions of Section 601 with respect to such program or activity by issuing rules, regulations, or orders of general applicability which shall be consistent with achievement of the objectives of the statute authorizing the financial assistance in connection with which the action is taken. No such rule, regulation, or order shall become effective unless and until approved by the President. Compliance with any requirement adopted pursuant to this section may be effected (1) by the termination of or refusal to grant or to continue assistance under such program or activity to any recipient as to whom there has been an express finding on the record, after opportunity for hearing, of a failure to comply with such requirement, but such termination or refusal shall be limited in its effect to the particular program, or part thereof, in which such noncompliance has been so found, or (2) by any other means authorized by law.

3-4. EDUCATIONAL ACCESS FOR THE HANDICAPPED*

The following testimony indicates some of the reservations expressed by state and local officials over the funding and reporting provisions of the Education for All Handicapped Children Act (P.L. 94-142). In essence, they correctly anticipated that the federal government would never pay its promised share of the cost of educating the handicapped. Additionally, they cite administrative inflexibility in the reporting requirements. At least one state cannot constitutionally comply with the organization and reporting mandates of the federal law. These federal requirements clearly determine much of the pattern of the state's own expenditures for educating the handicapped. Further, although report-

*Hearings before the Subcommittee on Select Education of the Committee on Education and Labor, U.S. House of Representatives, 95th Congress, 1st sess., Sept. 26 and 27, 1977. Washington, D.C. Government Printing Office, 1978.

ing may eventually become both uniform and effective, it is clear from the testimony that great inefficiencies are being introduced into the delivery of services at the state and local level. The speaker is Richard Flintrop, chairman of the Education Committee of the Wisconsin State Assembly and a representative of the National Conference of State Legislatures.

. . . [A] major obstacle to successfully implementing Public Law 94-142 is, I fear, a lack of commitment or will on the part of the Federal Government to carry out the law forthrightly and to amend it promptly where it proves flawed. The experience of the EDEA Title I program and other Federal education legislation suggests that the history of Public Law 94-142 may well be one of muddling through, or attempting to avoid conflicts between promise and reality rather than addressing them straight away. This, however, would be nothing more than a disservice to the children Public Law 94-142 purports to protect.

Frankly, Mr. Chairman, we are also fearful that the Federal Government may not follow through with the appropriations to fund Public Law 94-142 at its authorized levels. While States that accept Public Law 94-142 funding must bind themselves legally to educate all handicapped children according to Federal rules, the Federal Government is under absolutely no legal obligation to appropriate 1 cent in return. This is unfair and it provides no political incentive for the Federal Government to fund Public Law 94-142 to the maximum extent authorized. Furthermore, the fact that last year's child count figures were lower than anticipated also makes this an attractive option. I am further aware that the point had been made repeatedly in the last several months that there is no need for the Federal Government to increase its financial commitment to the education of handicapped children because States are liable to meet the basic requirements of Public Law 94-142 under their own State laws and under section 504 of the Rehabilitation Act. This proposition, from a strictly legal standpoint, is essentially correct. But it begs a basic issue: simply stated, many States and local educational agencies lack the economic wherewithal to do the job by themselves within a short period of time. While a handful of States have very handsome budgetary surpluses, they are not the norm.

Finally, I would like to comment on the last significant obstacle, namely the inordinate amounts of forms, certifications, and assurances which must be filed for this act. Mr. Chairman, I know that you have heard cries about Federal redtape many times, but I think the problems which Public Law 94-142 raises in this respect are unique and worth your careful consideration. Unlike almost all other major pieces of Federal education legislation, Public Law 94-142 was enacted substantially after most States had developed their own legislation in the same area. The result has been needless legal and administrative overlap, duplication and conflict. Records for the Federal program must be kept one way; records for State programs must be kept another. Federal due process requirements work one way; State requirements often work in another. This simply does not make sense. In other words, there is far too little flexibility on the part of the Federal Government to take into account adequately delivered programs at the State level.

It not only diverts far too much staff time and resources from the task of actually serving children, but also creates a legal crazy quilt which is an open invitation to little more than paper compliance.

Florida Constitutional and Statutory Conflicts with the Education for All Handicapped Children Act (P.L. 94-142)—Table produced by M. Bloom for the State of Florida

Conflicting Requirement: P.L. 94-142 requires administrative procedures from the LEA [local education authority] to the SEA (state education authority] before recourse to the courts.

Explanation of Conflict: The Florida Administrative Procedures Act does not provide for an appeal of a local school board's decision to the State Educational Authority. Such a procedure is considered excessively costly and time consuming to the parent. The Act provides for an informal hearing first, then a formal hearing, then recourse to the courts.

Conflicting State Legal Authority: Chapter 120, Florida Statutes.

Suggested Remedy: The language of P.L. 94-142 should provide generic requirements for adequate due process procedures.

Conflicting Requirement: requires the SEA to provide direct educational services to handicapped children when LEAs refuse to participate in handicapped programs or fail to adequately serve handicapped children.

Explanation of Conflict: The Florida Constitution and subsequent clarifying law provides that the Florida Board of Education (SEA) has only policy-making authority and it is the local school boards (LEA) which shall operate, control and supervise education programs, including programs for exceptional children, in the school district.

Conflicting State Legal Authority: Sections 2 and 4, Art. IX, Fla. Const.; Section 229.053, Florida Statutes; Section 230.03, Florida Statues; Section 230.23(4)(n)1, Florida Statues.

Suggested Remedy: The language of P.L. 94-142 should recognize the wide range of relationships which exist between SEAs and LEAs. Some SEAs which have direct statutory control over LEAs have, as a practical matter, little or no functional control over them.

3-5. THE COST AND CLUMSINESS OF FEDERAL BUREAUCRATIC CONTROL*

This exchange between Richard Flintrop of the Wisconsin State Assembly and Rep. Richard Brademas indicates clearly that Rep. Richard Brademas (Ind.) does not understand the nature of the federal system. He draws an analogy between local-state and state-federal fiscal relationships. But states created the federal government. The federal government can fund whatever it likes but cannot compel states as a matter of public law only to fund what the federal government would like. States, however, can choose to fund their social services in any way they choose as long as it is constitutional. In particular, they can choose to raise funds for state-defined or mandated services at the local level through the property tax, rather than through other mechanisms that might be statewide and more uniform in scope. State Representative Flintrop is not able to enlighten Mr. Brademas as to his error. This attitude toward state and local fiscal relations and the belief that the federal government has some right to command states to spend money in particular areas lead to increased federal control over and homogenization of social services.

Mr. Brademas: Let me ask you this question. I noted, Mr. Flintrop, that you said in the State of Wisconsin that you have a comprehensive special education act which you feel 94-142 [the Education for All Handicapped Children Act] was patterned after. Your law is fully as comprehensive, in some cases more so, as the Federal statute. Do I take it that

*Hearings before the Subcommittee on Select Education of the Committee on Education and Labor, House of Representatives, 95th Congress, 1st sess., Sept. 26–27, 1977. Washington, D.C. U.S. Government Printing Office, 1978.

you have a State statutory mandate in the State of Wisconsin to provide special education to handicapped children?

Mr. Flintrop: Yes; we do, Mr. Chairman. Our law was passed 2 years previous to enactment of the Federal legislation to be implemented fully by July 1, 1976. If we have had problems it is because the State superintendent has not wished to take a statutory role in aggressively seeking compliance with the law.

Mr. Brademas: Have you appropriated enough money to meet that statutory mandate?

Mr. Flintrop: We have appropriated a sum but it amounts to 70 percent of the cost of local education agencies. We will be moving to an excess cost formula in the next 2 years but at the moment it is categorical aid.

Mr. Brademas: At the moment you are not providing sufficient State funds to meet the needs of educating the handicapped children?

Mr. Flintrop: Correct. I would have to put that in the light of the fact that we fund generally 40 percent of the cost of primary and secondary education. Our commitment to the special education child is about 40 percent above that level.

Mr. Brademas: I make that point because I am sure that that is replicated elsewhere in the country. I think almost all of the States, with the exception of a few, now have statutory mandates for the education of handicapped children. Do they not, Mr. Hill?

Mr. Hill [Executive Director, Education Commission of the States]: Yes.

Mr. Brademas: Yet think probably it is also fair to say, otherwise we would not be here talking about this legislation, that you haven't had enough money from State and other resources to meet fully the commitment to educate handicapped children which your State articulated in either State statute or court order. Is that not a fair judgment?

Mr. Flintrop: Mr. Chairman, if I may, I think we have to address the fact that the scene is so different nationally. There are States like Wisconsin where in order to meet the Federal law all it means is that we are going to have to tinker a bit with the procedure for parental complaints to be filed and some other due process changes to be in compliance. In other States though they are an awful long ways from meeting, as a number of people here suggested, meeting the mandates of their State and Federal law. There are some States similar in size to Wisconsin that are appropriating one-tenth of the amount of State aid that we are. So the needs vary greatly.

While we recognize the need to seek full compliance with both our

State and Federal laws some States are in such economic condition right now it is virtually impossible to support the programs to the level which I think they frankly wish they could.

3-6. LIMITED EDUCATIONAL OPPORTUNITIES FOR WOMEN*

Title IX of the Educational Amendments Act of 1972 (P.L. 92-318) appears to prevent discrimination in the availability of educational and athletic opportunities to women. In this sense it does for women what Section 504 did for the handicapped and Title VI for minorities—opening access to educational and athletic programs supported in any part by federal monies. Notice, however, that much of the text of Title IX consists of a listing of exceptions to its coverage. In particular, although Title IX forbids discrimination on the basis of sex in programs receiving federal money, this ban applies only if the activity or institution is already organized for both sexes. Title IX does not require the abolition of single-sex high schools or colleges. Further, although statistics may be used in a Title IX complaint, quotas per se cannot provide direct evidence for one, nor may they be used as an aspect of a remedy. Section 902 clearly limits application of Title IX sanctions to the particular program that discriminates by sex and also receives federal funds. For several years, up until the Grove City College case of 1984, enforcement of Title IX by the Office of Civil Rights had been modeled on the enforcement of Title IV of the Civil Rights Act of 1964; that is, it was not limited to the program receiving federal funds.

Sex Discrimination Prohibited

Sec. 901 (a) No person in the United States shall, on the basis of sex, be excluded from participation in, be denied the benefits of, or be subjected to discrimination under any education program or activity receiving Federal financial assistance, except that:

(1) in regard to admissions to educational institutions, this section shall apply only to institutions of vocational education, professional education, and graduate higher education, and to public institutions of undergraduate higher education; . . .

*Educational Amendments Act of 1972 (P.L. 92–318) Title IX.

(3) this section shall not apply to an educational institution which is controlled by a religious organization if the application of this subsection would not be consistent with the religious tenets of such organization; . . .

(5) in regard to admissions this section shall not apply to any public institution of undergraduate higher education which is an institution that traditionally and continually from its establishment has had a policy of admitting only students of one sex.

(b) Nothing contained in subsection (a) of this section shall be interpreted to require any educational institution to grant preferential or disparate treatment to the members of one sex on account of an imbalance which may exist with respect to the total number of percentage of persons of that sex participating in or receiving the benefits of any federally supported program or activity, in comparison with the total number or percentage of persons of that sex in any community, State, section, or other area: Provided, That this subsection shall not be construed to prevent the consideration in any hearing or proceeding under this title of statistical evidence tending to show that such an imbalance exists with respect to the participation in, or receipt of the benefits of, any such program or activity by the members of one sex.

(c) For purposes of this title an educational institution means any public or private preschool, elementary, or secondary school, or any institution of vocational, professional, or higher education, except that in the case of an educational institution composed of more than one school, college, or department which are administratively separate units, such terms means each such school, college, or department.

Federal Administrative Enforcement

Sec. 902. Each Federal department and agency which is empowered to extend Federal financial assistance to any education program or activity, by way of grant, loan, or contract other than a contract of insurance or guaranty, is authorized and directed to effectuate the provisions of section 901 with respect to such program or activity by issuing rules, regulations, or orders of general applicability which shall be consistent with achievement of the objectives of the statute authorizing the financial assistance in connection with which the action is taken. No such rule, regulation, or order shall become effective unless and until approved by the President. Compliance with any requirement adopted pursuant to this section may be effected (1) by the termination of or refusal to grant or to continue assistance under such program or activity to any recipient as to whom there has been an express finding on the record, after opportunity for hearing, of a failure to comply with such requirement, but such termination or refusal shall be limited to the particular political entity, or part thereof, or other recipient as to whom such a finding has been made, and shall be limited in its effect to the particular program, or part thereof, in which such noncompliance has been so found, or (2) by any other means authorized by law. (86 Stat. 235)

3-7. FEDERAL CONTROL OF LOCAL EDUCATIONAL AND TAX POLICIES

The sweeping intent of Congress is demonstrated in the first article that follows. In general federal judges do not and cannot break down the political subdivisions created by state legislatures. This has been found true both for purposes of school integration in Detroit and for purposes of equalizing educational finance in Texas. However, when the political subdivisions have actively contributed to the segregation of schools, remedies may cross district lines. In this case, however, intent to discriminate must be shown.

In a parallel Title IV case, the city of St. Louis was required to tax itself to spend money on desegregation. At the same time, the state of Missouri was ordered by the federal courts to pay a portion of the cost of desegregating the schools in St. Louis and its suburbs. This case is currently under litigation. At issue is whether the court in pursuing Title IV remedies can take precedence over the state's right to tax and spend within its own boundaries for the general welfare and, in particular, for education. Specifically, does the state have the right not to tax when it so chooses? Can courts themselves tax?

Federal Judge Orders Consolidation Of Little Rock, Suburban Districts*

A federal district judge in Little Rock, Ark., has ruled that two largely white suburban school districts have contributed to student segregation in the city schools and thus should be consolidated with the predominantly black district.

Education Week, April 25, 1984, p. 14.

"In my view, public education in this community has reached a crisis stage," said U.S. District Judge Henry Woods in his April 13 order. "The problem cannot be avoided by equivocation or half-measures."

Judge Woods set a hearing for April 30 to begin working out details of the consolidation, which will affect approximately 56,000 students in the metropolitan Little Rock area.

Contributed to Segregation

In his 64-page memorandum and opinion, Judge Woods held that over a period of years, the suburban districts, in concert with other public and private agencies, acted in a manner that contributed to segregated housing and other conditions that resulted in increasing segregation in the Little Rock district.

For example, he noted that the districts accepted white students from Little Rock in 1959 when Governor Faubus closed the city schools following a U.S. Supreme Court desegregation order. Judge Woods also wrote that talks among the three districts regarding voluntary consolidation in the 1960s were broken off by the suburban districts following the city district's adoption of a full-scale desegregation plan. In addition, he noted that neither suburban district provides "compensatory" educational assistance for its black students.

Furthermore, Judge Woods wrote that the North Little Rock district has failed to hire and promote black teachers and administrators in numbers proportionate to their representation in the city and that it disproportionately classifies black students as educably mentally retarded.

The Pulaski County district, he continued, has failed in large part to comply with the provisions of a consent decree that settled a separate desegregation suit. Among other things, he noted the district has failed to guarantee racially neutral policies on the selection of school-construction sites, to establish a bi-racial council as ordered, and to seat two blacks on the county board as nonvoting, ex-officio members.

"The deficiencies in the Pulaski County and North Little Rock districts have had severe interdistrict effects," Judge Woods wrote. "The only long-term or even short-term solution to these problems is consolidation."

"Not only will this solution provide the basis for the establishment of a unitary school system, but it should provide economy in administration and transportation that will contribute toward a quality education for all students in this county," he concluded.

St. Louis Schools Seek Desegregation Funding*

St. Louis city and school officials are again tangling in federal court over the school district's request that a judge order two desegregation funding measures that were defeated by the city's voters last month.

State law required two-thirds approval by St. Louis voters for passage of a $63.5 million bond issue for capital improvements and a $34 million tax increase to support the areawide desegregation plan, but those measures drew only 58 percent and 52 percent support, respectively.

Facing a $41 million shortfall for its 1984–85 plan, the school board June 29 urged U.S. District Judge William Hungate to nullify the two-thirds voter approval requirement and order the defeated funding measures into place.

City and state officials are opposed, however, to the notion that Hungate has authority to order such revenue steps over the will of area voters and have asked the U.S. Supreme Court to bar court-ordered taxation in the case, under the constitutional separation of powers.

Indeed, the 8th U.S. Circuit Court of Appeals has authorized quite limited judicial authority to mandate a tax increase, Robert Dierker, associate city counselor, said yesterday. The appeals court said court-ordered tax increases are justifiable only after all other funding alternatives have been exhausted, he said, and the city within days will file court papers opposing the board in *Liddell* v. *Board* (72–100 c(3)).

The school board has clearly met the 8th Circuit standard for a court-ordered tax increase, it told Hungate, but such an order isn't even necessary in the case. The judge can merely invalidate the "supermajority" two-thirds voter approval requirement that has "impeded the implementation of the constitutionally required desegregation plans," said the school board motion.

Dierker called that argument "simply a deception. It is really a court-ordered tax increase." Missouri Attorney General John Ashcroft also will fight the board's request, state officials said. Meanwhile, the Justice Department is expected to file a Supreme Court brief on the matter July 22.

School Finance News, July 12, 1984, p. 4.

3-8. FEDERAL RULES AFFECTING LOCAL EDUCATIONAL PRACTICES*

This document, filed in the federal notices on July 18, 1970, is commonly referred to within the Office of Civil Rights as the May 25th memorandum. It is an early example of a short, ends-oriented regulation. It says, in effect, "Dear School District, do you have a bilingual problem? If so, or if you might, please check and let us know. Please tell us what you're doing about it. We assume you should be doing something rather than nothing. Please find out over time if what you're doing works. If not, change it." No means are stipulated.

The Office of Civil Rights went through about thirteen years of gyrations producing a means-oriented memorandum in the area of bilingual education. Finally, in 1983, a four-and-a-half page internal memorandum reaffirmed the enclosed policy. To prevent dissemination of the new memorandum as a regulation, the Office of Civil Rights insisted that the 1983 statement was merely a follow-up clarifying and restating the policy in the May 25th memorandum. In addition, it was directed not to external sources but to the Secretary of Education from the Office of Civil Rights. If the 1983 document—which is too long to include here— had been handled in any other way, it would have become a proposed regulation and subject to review by both the White House and the OMB. In the Reagan administration, this means that it would never have seen the light of day.

Identification of Discrimination and Denial of Services on the Basis of National Origin

The following memorandum has been sent by the Director, Office for Civil Rights, to selected school districts with students of National Origin–Minority Groups:

Title VI of the Civil Rights Act of 1964, and the Departmental Regulation (45 CFR Part 80) promulgated thereunder, require that there be no discrimination on the basis of race, color, or national origin in the operation of any federally assisted programs.

Title VI compliance reviews conducted in school districts with large Spanish-surnamed student populations by the Office for Civil Rights have revealed a number of common practices which have the effect of

*Federal Register 35, no. 139, July 18, 1970, pp. 11595–96.

denying equality of educational opportunity to Spanish-surnamed pupils. Similar practices which have the effect of discrimination on the basis of national origin exist in other locations with respect to disadvantaged pupils from other national origin–minority groups, for example, Chinese or Portuguese.

The purpose of this memorandum is to clarify D/HEW policy on issues concerning the responsibility of school districts to provide equal educational opportunity to national origin–minority group children deficient in English language skills. The following are some of the major areas of concern that relate to compliance with Title VI:

(1) Where inability to speak and understand the English language excludes national origin–minority group children from effective participation in the educational program offered by a school district, the district must take affirmative steps to rectify the language deficiency in order to open its instructional program to these students.

(2) School districts must not assign national origin–minority group students to classes for the mentally retarded on the basis of criteria which essentially measure or evaluate English language skills; nor may school districts deny national origin–minority group children access to college preparatory courses on a basis directly related to the failure of the school system to inculcate English language skills.

(3) Any ability grouping or tracking system employed by the school system to deal with the special language skill needs of national origin–minority group children must be designed to meet such language skill needs as soon as possible and must not operate as an educational dead-end or permanent track.

(4) School districts have the responsibility to adequately notify national origin–minority group parents of school activities which are called to the attention of other parents. Such notice in order to be adequate may have to be provided in a language other than English.

School districts should examine current practices which exist in their districts in order to assess compliance with the matters set forth in this memorandum. A school district which determines that compliance problems currently exist in that district should immediately communicate in writing with the Office for Civil Rights and indicate what steps are being taken to remedy the situation. Where compliance questions arise as to the sufficiency of programs designed to meet the language skill needs of national origin–minority group children already operating in a particular area, full information regarding such programs should be provided. In the area of special language assistance, the scope of the program and the process for identifying need and the extent to which the need is fulfilled should be set forth.

School districts which receive this memorandum will be contacted shortly regarding the availability of technical assistance and will be provided with any additional information that may be needed to assist districts in achieving compliance with the law and equal educational opportunity for all children. Effective as of this date the aforementioned areas of concern will be regarded by regional Office for Civil Rights personnel as a part of their compliance responsibilities.

Dated: July 10, 1970

J. Stanley Pottinger, Director, Office for Civil Rights

3-9. WHITE HOUSE REACTION TO THE FAILURE
OF REGULATORY REFORM

When President Reagan was inaugurated, the Department of Education withdrew its notice of proposed rule making regarding bilingual education. This did not affect the May 25th memorandum; it only affected the detailed, means-oriented proposed rule that had been developed and issued in 1980 pursuant to Northwest Arctic School District v. Califano. *It is no secret, however, that the power of the federal bureaucracy, particularly as it attempts to anticipate the informational and other needs of Congress, does not rest solely upon legislation and administrative regulations. Everything it does—and particularly its efforts to gather information pursuant to both congressional law and congressional committee needs—affects the operation of educational programs in school districts and states. These actions sometimes have the effect of reorienting the substance of programs around the information needs of the bureaucracy. One White House staffer was well aware of this and put out the following memorandum. The fact that neither the White House nor OMB succeeded in altering the subregulatory behavior of bureaucracies to any degree reinforces our picture of the close tie between individual bureaucracies and Congress. Moreover, the informa-*

tion needs of the White House, if it were to try to intervene in the sub-regulatory process, would be almost overwhelming.

White House Memorandum

March 3, 1981   To:——   From:——   RE: Bilingual Education

1) In doing the research for the National League of Cities Speech yesterday regarding the bilingual education program in Fairfax County, Virginia—provided me with an interesting background to bilingual education that you ought to be aware of.

2) While Secretary of Education Bell gave the impression for some that he was withdrawing the bilingual education regulations altogether—regulations which informs me he worked to enact by subregulatory memoranda in the Nixon administration—he really withdrew only the formal regulatory proposals for bilingual education leaving in force a host of subregulatory memoranda that serve to accomplish the same effect as codified regulations: mandatory bilingual education.

3) "The Mandate Millstone" has not been removed from school districts and will not be until there are changes at the subregulatory level because the previous mandate is still in force. These changes will be easier to make since the regulations were not codified. The withdrawal of the bilingual education regulations from the codification process was a proper move for the Administration to dismantle the mandate.

4) For the bilingual education mandate to be dismantled, and for individual districts to handle their own bilingual education affairs, the subregulatory memoranda must be superceded [sic] by new memoranda precluding the Department of Education from issuing bilingual education mandates.

4 Government Policy in Capital-Intensive Services

Government policies involving housing, transportation, and environmental improvement are determined very much like educational policies. All the policy areas evolve slowly and in response to the electoral needs of congresspeople. Few long-term or grand policy plans come from the federal government, yet in all these policy areas (as well as health and income maintenance; see Chapters 5 and 6), the episodic needs of congresspeople have produced workable results. Over time both education and capital-intensive policies have benefited organized groups in the usual sequential order: business and agriculture; professionals and labor; public sector professionals and bureaucrats; and consumers or targeted beneficiaries (see Chapter 1).

Just as federal education monies initially facilitated training for commerce and the national defense, monies spent on transportation initially facilitated the movement of goods among well-organized economic entities. Much federal money has been appropriated to develop rural, state, and interstate highway systems since 1916, the eve of U.S. entry into World War I. Parts of the federal bureaucracy developed a vested interest in maintaining and expanding public-sector activity supporting transportation, just as part of the Department of Education has a vested interest in directing monies to programs aiding the handicapped, the underachieving, and the non-English-speaking—the Army Corps of Engineers, for example, benefits from congressional appropriations for building canals, dikes, and harbors.

Housing is another policy area in which Congress has an electoral interest of long standing. In 1892 Congress appropriated $20,000 for a survey of four cities to determine the extent of slum housing in the United States (Public Resolution 52-22). The first substantial commitment of federal money to housing occurred under the Housing Act of 1937, which provided for low-rent housing and slum clearance. The act, however, was more concerned with the fiscal integrity of any federal investment and with getting rid of the blighting effects of slums than with providing housing for those who truly needed it (see Reading 4-1). The principal beneficiaries were the urban middle classes, whose property values were affected by the slum blight, and the public and private purveyors of the capital used for construction. The Federal Housing Authority (FHA), established under the 1937 act, had to act through state and local housing authorities; only the latter were able to exercise eminent domain to obtain the land necessary for building (*United States v. Certain Land in the City of Louisville, Jefferson County, Kentucky,* 1935).

Improving the environment is the most recent goal of federal capital expenditures. Since large metropolitan areas produce both human and industrial wastes, large influxes of capital have been necessary to prevent the degradation of air, water, and even soil fertility in many parts of the country. Federal legislation and expenditures on environmental protection are now necessary; the scale of activity is so large that few private investors will make up-front capital commitments to activities benefiting the environment even if they are profitable in the long run.

The evolution of federal financing of highway and housing construction and environmental improvement repeats patterns that we have observed in education (Chapter 3) and other policy areas. First, the monies are channeled through state or local governments—the former in the case of the federal highway system. State highway departments or their nominal equivalents contract with local contractors to build various parts of the state and interstate system. This is paid for with various mixes of federal and state money.

A second common feature is the increased involvement of planners in setting the initial program agendas. After 1949, planning on the part of local governments was required before they could receive federal housing or highway funds (see Reading 4-2). The requirements of federal housing, transportation, and highway legislation contributed to the now extensive planning profession.

Many of the details of local-level programing using federal dollars are consequences of negotiations among planners at different levels in the federal system. Program authority may be delegated not only to more local, geographically based political units, but to nonelected professional groups. This functional delegation is found in federal education programs involving the handicapped (Chapter 3). In the case of highways, however, the delegation is explicit in the statute, and some federal monies are earmarked for planning. Examples include the 1954 urban renewal legislation, the Education of All Handicapped Children Act (see Chapter 3), and the 1964 Community Mental Health Centers Act (see Chapter 5).

The funding of both federal highway and housing programs reflects the tendency of all targeted federal programs to increase in scope with reauthorization. Highway monies fund many programs, including access to rural areas for farmers, the interstate highway system, the state truck road system, and, since 1963, urban mass transit and highway beautification. In the case of federal aid to rural housing, the scope of the aid broadened from the original target of form-related buildings to include all buildings in rural areas. Housing and urban development acts passed since 1974 contain provisions related to housing, urban transport, highway development around urban areas, beautification, civil liberties, and many smaller concerns tacked on by congresspeople. This expansion parallel-similar processes in federal involvement in education (Chapter 3) and in health (Chapter 5).

Federal loan guarantees and other means of securing the integrity of invested capital have a long history in the areas of transportation and housing. Banks received guarantees when they made loans to construct the first two transcontinental railroads. Recently, automobile companies, notably Chrysler, have received loan guarantees, as much to maintain employment in the electoral districts in which the auto industry is found as to prevent bankruptcy per se. Federally guaranteed home mortgages have encouraged home ownership and benefited the construction industry since the Great Depression.

The highly physical product of federal policies in housing, transportation, and environmental improvement has little bearing on the policy tools available to Congress. As in the case of education, water, sewage, housing, and transportation projects have been used to force states to enact their own laws or spend their own monies in federally directed ways or suffer withdrawal of some federal funding. An example of such negative regulation is the enactment of the fifty-five MPH speed limit. The magnitude and fiscal importance of negative regulation are less in federal capital expenditures than in federal support for education. Yet in each of these very different areas, negative regulation has become an important policy tool of Congress in the past several decades.

Context

In 1891 New Jersey was the first state to establish a program of assistance for the development of county roads. The federal government did not follow suit until 1916, when Congress authorized $75 million for road construction over the next five years. This money was to be provided to state road departments (of which there were thirty-nine) on a straight matching basis; states had to spend a dollar on roads for every dollar of federal money spent. By 1921 the first of two basic divisions developed to plague those who lobbied for greater federal expenditure on public highways. This division was over the amount of money to be spent on rural versus primary interurban roads. Particularly in rural states, state legislatures and the state congresspeople were reluctant to spend state matching monies on roads connecting cities. But if a state emphasized rural roads, it sacrificed federal funds, which were targeted at interurban and interstate mileage because the representatives of eastern, urban, and oil-producing constituencies promoted and determined the details of federal aid to highways at that time.

The second basic division was over who was going to pay and who was going to benefit from the interurban and interstate system. There was general agreement among users that the money they paid for gasoline taxes, licenses, and so on should be spent on roads. The basic disagreement was between truckers on the one hand and farmers on the other. Just how much money was to be spent on rural roads versus interurban connections? The oil industry supported both sides; the producers of gasoline wanted more travel, and they also wanted gas taxes collected by states to be spent only on highways. (In the 1920s and 1930s such taxes often went to supplement general state revenues.)

In the federal highway administration, the principle that roads should be built for the convenience of those who paid for them was central. In the 1920s and 1930s state and federal engineers increasingly took over from local officials the supervision of planning and building highways. Actual planning was somewhat local; building was entirely local. There are now national rules and conditions for receiving national monies.

Another feature of federal involvement was the conception of a highway building as a vehicle for macroeconomic control. Herbert Hoover considered it a positive form of economic stimulation (Rose 1979, p. 10); Franklin Roosevelt, however, was uncertain of its fiscal impact and did not significantly increase the federal budget for highway construction during the Depression. Until Roosevelt had to plan for the war effort in the late 1930s, interstate highway construction was only one of many projects employed to stimulate the economy.

Roosevelt also attempted to use highway construction to obtain funds for the federal government. He wanted to condemn excess lands along federal rights-of-ways and sell these lands at a profit to private enterprise or state and local governments. He saw this as a budget-balancing measure, thus reflecting his generally conservative view of large budget deficits. Congress actually considered such legislation in 1936 (*Congressional Record*, 86, p. 10, p. 11150).

For three reasons, highway development came under the increasing control of the planners rather than politicians before World War II. First, there was a diversion of state gasoline taxes to schools and welfare for which politicians took credit; what was left of the taxes was spent on highways and was usually allocated by state highway departments. This diversion was stopped by the highway lobby in a few states. Second, disagreement over what highway funds were to be spent on meant that politicians could not easily make opposing constituencies happy with a particular highway expenditure. Finally, a 1922 law established the criteria and percentages for the allocation of federal highway spending in advance of congressional appropriations. This meant that planners in the Bureau of Public Roads and various state highway officials could bargain and determine the relative allocations of federal highway monies while Congress still controlled the absolute amount spent. This prevented successive administrations from using allocations of highway monies to states and localities as tools in electoral campaigns.

The first systematic federal involvement in housing occurred during the presidency of Franklin Roosevelt. The most significant event was the provision of loan guarantees through the FHA. Title I of the National Housing Act of 1934 created the FHA and authorized it to insure banks, trust companies, and so on against losses on loans for alterations, repairs, and improvements on houses and certain other properties. To some extent much federal housing legislation since 1934 has represented efforts to update, fine-tune, and expand the activities of this insurance program and to create secondary markets in the mortgages insured under this legislation. These markets recycle private-sector dollars involved in the program by packaging them as instruments that can be purchased by anyone holding capital. The federal government guarantees the instruments. The entire process benefits the middle-class house purchaser and lenders of capital.

Before World War II federal expenditures on public support for housing were small. The principal component of the federal housing program was the FHA guarantee of mortgages. The insurance was intended to assist in providing adequate housing for families of low or moderate income particularly in suburban or outlying areas" (National Housing Act, Sec. 8A, June 27, 1934). The unemployed and those on welfare were not eligible for FHA loans. This program was designed for the deserving and usually working class, a group that would in the 1980s probably be termed middle class. This reflects the tendency of legislatures to reduce risks in the marketplace for businesses that are providing services to already mobilized sets of voters. Banks, insurance companies and the like are insured against the default of working-class, employed buyers.

Congress never intended to redistribute economic opportunities or alter patterns of residence with FHA home loan guarantees. This is illustrated in the FHA underwriters' manual, which warns official not to insure property unless there is protection from the presence of "inharmonious racial groups." The act intended to stabilize neighborhoods through the conversion of rental properties to neighborhoods of homeowners. Mortgage guarantees were aimed at the suburbs and outlying areas, indicating that they were intended to benefit banks, insurance companies, and white, not minority, homeowners. The National Association of Real Estate Boards encouraged a similar point of view when it declared in its 1924 Code of Ethics (Article 3A) "a realtor should never be instrumental in introducing into a neighborhood a character of property or occupancy, members of any race, nationality or individuals whose presence will clearly be detrimental to property values in the neighborhood". The preservation of property value and the stabilization of neighborhoods through expansion of homeownership appeared to be the objective of Congress and the Federal Housing Administration in the implementation of the 1934 Act (Friedman, 1969. pp. 134–37) (See Reading 4-3).

Federal involvement in housing and highway construction was dominated by the needs of World War II during the period from 1940 to 1945. After World War II federal rent control remained in effect through the ending of the Korean hostilities in 1953. The 1949 Housing Act provided monies for slum clearance and urban redevelopment on a somewhat larger scale than occurred in 1937 and 1938. After the war a number of states followed the lead of Pennsylvania and constructed toll roads. These four-lane highways were later included in the federal interstate system. Few housing programs were started in 1954–55 (Table 4.1) because of the lack of materials for home building, the need for construction of military bases, and the lack of agreement within the highway lobby as to the proper allocation of federal funds for highway users.

By that time the United States faced a situation in which new housing had been largely unavailable for over ten years. Economic development beyond recovery from the war was thwarted by the inability to transport goods and services between cities without running into serious traffic bottlenecks. Additionally, downtown areas of large cities were dying;

TABLE 4-1   **Low-Income Public Housing Under Housing Act of 1949 (and 1954 Amendments): Units Subsidized by the Federal Government**

Calendar Year	Units	Calendar Year	Units
1950	78,248	1965	26,281
1951	88,929	1966	43,514
1952	41,513	1967	70,277
1953	10,406	1968	77,801
1954	—	1969	108,783
1955	29,965	1970	101,932
1956	43,097	1971	58,228
1957	5,391	1972	80,319
1958	24,293	1973	33,453
1959	29,770	1974	22,438
1960	11,437	1975	12,858
1961	27,867	1976	4,286
1962	25,094	1977	3,440
1963	36,031	1978	9,371
1964	37,429	1979	59,186
		1980	41,876

TOTAL = 1,243,513

Source: U.S. Department of Housing and Urban Development, *HUD Statistical Yearbook: 1980* (Washington, D.C.: Government Printing Office, 1981), p. 255.

the United States was already experiencing the exodus of the employed middle class from the inner city. Organized interests turned to the Congress for aid in developing the capital-intensive infrastructure needed to facilitate economic activity. In this sense very little had changed since 1789.

Agenda

The Housing Act of 1954 and the National Interstate Highway Act of 1955 represent two responses to the needs of organized groups in business, agriculture, and defense. The Interstate Highway Act authorized monies to connect major urban areas. It did not initially provide benefits for rural areas. The Housing Act expanded the money available for planning grants, extending aid to municipalities with populations under 25,000 and authorizing 35,000 units of low-rent public housing (See Table 4-1). New public housing was explicitly tied to slum clearance and the development of an urban redevelopment or renewal plan. The number and types of housing eligible for the FHA Section 203 mortgage insurance program expanded. The 1954 Housing Act is a classic case of a reauthorization designed to provide more constituency-relevant benefits for more congresspeople. At the same time, it provided less housing than the pre–Korean War legislation. The President was in favor of the act because it continued the flow of federal monies into areas that could stimulate the economy during the recession that followed the end of the Korean War. A major part of the expansion occurred through increased aid for housing in rural areas and suburbs in both the 1949 and 1954 acts. Like most legislation that distributes benefits to congressional districts, party affiliation was not tremendously important in the passage of either act. Housing bills that provide benefits for both urban and rural constituencies are seldom controversial except to extreme fiscal conservatives. Only when housing is viewed as a burden on the budget-balancing activities of the executive is there active debate and controversy over federal funding.

Eisenhower's 1959 budget message recommended increased interest rates on FHA, Veterans' Administration (VA), and college housing loans and additional urban renewal grant funding. It also recommended the extension of FHA loan commitments to nonresidential urban renewal projects, new FHA mortgage insurance programs for housing the elderly, and a gradual increase in the state and city share of urban renewal costs to appease concerns for fiscal integrity. Congress passed more extensive legislation without provision for increasing interest rates or efficiency of spending. Eisenhower vetoed the original housing act of 1959. He won this exercise in budgetary control, and a compromise act closer to his recommendations passed on the third attempt. Similar to the Housing Act of 1954, this act took forty-seven sections to respond to and provide benefits for congressionally targeted constituency groups. Fine-tuning determined exactly what activities would be funded and who would benefit in which constituencies from the moderately larger federal housing program. Slight additions included the authorization of $10 million more for federal matching grants to assist state and urban planning and the new eligibility of nonprofit student housing cooperatives for college housing loans. The act encouraged statewide planning to improve efficiency and to force planning and program development to the state level so that program information would be readily available to Congress (compare the state-level programmatic administration of Title I described in Chapter 3).

By the late 1950s urban renewal funds were distributed to many congressional districts; however, the funds were not a major stimulator of the economy. Under the most optimistic of assessments, less than 0.1 percent of monies spent on public- and private-sector building, maintenance, and repair from 1950 to 1960 were associated with urban renewal programs. During this period the amount of low-rent housing decreased and the amount of high-rent housing increased. Private enterprise had achieved a net increase of 803,000 units occupied by nonwhites and a decrease of 537,000 in the number of substandard units involved. It is likely that the private sector was working better than the public sector with regard to the housing of racial minorities.

Building, remodeling, and maintenance would occur in the United States, particularly in urban areas, with or without the existence of urban renewal programs (Anderson, 1964, esp. chap. 11). It would be fair to say that the major effect of the federal urban renewal program was to cause shifts in the timing and location of some construction activity and to provide a useful tool for particular interests to get rid of city slums. The 1938, 1949, and 1954 public housing and urban renewal legislation emphasized the eradication of slums to benefit the wealthy more than the building of new housing for the poor. Urban renewal programs allowed public authorities or their private proxies to use eminent domain to get rid of slum housing. Other legislation provided housing and mortgage support for the middle class and the working poor. Other initial beneficiaries, as noted above are the construction companies and financial intermediaries that lend money. Later ones include the deserving poor (for more on this distinction see Chapter 6), businesses and organized craftspeople, and the middle class generally.

This pattern is repeated in the National Interstate Highway Act of 1955. The object was to develop efficient highways for the expansion of the economy and the needs of the military and civil defense. As in the NDEA of 1958 (see Chapter 3), national defense was used to pry open a new area of federal activity. In the case of highway construction, however, the goal was an accommodation among all the interest groups that favored highway construction and wanted to minimize the cost of such construction to their own constituents. Highway construction fell well within the purview of Congress under Article I, Section 8, and was already represented by ongoing programs at the federal level.

The plans produced by the executive branch were not the ones passed by Congress in 1955. The original proposal was for a somewhat federalized agency to plan, construct, and finance the interstate highway system. Both program and financial impetus would come from the federal government, but states would pay 10 percent of the monies for intrastate construction. Both truckers and farmers resisted this proposal. Over the preceding twenty years, both groups had worked to obtain influence in state legislatures and state highway departments. They were not about to give up their access to the state appropriation and planning processes so that some national body could rationalize an interstate highway system in the interest of other groups. The House of Representatives, as a locally elected body, responded to this concern. The 1955 act requires states to come forward with the planning and construction initiative. State plans must fit into a national plan, however, prompting some degree of intergovernmental bargaining between national and state planners. Where there is a disagreement about the planning of the interstate system, Congress can intervene. This has happened on a number of occasions: the fact that the interstate highway system goes through Scranton, Pennsylvania, and not Ithaca, New York, reflects the influence of Dan Flood, a representative from the Scranton area who served on the House appropriations committee in the late 1950s.

Under the 1955 legislation the federal government could not force states to build interstate highways. Components of the interstate system remained unfinished for years because state legislatures would not appropriate their 10 percent share of the cost. An outstanding example is

Interstate 70 through West Virginia, which was completed approximately fifteen years after the remainder of the highway. The practice of state contracting and local construction, justified as expanding commerce and helping to provide for the national defense, could be used selectively by Congress and the President to provide particularized employment and other economic benefits to congressional districts. When state governments whose legislatures were locally elected were ready to provide their share of funding for the interstate system, federal funding for those same parts of the system could usually be arranged.

Finally, a central feature of the highway program under the 1955 act was the dedication of the federal gasoline tax to a trust fund for the building of the interstate highway system. The corporation that managed the trust fund was authorized to issue bonds for up to $30 billion, not because Congress anticipated deficit financing of the highway system , but rather to even out the cash flow available to the corporation.

The 1955 National Interstate Highway Act was the last major piece of legislation in the area of highway construction in the 1950s (see Reading 4-4). Like the 1954 Housing Act, it laid the basis for federal expenditures "in the national interest" that would be responsive to already well-organized groups in the economy: builders, unions, farmers, oil companies, truckers, the Department of Defense, and those planners at the national level interested in using highway and home construction for macroeconomic ends.

The inherent instability of such legislated programs is manifested when new groups enter the political arena. Minorities, the poor, or consumers organize at the local and congressional level and exert pressure to expand the population benefitted by previously existing legislation and extend the basic thrust and purpose of the legislation itself.

The old beneficiary groups, however, do not just fade away. Farmers, for example, did not want to be and are not a prime beneficiary group under the 1955 Interstate Highway Act. Yet farmers pay taxes, and as the interstate system nears completion, they make their presence known (see Reading 4-4). Farmers will continue to receive benefits from rural housing and highway legislation whenever the urban poor receive support for public housing and mass transit. The evolution of the relationship between organized groups and congressional responsiveness is characterized by continual addition and complication, not replacement (see Chapter 1).

By 1961 there was pressure to expand housing for the elderly, to provide housing for the poor, to engage in demonstration grants and a greater degree of planning for the use of space in urban areas. The planning and funding of federal transport and housing programs began to merge. How people in the city and suburbs were transported and where urban highways were placed affected the economic well-being and employability of populations in metropolitan areas. Often highway and housing plans affecting urban populations centered on the use of physical space, but the federal and state governments found that these new groups made demands that could not be ignored.

Process

In response to the physical needs of metropolitan areas and the electoral needs of the members of Congress representing them, in the early 1960s the federal government encouraged the planning and development of mass transit systems. In fiscal year 1961 monies were committed to both metropolitan planning and planning mass transit systems. In 1964 and 1968 federal support for such planning was extended in scope and increased to cover two-thirds of the costs involved. The Urban Mass Transportation Act of 1964 required metropolitan transport planning and evaluation as a condition of receiving federal funds (see Reading 4-7). The 1964 act was also significant because it permitted the dedication of some highway trust fund monies to mass transit. Today this amount is a carefully circumscribed.

The 1964 changes were possible because of a rapidly expanding economy. Not only were federal revenues increasing, but so were highway trust fund revenues as people drove more. During this period of growth, it was almost impossible not to expand the number of beneficiaries of federal highway programs, although the traditional highway lobbies resisted. That this expansion took so long attests to the power in many local areas of the highway and gasoline lobbies. Through the mid-1970s, the interstate highway fund amply provided for the construction of the system designed in 1955. There was little controversy surrounding this activity until the interstate system was almost complete. At that point the interests that had lost out in the 1955 act— farmers and residents of small towns—reestablished their claim on part of the highway money. Although rural roads had been funded all along, it was only in the 1970s that urban transport was recognized as a priority. One can see the balancing of the interstate and noninterstate systems by looking at actual outlays for the two systems (Table 4-2). In

TABLE 4-2   **Highway Program Levels for Trust Fund, General Fund, and All Programs, Measured by Outlays; Fiscal Years 1957–77 (in millions of dollars)**

	1957	1958	1960	1962	1964	1966	1968	1970	1972	1974	1976	1977
Outlays												
Trust fund programs												
Interstate	211	673	1,861	1,914	2,635	2,979	3,207	3,286	3,467	3,017	3,435	2,950
Noninterstate	755	839	1,079	870	1,010	986	964	1,092	1,223	1,582	3,086	3,197
Total trust fund	966	1,512	2,940	2,784	3,645	3,965	4,171	4,378	4,690	4,599	6,521	6,147
General fund programs	126	125	127	136	162	235	348	434	548	528	589	615
Total	1,092	1,637	3,067	2,920	3,807	4,200	4,519	4,812	5,238	5,127	7,109	6,762

Source: Clifford W. Woodward 1978 Trends Federal Domestic Transportation Programs, Revenue and Expenditures by State Fiscal Years, 1957–1975. Washington D.C. U.S. Department of Transportation.

1957 the outlays for the interstate system were $211 million, as contrasted to $755 million for the noninterstate system. By 1965 the interstate system consumed a little over $3 billion and the noninterstate system a little over $1 billion. This ratio was roughly maintained until the early 1970s. In 1972, however, the gap began to close. In 1976 the noninterstate total became two-thirds the size of the interstate total and in 1977 surpassed it.

To administer these programs and to provide organized constituents with a single locus for contact with the bureaucracies managing them, Congress created the Department of Housing and Urban Development (HUD) in 1965. It assumed jurisdiction over most housing programs. The Department of Transportation (DOT) was created in 1966 and assumed responsibility for the interstate highway system (see Chapter 2). In creating the two agencies, Congress recognized that organized urban constituents would set some of the agenda for congressional action in the near future (compare the creation of the Department of Education, discussed in Chapters 2 and 3). HUD and DOT were to coordinate their programs in the newly emerging area of mass transit. HUD also took over already existing water and small sewage projects that had evolved as part of HEW's response to public concern about the effects of pollution on the environment.

Federal capital construction programs affecting the environment emanate from three sources. First, earlier federal housing and highway activities required planning so that they would not affect the quality of air or water nearby. A poorly constructed highway, for example, can alter drainage patterns and make groundwater undrinkable. Second, economic expansion in the 1950s and 1960s created waste and pollution that could raise the cost of providing water to public and private suppliers. Finally, by the 1950s consumer groups had begun to organize at least on the local level, and they had advocates in Congress, particularly senators (like Edmund Muskie) from rural northeastern states affected by the industrial pollution of the mid-West. Congresspeople found that requiring clear air and water benefited many organized groups (non-manufacturing industry, professionals, organized middle-class consumers, building and transportation trades, etc.), particularly when Congress helped to pay for such clean ups. Coal-burning utilities and some manufacturers were among the groups disadvantaged by such legislation, but they could often pass increased costs on to domestic (but not overseas) customers.

Substantive federal support for cleaning up the environment began in 1959 with the appropriation of $50 million to support the development of municipal waste-water treatment plants. In 1962 a portion of the federal highway mónies were dedicated to beautification of the areas around highways. In 1965 gas emission controls were established. The major pieces of legislation affecting the quality of the air were passed in 1967 and 1970. The 1970 Clean Air Act actually gave citizens standing to sue the federal government or any public or private party for contributing to the deterioration of the water or air in any national park or forest. This meant that any new industrial process could be litigated. n 1972 the Water Pollution Control Act vastly expanded the amount of capital the federal government put into the treatment of waste-water (see Table 4-3).

TABLE 4-3   **Federal Construction Grants for Municipal Waste-Water Treatment, 1964–77 (in millions of dollars)**

	Authorized	House Appropriation	Senate Appropriation	Actually Spent
1964	100	90	85	66
1965	100	90	84	70
1966	150	121	118	81
1967	150	150	131	84
1968	450	203	191	122
1969	700	214	201	135
1970	1,000	800	424	176
1971	1,250	1,000	1,152	478
1972	2,000	2,000	860	413
1973	7,000[a]	3,900[b]	2,989	684
1974	6,000	3,000	2,608	1,553
1975	6,000	4,000	4,131	1,938
1976[c]	0	9,000	4,853	3,347
1977	7,700	1,980	7,168[d]	3,546
Total	29,600	25,548	24,996[e]	12,696

Source: Environmental Protection Agency, Office of Planning and Management, *Activities of the Grants Assistance Programs* (Washington, D.C.: Environmental Protection Agency 1977).
[a]Includes $2 billion for reimbursement to municipalities for prior construction.
[b]Includes $1.9 billion for reimbursement to municipalities for prior construction.
[c]Includes transition quarter.
[d]Includes $0.5 billion for reimbursement to municipalities for prior construction.
[e]Includes $2.3 billion for reimbursement to municipalities for prior construction.

Cleaning up the environment costs a great deal of money. An important corollary is that the amounts involved are so large that the federal government is going to have to put up much of the money. No congressional legislation or subsequent regulations can extract nonexistent funds from state and local governments. Hence, neither small carrots (grants) nor big sticks (negative regulation) can be relied on exclusively to prompt state and local spending in amounts adequate to clean up public air and waters. Large federal grants became necessary.

As in education (Chapter 3) and health (Chapter 5), environmental programs expand and new programs come into place when the economy is expanding. However, a downturn in the economy does not stop resources from going into the new programs. Great expansion of highway, housing, and environmental programs occurred in the 1960s. These commitments had to be funded in the 1970s, when the economy grew much more slowly. In the case of capital construction, the time from the promise of capital commitment to actual construction of a project may take years. Once started, however, construction programs are supported by local governments, the construction industry, the ecology lobby (where relevant), and congresspeople concerned about localizing the benefits of federal expenditures. Hence, federal spending on environmental improvement expanded rapidly in the 1970s.

The Clean Water Act of 1980 (see Reading 4-5) illustrates several features of the way Congress writes legislation. Congress often prefers indirect to direct aid. In the process of cleaning up steams and the air, financial institutions and other companies will obtain business and make profits. This is consistent with the general rule that whenever new groups obtain benefits, groups that are already represented in locally based legislatures retain and even expand their legislated benefits.

The riots of the 1960s clearly demonstrated that urban renewal and other federal and state programs had not alleviated the sometimes deplorable living conditions found in the inner cities. Partly in symbolic response, Congress in 1966 passed the Model Cities program. Within a year or two it became evident that the executive branch and Congress had different conceptions of the program. The former said that the key to success was the coordination of federal expenditures in urban areas. To Congress, however, Model Cities was just another case of distributed urban aid (Friedman and Kaplan, 1975, pp. 190–93). Although it voted additional monies, the necessary coordination was never forthcoming, not because coordination was not desired at the highest levels, but because there is little incentive for those at the middle levels of the federal bureaucracy to give up already established lines of communication to congressional committees and local governments in order to coordinate activities with people outside their own hierarchy. The more pressure for coordination comes from the top, the more resistance is likely from risk-adverse middle-level bureaucrats. Clearly the program did not work as the executive branch had intended (see Chapter 2).

The 1974 Housing and Community Development Act provides funds for urban development (see Reading 4-6), 80 percent of which are to go to urban areas. Metropolitan areas receive these funds on an entitlement basis through the large cities block grant. Among the few conditions are that each area must have a housing survey and a three-year plan and provide details concerning the proposed use of federal money. In effect, the 1974 act is a block grant to large cities. A similar block grant to small cities and towns is administered through state governments (except in New York and Maryland). Additionally, urban development action grants (UDAGs) are administered by the federal government to local areas on the basis of competitive application. Only about 20 percent of the applications are funded.

This system has been in place about ten years now, and as a consequence the flow of funds is fairly regularized. Local areas employing planners who keep abreast of the activities and goals of their peers at HUD are most likely to get UDAG's and urban renewal funding. Since the larger allocations in this area are now block-granted and the smaller ones are provided to small cities and local governments on an application basis, the politics of obtaining federal funding in this area has in effect been delegated to negotiation competition among professionals.

At the same time that housing and urban development funds were becoming increasingly like block grants, the reverse process was occurring. Congress and the executive simply could not resist continual changes in the conditions and the targets of the grants (see chapter 3 reading 2-9). In the 1974 act applications for small cities block grants had to show that 75 percent of the impact of the requested monies would benefit low- and moderate-income individuals, as determined by the scoring done at HUD regional evaluations. HUD dropped other regulations as well. In 1984 Congress explicitly legislated that community development funds must be spent so that 51 percent of the beneficial impact goes to low- and moderate-income individuals; otherwise applications cannot be considered. Congress thus reasserted its need to control the flow of federal monies to electorally reluctant beneficiaries. This process parallels the increased congressional tampering with the conditions of the federal education block grant (Chapter 2).

Small cities block grants and UDAGs are two of the many instances in which the professional norms shared by those employed by federal, state, and local governments and by the private sector have evolved to determine the context in which federal programs are implemented. Congress appropriates funds for UDAGs. The actual recipients of the funds are largely determined by the contestants' ability to develop programs that reflect values shared by administrators and planners in HUD and its regional offices. However, all areas have an opportunity to compete, and this opportunity is an electoral benefit to locally elected congresspeople.

Consequences

The Urban Mass Transportation Act of 1964 and the Housing and Urban Development Act of 1974 together created a complicated set of interactions among local and state governments on the one hand and local planning bodies that receive their funds from the federal government on the other. This can often create a tension between the responses of the planning bodies to federal regulations and the political needs of local governments in allocating the time and money for planning, housing, and transportation. This tension is resolved through negotiation and not legislation. County government cannot legislate that local planning bodies funded with federal monies ignore the federal laws that provide the funds. Federal- and state-level officials cannot ensure that local planning is done without the cooperation of local governments. This reflects a fundamental characteristic of policy as it is implemented at the local level in the United States. Where implementation involves money, planning, and administration by a number of levels of government, the resulting policy is almost never legislated; rather, it represents a negotiated compromise between the legislative needs of politicians at different levels and the bureaucratic needs of administrators at different levels (see Reading 4-7).

One consequence of the extension of federal involvement in housing and transport is that its effect on the federal budget as a whole is more visible. When the economy and federal tax revenues are declining, there is a temptation to cut spending for these domestic items. In 1971 and 1972 Nixon tried to "impound" monies that had been appropriated for highway construction and other purposes. This action later declared an unconstitutional assumption of legislative authority, gave rise to the Congressional Budget and Impoundment Control Act of 1974 (see Chapter 2). There are many other, more incremental ways to control spending, however, particularly on housing (see Reading 4-8).

A second consequence of federal involvement in transport, at least, is a quasi nationalization of transportation infrastructure with the purpose of preserving inefficient capital facilities of national importance. The two principal instances of this are the creations of Amtrak and Conrail. Amtrak came into being as a consequence of a rapid sequence of steps taken by the consolidated Penn Central Railroad and others to preserve assets. In 1970 Penn Central filed for reorganization under Chapter 11 of the Federal Bankruptcy Act. Under reorganization it became clear that it had to dump its passenger train service. This was also true of the money-losing Lehigh Valley and Reading Railroad. In early 1970 petitions to cut service for almost all passenger lines were filed at once. Many of these petitions could have been filed as early as 1958, since the lines were already losing money then (Saunders, 1978, pp. 298–99). The loss of passenger service to so many towns and cities panicked Congress. Various pieces of emergency legislation passed in 1970 loaned money to railroads that were incurring losses. Finally, the railroads' inability to repay debts resulted in the establishment of a National Railroad Passenger Corporation on May 1, 1971. This legislation took no capital stock, except passenger cars, away from Penn Central and other cystems: Amtrak rented track from the various private railroads. The public sector took over the clearly unprofitable passenger-oriented parts of a private-sector corporation because these parts provided identifiable services to constituents in many cities and towns in the Northeast.

The establishment of Conrail was conceptually somewhat more complicated. In this instance, unprofitable firms were taken over by the government. Profit-making railroads appeared to be unwilling to take over segments of the freight traffic of Penn Central or the other railroads that were losing money on commercial traffic. Nationalization was one way to preserve rights-away, tracks and facilities for national defense or other purposes. In the United States, however, one cannot talk about nationalization. That is why the government will never take over a company per se. The government's business is not business, but to facilitate business, independent of direct legislative and executive control. Other countries, like Canada and France, could nationalize railroads that failed. Parallel actions in the United States could not be formally labeled.

Congress could not allow the railroads' basic capital facilities to lie unused and to deteriorate. Major institutional holders of railroad stock would bring strong pressure on both the executive and the legislative branches of government to ensure that such capital holdings did not become suddenly valueless. Southern and western congresspeople did not want to cut off the flow of goods by rail into the Northeast. The Union Pacific Railroad wrote parts of the bill. First National City Bank supplied data about finance. Banks supplied most of the money, although the solvency of the rail corporation was guaranteed by the federal government. Banks succeeded in trading the obligations they held from Penn Central, which might not be honored in bankruptcy, for loans that were, in effect, to the federal government. The amount of the loans was increased to reimburse stockholders.

These experiences and the Chrysler bailout (Chrysler maintained capital holdings and employment in a number of congressional districts) are significant examples of the use of politics to insure private corporations and even unions against the risks of the marketplace. As was pointed out in Chapter 1, congressional legislation in almost all policy areas initially benefits and never ignores these engaged in commerce. These benefits includes transfers and investments of private-sector capital as well as the facilitation of trade itself.

Another consequence of federal funding of state activity in transportation and housing is that Congress can redirect state and local priorities. Existing federal grants can be withdrawn, if states and localities do not enact particular regulations or fund specified programs. This sort of negative regulation is a way of bypassing the federal structure of government. The federal government often cannot legislate with respect to economic activity that occurs entirely within states. However, Congress can put conditions on the money it appropriates that force state-level legislation or spending into line with congressional desires. A state legislature may have to choose between turning away federal money or passing legislation opposed by a number of constituencies within the state. Congress has, for example, attached receipt of highway monies to the establishment of state speed limits and a higher drinking age and to the use of seatbelts and mandatory child restraints.

Soon after the Arab oil embargo in the early 1970s, Congress passed a law that penalized all states that did not lower their speed limits to fifty-five MPH. To ensure enforcement, Congress required that surveys be taken of the proportion of people driving under that limit in each state. If the proportion was high, Congress provided incentive grants; if the state chose not to pass or enforce the new limit, Congress withdrew a portion of its highway funding. Similarly, states must pass legislation requiring that young children be in approved child restraint carriers when in a moving vehicle (see Reading 4-9). Like most elements of public safety, the speed limit and the drinking age are for states to legislate (see Readings 4-10, 4-11). Congress, however, responds to recently organized groups by attaching new forms of required state behavior to already existing federally funded programs, as occurs in education (see Chapter 3). In both cases Congress commits little or no money to new programs; rather, it attaches the receipt of "old" monies to state performance of new tasks.

As a consequence of generations of congressional activity, housing and transport policies funded by the federal government are particularly complicated when implemented at the local level. This is because of the other purposes and goals the federal government has used these programs to facilitate. Amendments promoting the civil rights of minorities have been added to already existing federal support for housing and transport. Title VI of the Civil Rights Act of 1964, for example, requires that public housing be racially integrated and that a particular effort be made to house minority families. The Housing and Urban Development Act of 1968 amends the 1964 net by requiring some degree of preferential minority hiring in the construction of houses in the public sector. The National Environmental Policy Act requires that all proposed housing built with federal monies include an assessment of the effect of such housing on the immediate physical and social environment. The Federal Relocation Act of 1970 requires that there be no discrimination against minorities or others in the relocation of those displaced by federal housing programs. All of these requirements can sometimes come into conflict with the timely use of federal funding to alleviate what local officials perceive as immediate and pressing needs and provide congresspeople with current electoral benefit. This makes the regulation or negative regulation of behavior much more difficult than the regulation of state- and local-level spending or building.

President Kennedy's executive order of 1961 forbidding discrimination in the construction or use of facilities built with federal funds is fairly well enforced when the federal government is actually involved in the construction (military housing and bases, for example). When large sums of money are involved in building sewage plants, public housing (through private contractors), or interstate highways, however, Congress wants the money to be spent expeditiously to provide employment and other tangible benefits to constituents. Hence, one should not be surprised at the limited enforcement of civil rights regulations by national-level officials. In principle, HUD has the power to withdraw federal funds from public housing or public programs when racial discrimination occurs. It has threatened to do so in only one case to date (U.S. Commission on Civil Rights, 1979).

Although negative regulation involving emission control standards, drinking age, and child restraint systems may appear to limit the powers of state governments and the private sector, federal grants promoting transportation and housing benefit private-sector economic activity. Federal legislation can increase the powers of the states as well. Much of the on-site enforcement of the minority housing, integration, and environmental protection regulation rests with states and localities. States monitor and even mandate the housing and transportation projects of local government and the private sector, just as they ensure that the handicapped have equal access to educational opportunity (Chapter 3). Before the housing and highway legislation of the last two decades, many states exercised little control over the housing, transport, poverty or even education policies of local governments. Legislation of the 1960s and 1970s has thus led to greater state control over transport and housing construction in both the public and the private sectors. Clearly, increases in federal power need not decrease state power.

Capital-intensive programs like the building of highways and housing resemble the provision of educational services in a number of ways. Capital expenditure for the benefit of the poor is channeled through already existing private sector institutions, as opposed to direct grants by the federal government. There is a varying but constant emphasis on using guaranteed loans and rates of return to encourage the private sector to provide housing for poor and moderate-income individuals. Direct benefits, like highway funding and federal education programs, can later be used by Congress for negative regulation. In the area of housing, however, it is much more difficult to thwart private-sector activity once loan guarantees, subsidies, and rates of return have been provided. This means that it is also more difficult to use subsequent legislation to ensure that housing so provided meets federal standards for minority hiring, racial integration, and environmental protection. It is only with the rapid expansion of federal involvement in welfare in the 1970s that direct *cash* transfers have been made to the poor for housing rentals (see Chapter 6).

Yet in spite of the patchwork quality of policy evolution in these areas, federal involvement has frequently been successful in responding to the most clearly felt citizen needs. This is just what a locally elected Congress with a structure that facilitates the delivery of constituency-oriented benefits leads to.

Readings

4-1. HOUSING BENEFITS FOR THE MIDDLE CLASS AND THE DESERVING POOR*

This excerpt from the annual report of the U.S. Housing Authority and the reading that follows illustrate three aspects of federal policy in the area of public housing. The first is that the poorest and most needy people in the American population are not the only intended beneficiary group. Second, there is great concern with the fiscal integrity of public housing projects. Congress prefers to have local governments develop and administer the programs and to have the private sector entirely responsible for construction. No public-sector corporation is established to build the units for which funds have been appropriated by Congress. Finally, Congress and the federal housing agency (FHA) are somewhat more concerned with clearing slums than with rehousing individuals. All of these principles will extend through subsequent public housing legislation.

. . . Comparison with the family incomes statistics of the National Resource Committee shows that all the approved southern projects will serve families with income ranges well within the lowest third income

---

*Annual Report of the United States Housing Authority, 1938 (Washington, D.C.: Government Printing Office, 1938), pp. 6, 23.

group in northern urban areas. In other words, the program will serve only the lowest income group and will supply decent housing to families having only about half the income that they would need to rent or purchase modern homes supplied by private enterprise. It will reach into the lowest ranks of those employed in normal industry and will also serve those on relief and in public employment who are receiving allowances which meet a bare minimum subsistence level. In short, it will reach down to the vast majority of those now forced to live in the slums. But if a family has no income, or an income absolutely inadequate for minimum subsistence then there is not a practical and non-Utopian way to furnish it with decent housing until it receives such minimum income, either from public or private sources.

The elimination of slums under the United States Housing Act does not depend in any sense upon whether the new housing projects are build upon slum sites or upon new or relatively vacant sites. Wherever the new construction takes place, the act requires "the elimination by demolition, condemnation, and effective closing, or compulsory repair or improvement of unsafe or unsanitary dwellings situated in the locality or metropolitan area, substantially equal in number to the number of newly constructed dwellings provided by the project."

In most cases, the elimination of the necessary number of dwellings, other than on the site of the new project, is accomplished by localities through exercise of their police powers. All local governments have the inherent right to condemn, close or force the repair of dwellings which menace public health, safety or morals. In spite of two generations of public pressure, however, these powers have laid dormant in most communities. For one thing, no means existed for providing decent low-rent homes into which dispossessed families could be moved. But, Congress has not only provided the machinery for building the new-low rent homes—it has also recognized the necessity of permitting the "equivalent elimination" to be carried out through the exercise of local police power. The U.S.H.A. program thus enables cities and towns to compel compliance with local sanitary and building codes and to close up firetraps and slum buildings, in a word, to enforce the law.

4-2. EFFECTS OF HOUSING PROGRAMS
ON ECONOMIC GROWTH*

Again in 1949 we find that the elimination of slum dwellings is at least as important as the provision of low-rent public housing. Title III of the Housing Act of 1949 (P.L. 81-171) for the first time gives the President some discretion about how many public units can be built in a year. The rationale for this flexibility is that public construction can serve as a tool for managing the economy. Housing is a "high multiplier" activity; that is, the construction of housing generates many other jobs as well. The President can vary the number of units constructed according to the perceived need to stimulate the economy or control federal expenditures. This act also requires state and local governments to develop housing plans, rules, and income limits as a condition of using federal funding for housing construction.

Title III: Low-Rent Public Housing

Since public low-rent housing is intended to raise the standards of housing in the community, the law makes the provision for the elimination of substandard dwellings in connection with public housing projects.

Where public housing is built on a a slum site, this is accomplished when the site is cleared. Otherwise in urban areas, unsafe or unsanitary dwellings must be eliminated substantially equal in number to the number of new dwellings provided by the project. This must be done within 5 years after the project is completed, unless deferred because of an acute shortage of housing for low-income families in the locality.

The law permits PHA [Public Housing Authority] to authorize construction of 135,000 units a year for six years. The President can step up the rate to 200,000 units a year or slow it down to 50,000 units a year if economic conditions warrant. Much will depend, of course, on how quickly the localities undertake their programs, complete programs, acquire sites, and get construction under way. It is expected that about 50,000 units will get under construction in the next 12 months.

Only low income families are eligible to be admitted and live in low-rent public housing projects. Each locality will establish income limits

*Summary of *the Housing Act of 1949* Washington D.C.: U.S. Government Printing Office, 1949.

for admission and continued occupancy to make sure that tenant families fall within the low-income group. Other factors also figure in determining eligibility. These include requirements of citizenship, residence in substandard housing, and preferences for veterans and persons displaced by public slum clearance and urban redevelopment projects. . . .

Title I: Slum Clearance and Community Development and Redevelopment

This title authorizes the Housing and Home Finance Administrator to make loans and grants to localities to assist locally initiated, locally planned, and locally managed slum-clearance and urban redevelopment undertakings. A local public agency would, after public hearing, acquire (through purchase or condemnation) a slum or blighted or deteriorating area selected in accordance with a general city plan for the development of a locality as a whole. The local public agency would then clear the land and make it available, by sale, or lease, for private or public redevelopment or development in accordance with a predetermined local redevelopment plan for the area.

4-3. FEDERAL SUPPORT FOR HOUSING DISCRIMINATION*

The reading excerpts below illustrate some of the legal and structural variables that operate against the integration of housing, either public or private. In the excerpt, from the 1959 hearings on housing of the Commission on Civil Rights, the commission finds that the explicit and later de facto policies of the FHA have contributed to the segregation of public and private housing in the United States. The second excerpt, from a study of housing segregation, notes the banking community was, at best, a reluctant or neutral follower that would not use its lending resources to promote integrated housing. These legal and formal, financial and professional barriers to integration presented a formidable obstacle to any minority person who wanted to buy housing in a white area in the immediate postwar period.

Housing policies of the Federal Government have done much, both directly and indirectly, to sustain and strengthen racial segregation in

Hearings before the National Commission on Civil Rights, Washington D.C. U.S. Government Printing Office 1959, p. 66.

housing. While vastly assisting and stimulating the production and distribution of housing, the Federal agencies, public housing excepted, have made no significant attempt to insure the availability of Federal housing benefits on equal terms to all Americans. One of the effects of the Federal mortgage insurance or guarantees is to make large scale building operation financially feasible; a corollary effect is to give the private builder the power to discriminate and segregate over wider areas than ever before. Hence, we have seen, in the postwar period, the emergence of huge new communities without a single Negro resident, at least at the outset. Racial segregation is probably nowhere more complete than in federally assisted new private housing developments.

At one time and for a period of years, the Federal Housing Administration advocated the permanent exclusion of nonwhites from white subdivisions and ajoining territory by means of race restrictive convenants. Racial segregation was virtually one of the conditions of obtaining an FHA insured loan. These policies have long since been abandoned in favor of a policy of neutrality or nonresponsibility toward the question of nondiscrimination. Formal neutrality, however, has the practical effect of supporting existing practices. It also represents a more real sanction, for if the Government, expressing public policy, sees nothing wrong in racial discrimination, how can private persons be censured for practicing it?

The public housing program, also, has probably done more to increase than diminish segregation, notwithstanding the open-occupancy policies of many local authorities. Federal policy, as in the private field, leaves to local agencies the decisions of whether to segregate or not.

Local public agencies and officials, particularly in suburban communities, often use their discretionary powers over land use and building to prevent the entry of minority groups into areas reserved for white occupancy. Our studies have found evidence of frequent abuses of governmental powers to restrict the housing opportunities of nonwhite minorities in ways not accessible to judicial review, and under the cover of legitimate purposes.

Public Relations and Segregation*

In an earlier period the property value motive was probably the dominant one. More recently, as the effects of mixed occupancy on property

*From David McIntire, *Residence and Race* (Berkeley and Los Angeles: University of California Press, 1980), p. 225.

values have become debatable, reasons of public relations have become for many if not for most lenders the principal motive for withholding loans to nonwhites in white neighborhoods. The shift of emphasis in motive is important because the factors of public relations do not exert a uniform force in all areas nor upon all lenders. Usually, too. there is room for differing judgments about the nature and extent of adverse reaction to a particular loan and consequences for the lending institution. As a result, lender policy on the issue has tended to become rather vague and variable. This is illustrated in the comment of a Cleveland banker speaking more or less for all banks in the city:

> We do not finance the first Negro purchaser in a white area for public relations reasons. White resentment in the area would be great, probably resulting in account cancellations and discontinuance of other business. However, we do not insist that neighborhoods be 50 percent colored, or insist on any arbitrary statistical line before lending to Negro applicants. Depends on circumstances (Quote from *The Cleveland Press,* September 8, 1956.)

4-4. HIGHWAYS AND THE NATIONAL DEFENSE

The national highway program of 1955 (H.R. 4260) resembles the 1958 NDEA (chapter 3). Both pieces of legislation, like many others, invoke the national interest and then authorize the spending of federal funds to facilitate this interest. In the case of both NDEA and the national highway program, commerce and the national defense were cited. This 1955 act places considerable emphasis on the development of an interstate, as opposed to a rural, highway system.

Sec. 2 . . . It is hereby declared to be in the national interest to foster and accelerate the development of a modern, adequate, safe and efficient system of highways deemed essential for the expression of the economy and the changing concepts of the military and civil defense of the United States. It is further declared to be desirable that the development of such a system of highways be continued through the cooperation and joint efforts of the Federal Government, the States, and local subdivisions thereof. It is hereby found that those essential highways are in fact adequate to meet the needs of interstate commerce and the national civil defense, and that the most important portion of such highways are or should be, located on the National System of Interstate Highways.

Accordingly it is the objective of this Act to complete the construction of the National System of Interstate Highways within the next ten years to such standards as will produce safe highways adequate to handle the traffic needs for at least the next twenty years. This objective will be reached only by means of a program which will presently assure the financing of a system as a whole, and provide for prompt acquisition of necessary rights of way. It is hereby declared to be the policy of Congress to continue or impose such taxes as may be necessary to meet this objective.

(b) It is hereby declared to be in the national interest to accelerate the construction of the Federal-aid highway systems, including the National System of Interstate and Defense Highways, since many of such highways, or portions thereof, are in fact inadequate to meet the needs of interstate commerce, for the national and civil defense.

It is thereby declared that the prompt and early completion of the National System of Intersate and Defense Highways so named because of its primary importance to the national defense and hereafter referred to as the "Interstate System" is essential to the national interest and is one of the most important objectives of this Act. It is the intent of Congress that the Interstate System be completed as nearly as practicable over the period of availability of the thirty-four years' appropriations authorized for the purpose of expediting its construction, reconstruction or improvement, inclusive of the necessary tunnels and bridges, through fiscal year ending September 30, 1990, under section 108(b) of the Federal Highway Act of 1956 (70 Stat. 374), and that the entire system in all the States be brought to simultaneous completion. Insofar as possible in consonance with this objective, existing highways located on an interstate route shall be used to the extent that such use is practicable, suitable, and feasible, and shall be given equal consideration with the needs of interstate commerce.

Federal-State Relationship

The authorization of the appropriation of Federal funds or their availability for expenditure under this chapter shall in no way infringe on the sovereign rights of the States to determine which projects shall be federally financed. The provisions of this chapter provide for a federally assisted state program.

4-5. BUSINESS BENEFITS OF THE CLEAN WATER ACT

The Clean Water Act (P.L. 95-217) illustrates that even in 1980 federal aid to states and localities often took the form of loan guarantees rather than direct grants. Again, financial lending institutions benefit as well as state and local governments. Section 309 illustrates the lengthy procedures that the administrators of the Environmental Protection Agency (EPA) must go through in order to force states to remedy systematic violations of the environment within their boundaries. Even private corporations cannot be effectively punished for violating the environment. In Section 508 we see that a corporation must convicted (not just accused) of a violation to become ineligible to be a supplier to the federal government. Throughout this act administrators are carefully discouraged from using excessive zeal or speed in altering the practices of state and local governments or the private sector. In the long run there will be benefits for the environment. In the short run adverse publicity affects a polluter's behavior more than the sanctions of the law.ql

. . . Sec. 213 (a) Subject to the conditions of this section and to such terms and conditions as the Administrator determines to be necessary to carry out the purposes of this title, the Administrator is authorized to guarantee, and to make commitments to guarantee, the principal and interest (including interest accruing between the date of default and the date of payment in full of the guarantee) of any loan, obligation, or participation therein of any State, municipality or intermunicipality or interstate agency issued directly and exclusively to the Federal financing bank to finance that part of the cost of any grant-eligible project for the construction of publicly owned treatment works not paid for with Federal financial assistance under this title (other than this section), which project the Administrator has determined to be eligible for such financial assistance under this title, including, but not limited to, projects eligible for reimbursement under section 206 of this title. . . .

Section 309 (2)   . . . [W]henever, on the basis of information available to him, the Administrator finds that violations of permit conditions or limitations as set forth in paragraph (1) of this subsection are so widespread that such violations appear to result from a failure of the State to enforce such permit conditions or limitations effectively, he shall so notify the State. If the Administrator finds such failure extends beyond the thirtieth day of such notice, he shall give public notice of such finding. During the period beginning with such public notice and ending when such State satisfies the Administrator that it will enforce such conditions and limitations (hereafter referred to in this section as the period of "federally assumed enforcement") except where an extension has been granted under paragraph (5) (8) of this subsection the Administrator shall enforce any permit condition or limitation with respect to any person—

(a) by issuing an order to comply with such condition or limitation, or

(b) by bringing a civil action under subsection (b) of this section. . . .

Federal Procurement

Sec. 508 (a) No Federal agency may enter into any contract with any person, who has been convicted of an offense under section 309 (c) of this Act, for the procurement of goods, materials, and services if such contract is to be performed at any facility at which the violation which gives rise to such conviction occurred, and if such facility is owned, leased, or supervised by such a person. The prohibition in the preceding sentence shall continue until the Administrator certifies that the condition giving rise to such conviction has been corrected.

(b) The Administrator shall establish procedures to provide all Federal agencies with the notification necessary for the purposes of subsection (a) of this section.

(c) In order to implement the purposes and policy of this Act to protect and enhance the quality of the Nation's water, the President shall, not more than one hundred and eighty days after the enactment of this Act, cause to be issued an order (1) requiring each Federal agency authorized to enter into contracts and each Federal agency which is empowered to extend Federal assistance by way of grant, loan, or contract to effectuate the purpose and policy of this Act in such contracting or assistance activities, (2) setting forth procedures, sanctions, penalties, and such other provisions, as the President determines necessary to carry out such requirement.

(d) The President may exempt any contract, loan, or grant from all or part of the provisions of this section where he determines such exemption is necessary in the paramount interest of the United States and he shall notify Congress of such exemption.

4-6. HOUSING FUNDS AS URBAN ENTITLEMENTS

The Housing and Community Development Act of 1974 (P.L. 93-363) was intended to provide some development monies to almost everybody. After meeting only a few conditions, cities receive their community development monies almost as an entitlement. Smaller urban and rural areas must compete for 20 percent of the total funds allocated. This law replaces a variety of other programs, including Model Cities and many programs involving urban renewal. These programs had grown so extensive in terms of their beneficiary groups that the block grant approach of the current law was the next natural step. All large urban areas needed funds, so the trials and costs of competition were removed.

Title I—Community Development

Sec. 101 (a) The Congress finds and declares that the Nation's cities, towns, and smaller urban communities face critical social, economic and environmental problems arising in significant measure from—

(1) the growth of population in metropolitan and other urban areas, and the concentration of persons of lower income in central cities; and

(2) inadequate public and private investment and reinvestment in housing and other physical facilities, and related public and social services, resulting in the growth and persistence of urban slums and blight and the marked deterioration of the quality of the urban environment.

(b) The Congress further finds and declares that the future welfare of the Nation and the well-being of its citizens depends on the establishment and maintenance of viable urban communities as social, economic and political entities, and require—

(1) systematic and sustained action by Federal, State and local governments to eliminate blight, to conserve and renew older urban areas, to improve the living environment of low and moderate income families, and to develop new centers of population growth and economic activity;

(2) substantial expansion of and greater continuity in the scope and level of federal assistance, together with increased private investment, and in support of community development activities; and

(3) Continuing effort at all levels of government to streamline programs and improve the functioning of agencies responsible for planning, implementing, and evaluating community development efforts.

(c) The primary objective of this title is the development of viable urban communities, by providing decent housing and a suitable living environment and expanding economic opportunities, principally for persons of low and moderate income. Consistent with this primary objective, the Federal assistance provided in this title is for the support of community development activities which are directed toward the following specific objectives—

(1) the elimination of slums and blight and the prevention of blighting influences and the deterioration of property and neighborhood and community facilities of importance to the welfare of the community, principally persons of low and moderate income;
(2) the elimination of conditions which are detrimental to health, safety, and public welfare, through code enforcement, demolition, interim rehabilitation assistance, and related activities;
(3) the conservation and expansion of the nation's housing stock in order to provide a decent home and a suitable living environment for all persons, but principally those of low and moderate income;
(4) the expansion and improvement of the quantity and quality of community services, principally for persons of low and moderate income, which are essential for sound community development and for the development of viable urban communities;
(5) a more rational utilization of land and other natural resources and the better arrangement of residential, commercial, industrial, recreational, and other needed activity centers;
(6) the reduction of the isolation of income groups within communities and geographical areas and the promotion of an increase in the diversity and vitality of neighborhoods through the spatial deconcentration of housing opportunities for persons of lower income and the revitalization of deteriorating neighborhoods to attract persons of higher income;
(7) the restoration and preservation of properties of special value for historic, architectural, or aesthetic reasons.

4-7. FEDERAL CONTROL OVER LOCAL TRANSPORTATION PROJECTS

This resolution of the Binghamton (N.Y.) Metropolitan Transportation Study Policy Committee (no. 76-3) represents the city's compliance with various federal statutes that require comprehensive planning as a condition for receipt of federal mass transit money. Whether planning and evaluation actually occur and influence the spending of federal monies depends upon complex negotiations among local and county legislators, executives and planners, state-level planners, and federal program officers and planners. For details about how a community puts together many sources of federal and state funding into one community development package, see table 4-4.

Resolution Endorsing the Unified Operations Plan (Prospectus) for the Binghamton Metropolitan Transportation Study Area

WHEREAS, the Binghamton Metropolitan Transportation Study Policy Committee has been designated by the Governor of New York State as the Metropolitan Planning Organization responsible for the comprehensive, continuous, cooperative transportation planning process for the Binghamton metropolitan area, as required by Section 134 of Title 23, U.S. Code, and the Urban Mass Transportation Act of 1964 as amended, and

WHEREAS, Chapter 1, Part 450, Subpart A, 23 CFR and Chapter VI, Part 613, Subpart B, 49 CFR state that the urban transportation planning process shall include the development of a prospectus which shall establish a multi-year framework within which the unified planning work program is accomplished, and

WHEREAS, the prospectus shall include a summary of the planning process; a general description of the status and anticipated accomplishments of each element of the urban transportation planning process including procedures for carrying out those elements; a description of the functional responsibilities of each participating agency; and a cooperative agreement containing the understandings required by Federal regulations; and

WHEREAS, at its January 27, 1976 meeting the Binghamton Metropolitan Transportation Study Planning Committee recommended endorsement by the Policy Committee of the Unified Operations Plan for the Binghamton Metropolitan area.

TABLE 4-4   City of Binghamton Tenth Year Community Development
Program: Detailed Budget Breakdown

Housing Program		$ 785,000
A. Deferred Loan Program	200,000	
B. Rehabilitation Loan Program	250,000	
C. Investor Owner/Mixed Use Program	100,000	
D. Demolition Grant Program	10,000	
E. Physically Handicapped Assistance	10,000	
F. Housing Division Staff	215,000	
Economic Development Program		300,000
A. BLDC Economic Development Program	220,000	
B. BLDC Administration	20,000	
C. Economic Development Staff	60,000	
Neighborhood Redevelopment Program		350,000
Street Reconstruction		400,000
Public Service Programs		271,200
A. Talent Search	91,000	
B. Inner City Nursery	14,000	
C. Services for Older Persons	70,000	
D. Urban 4-H	7,500	
E. Day Nursery	22,500	
F. Susquehanna School	6,500	
G. PROBE	14,700	
H. BCCDC	41,000	
I. Staff	4,000	
Parks & Recreation		
A. Recreation Park		100,000
Planning and Environmental Design		20,000
General Administration		300,000
Contingency		44,800
		$2,571,000
Anticipated Program Income		
Housing Program:		
A. Rehabilitation Loan Program		80,000
Economic Development Program		
B. BLDC Economic Development Program		100,000
Total Tenth Year Program		$2,751,000

BE IT THEREFORE RESOLVED that the Binghamton Metropolitan Transportation Study Policy Committee endorses the Unified Operations Plan for the Binghamton Metropolitan area.

4-8. COMPLIANCE WITH FEDERAL RULES VERSUS DELIVERY OF BENEFITS*

Localized political demands often prompt local housing authorities to develop rules and subsidies that are inconsistent with the federal legislation under which they receive funds. The following reading reports the federal government's claim that Newark, New Jersey, and other authorities had done just that. Local authorities made more money from the investment of federal funds than was anticipated because interest rates were considerably higher in 1984 than when the allocations were made to local authorities. Undoubtedly the local authorities have already committed the funds and will resist all efforts to recover them.

The Federal Department of Housing and Urban Development has begun a drive to recover millions of dollars it paid to local housing authorities in recent years.

In its largest claim, the department seeks to recover $6.37 million from the housing authority in Newark. It also seeks $1.1 million from the New Haven authority. Other large claims are against Minneapolis, Boston and San Francisco. The department plans to recover the money by reducing future operating subsidies to these housing authorities.

The operating subsidies are designed to compensate for the below-market rents local housing authorities charge their tenants, who by law cannot pay more than 30 percent of their income for rent. The housing authorities, which own and manage public housing complexes, annually estimate their income from rents, investments and other sources, and compare those figures to projected expenditures. The department then pays most of the difference.

The department asserts that some authorities earned higher income from investments than they had originally estimated or miscalculated their estimates of income from the rents paid by tenants.

The public housing authorities normally buy securities such as Treas-

*"Local Housing Bodies Contest Move By U.S. to Recover Subsidy Funds," *New York Times*, Oct. 7, 1984.

ury bills with funds not immediately needed for operations. The interest earned goes into their budgets, which in some instances did not reflect reasonable projections of interest income, departmental officials have contended.

The department is examining the investment income of housing authorities since December 1980 and rental income since December 1981. Where it determines that an overpayment was made, the department is reducing the current operating subsidies by that amount.

Local housing authorities have contended that the policy is illegal and unfair, and will reduce the amount they have available to spend on public housing. They have sought unsuccessfully to have the department abandon the plan.

"Public housing authorities are outraged over HUD's attempt to change rules retroactively," said Robert McKay, executive director to the Council of Large Public Housing Authorities. "HUD is disregarding the fact that funds received in those years were used to cover essential and authorized expenditures."

Joseph F. Laden, director of the public housing authority in Albany and president of the Public Housing Authorities Directors Association, said the budgets being adjusted had already been approved by the department. By seeking to recover the funds the department is retroactively changing the rules under which they were provided, he contended.

About a dozen housing authorities that have had money deducted from their subsidies filed the suit Friday to have the recovery policy declared unlawful and to prevent the department from continuing it. The suit also seeks to have any funds cut from the subsidies restored.

"HUD is trying to destroy public housing by creating an administrative nightmare and to reduce the amount of money to pay for utilities and essential services, and to maintain the buildings decently," said Florence W. Roisman, an attorney representing the housing authorities.

4-9. CHILD RESTRAINTS AND FEDERAL HIGHWAY MONIES

Child restraints offer another example of negative regulation. Under P.L. 98-363, enacted July 17, 1984, states must develop and implement a comprehensive program concerning the use of child restraint systems. Until an adequate system is in place in each state, the state must spend a certain portion of its federal highway money putting such a system into place. In effect Congress is penalizing a state 8 percent of its high-

way funds until a child restraint system is required as a matter of state law.

Be it enacted by the Senate and House of Representatives of the United States of America in Congress assembled, That (a) section 203 (a)(1) of the Surface Transportation Act of 1982 is amended to read as follows:

Sec. 203. (a)(1) There is hereby authorized to be appropriated for carrying out section 402 of title 23, United States Code (relating to highway safety programs), by the National Highway Traffic Safety Administration, out of the Highway Trust Fund (other than the mass transit account), $126,500,000 for the fiscal year ending September 30, 1986.

(b) Section 203 (a) of such Act is amended by adding at the end thereof the following new paragraph:

(4)(a) Each State shall expend each fiscal year not less than 8 per centum of the amount appropriated to it for such fiscal year of the sums authorized by paragraph (1) of this subsection, for developing and implementing comprehensive programs approved by the Secretary of Transportation concerning the use of child restraint systems in motor vehicles. Upon request of the Governor of any State, the Secretary may reduce the amount required to be expended by the State for any fiscal year under the preceding sentence if the State demonstrates to the satisfaction of the Secretary that the percentage of children under the age of four travelling in motor vehicles in the State who are properly restrained by a child restraint system is greater than 75 per centum.

(b) No project for developing and implementing a comprehensive program concerning the use of child restraint systems in motor vehicles may be approved by the Secretary of Transportation in the fiscal years ending September 30, 1985, and September 30, 1986, unless the State applying for approval of such project enters into such agreements with the Secretary as the Secretary may require to ensure that such State will maintain its aggregate expenditures from all non-Federal sources for such programs at or above the average level of such expenditures in its two fiscal years preceding the date of enactment of this paragraph. P.L. 98-363

4-10. A NATIONAL MINIMUM DRINKING AGE

*Congress has attempted to establish a national minimum drinking age
by selectively withholding federal highway funds. Only states can legislate drinking age, but if they should not mandate the age of twenty-one,
they will lose federal funding as described in P.L. 98-363.*

Sec. 158 (a)(1) The Secretary shall withhold 5 per centum of the
amount required to be appropriated to any State under each of sections
104 (b)(1), 104 (b)(2), 104 (b)(5), and 104 (b)(6) of this title on the first
day of the fiscal year succeeding the second fiscal year beginning after
September 30, 1985, in which the purchase or public possession of any
alcoholic beverage by a person who is less than twenty-one years of age
is lawful.

(b) The Secretary shall promptly apportion to a State any funds which
have been withheld from apportionment under subsection (a) of this
section in any fiscal year if in any succeeding fiscal year such State
makes unlawful the purchase or public possession of any alcoholic beverage by a person who is less than twenty-one years of age.

(c) Sec. 408 (e) of title 23, United States Code, is amended by adding
at the end thereof of the following new paragraph: (3) For the purposes
of this section, a State is eligible for a special grant if the State enacts a
statute which provides that—

(A) any person convicted of a first violation of driving under the
influence of alcohol shall receive -(i) a mandatory license suspension for a period of not less than ninety days; and either (ii)
(I) an assigment of one hundred hours of community service; or
(II) a minimum sentence of imprisonment for forty-eight con-
secutive hours;

(B) any person convicted of a second violation of driving under the
influence of alcohol within five years after a conviction for the
same offense, shall receive a mandatory minimum sentence of
imprisonment for ten days and license revocation for not less
than one year;

(C) any person convicted of a third or subsequent violation of driving
under the influence of alcohol within five years after a prior conviction for the same offense shall—(i) receive a mandatory minimum sentence of imprisonment for one hundred and twenty

days; and (ii) have his license revoked for not less than three years; and

(D) any person convicted of driving with a suspended or revoked license or in violation of a restriction due to driving under theinfluence of alcohol shall receive a mandatory sentence of imprisonment for at least thirty days, and shall upon release from imprisonment, receive an additional period of licence suspension or revocation of not less than the period of suspension or revocation remaining in effect at the time of the commission of the offense of driving with a suspended or revoked license.

4-11. THE STATES AS LABORATORIES FOR EXPERIMENTS IN GOVERNANCE*

Clearly both President Reagan and Congress have bowed to pressure groups advocating a national minimum drinking age of twenty-one. Reagan's comments in the article that follow are inconsistent with his general view of federalism. The essence of federalism is a willingness to have a potpourri of laws relating to the same topic across the states: the perceived needs of states differ, and hence state legislatures pass different laws in a given policy area. Here the pressure of organized groups in congressional districts has overcome the natural reluctance of the President and Congress to tell states what they must legislate in terms of social policy. The use of the power of the federal purse in negative regulation does not distinguish the conservative from the liberal.

President Reagan, appealing for cooperation in ending the "crazy quilt of different states' drinking laws," today signed legislation that would deny some Federal highway funds to states that keep their drinking age under 21.

Mr. Reagan indirectly acknowledged that he once had reservations about a measure that, in effect, seeks to force states to change their policies. In the past, Mr. Reagan has taken the view that certain matters of concern to the states should not be subject to the dictates of the Federal Government.

*Excerpts from "Reagan Signs Bill Tying Aid to Drinking Age," *New York Times*, July 18, 1984.

"It's a grave national problem, and it dictates all our lives," he added. "With the problem so clear-cut and the proven solution at hand, we have no misgiving about this judicious use of Federal power."

Under the law Mr. Reagan signed today, the Secretary of Transportation is required to withhold 5 percent of Federal highway construction funds from those states that do not enact a minimum drinking age of 21 by October 1, 1986. The Secretary is required to withhold 10 percent of the funds for states that do not act by Oct. 1, 1987.

The amount at stake ranges from $8 million for the smallest states to $99 million for the largest, including New York State. The amounts withheld would be returned once a state raised its drinking age.

The bill that was approved by Congress would penalize states that failed to enact a minimum drinking age of 21 years and reward states with mandatory sentencing for drunken drivers. Although it passed with overwhelming support on Capitol Hill, even some of those supporting the measure said privately that it was coercive.

Mr. Reagan called the movement against drunk driving part of a "rebirth of an American tradition of leadership" in which movements start from the grass-roots levels. "It began in the community, it spread to state governments and now it's won wide support here in our nation's capital," he said.

4-12. THE ELECTORAL BENEFITS
OF FEDERAL HIGHWAY AID*

The following article describes what happens when Congress uses a particular program, in this case federal highway aid, to provide electorally relevant benefits to states and congressional districts and vehicle for fiscal control. A large number of both Democratic and Republican congresspeople, members of both House and Senate, anxiously await the end of attempts by fiscal conservatives to hold highway expenditures hostage until the total amount is decreased. Soon after this article appeared, the funds were released.

---

*"Congress Standoff Delays Road and Transit Funds," *New York Times,* Oct. 14, 1984.

A standoff between the House and Senate over the terms for spending some Federal funds of highways and mass transit has delayed allocation of $7 billion in Highway Trust Funds to the states until 1985.

Officials of Connecticut, which is to receive $230 million from the trust fund, said nine major projects would be held up because the Federal money was delayed. The projects include reconstruction and widening of about fifteen miles of Interstate 91 between Hartford and the Massachusetts state line.

A New Jersey representative said that the state was to receive $214 million but that the delay in getting the money might hold up four interstate projects. Other states waiting for money are California, $470 million; Florida, $368 million; Pennsylvania, $350 million; Louisiana, $244 million; Washington, $237 million; Massachusetts, $213 million and Vermont, $207 million.

An annual Transportation Department report on anticipated Interstate System spending that has to be approved by Congress became entangled in a web of proposals and counterproposals as Congress rushed toward adjournment.

Senator Jake Garn, Republican of Utah, chairman of the Banking Committee, which has jurisdiction over mass transit, opposed a House proposal, attached to the report, to release an extra $400 million in mass transit funds.

There was disagreement over how many states' favorite projects should be attached to the report and whether their financial formula should be revised. The House had proposed 100 percent financing with no maximum. The Senate wanted far fewer projects, with costs shared by the states and a maximum price tag on each.

Further delaying the release of the interstate highway funds were differences over whether the distribution formula should be revised to allot more money to states whose roads freeze severely.

Several Senators adamantly advanced the Reagan Administration's position that far less money than the House had sought should be approved for the 1.8 mile Central Artery reconstruction project in Boston. The expressway job is sometimes called the "Speaker's Project." One of its prime backers is Speaker Thomas P. O'Neill, Jr.

Several attempts were made in the final hours of the Congressional session to free the $7 billion Interstate Cost Estimate report from the other items by calling it to the floor of each chamber by unanimous consent. But there was no unanimity in either chamber.

"This was a very serious breach in the continuation of our Federal highway aid program," said Senator Jennings Randolph, Democrat of West Virginia, the ranking minority member of the Senate Environment and Public Works Committee. Senator Randolph, considered a founder of the Interstate System, said the development "does not bode well for the future."

He was alluding to what some see as a trend in Congress over the past year to use the cost estimate report as a vehicle for getting other programs approved. Since the report is now approved in the form of a bill, it is easy to add items as the bill makes its way through Congress.

5 Health Policy

Federal health policy shares with education policy an end-product of service to individuals rather than a physical good. Unlike the case of education, however, the federal government can involve itself directly in health policy and set some rules independent of grants of money. No constitutional reservations limit federal involvement in providing for the general welfare. In spite of this the forms and outcomes of the health policy process are surprisingly similar to those of the education process. Federal policy is often implemented and modified through more localized public- and private-sector entities, and negative regulation is increasingly employed. The forms of federalism are observed, particularly in the allocation of federal monies for medical education. In these ways federal health policy resembles policy promoting commerce or a clean environment (Chapter 4), even though the latter areas are capital- rather than service-intensive.

The evolution of the federal government's entry into health care parallels the policy evolution that occured in transportation, environmental protection, and education. Military needs prompted the first federal involvement in the provision of health care, and other early areas of federal concern were capital construction and research. Organized professional groups, builders, and those engaged in commerce generally benefited directly from these activities. Federal funds for health care (as for welfare generally) were channeled largely through state governments (compare Chapter 6).

Health policy at all levels evidences a greater degree of professional involvement than do the other policy areas so far explored. Medical societies are organized at the state level and endowed with public authority and responsibility through state law. Yet many state policies and federal reimbursement procedures use "voluntary" standards that are nationally derived. Hospital accreditation and medical school curricula, for example, must be sanctioned by a private, professionally derived, national board. In Britain national health policy has a centralizing and homogenizing effect on policy and service variations; medical societies are nationally organized in order to deal with the strong, national parties that make health and other policy.

Federal involvement in health care channels large amounts of money to the private sector. Private contractors build hospitals, including VA hospitals; the private sector even determines the rates paid to professionals employed in VA hospitals. Only doctors actually in the military have pay and benefits largely determined by the payer. As in other cases we have examined, then, federal involvement maintains and reflects the national history of service provision through states and localities (the federal aspect of our system). It also preserves the independent standing of professional service deliverers and their ability to organize and influence rates of remuneration and conditions of service. Finally, the federal government channels health monies and benefits through professional intermediaries or the private sector to the patient, or welfare recipient, student, and so on.

Negative regulation is directed to two principal ends. Since the 1960s, continued eligibility for federal funds under Medicare, Medicaid, and other legislation has been contingent on meeting standards developed in response to the organized needs of the elderly, the ill, the mentally ill, and the mentally retarded. Second. recently Congress has employed negative regulation as a vehicle for cost control, requiring states to keep their Medicaid fraud rates down or lose some Medicaid reimbursements. Reimbursement amounts are determined after negotiations between the professional providers and the federal government. Regional planning agencies must approve federal funding of loan guarantees for hospital building or the purchase of equipment in order to prevent needless overinvestment. Failure to plan may threaten the flow of federal funds to a state's service providers and hospitals. Congress does not, however, use negative regulation to provide direct benefits to groups in order to facilitate incumbency, as occurred in the case of education. Rather recent negative regulations have been used to control the spending of federal monies by state and local governments and private health care providers.

Context

Federal involvement in health care began in 1979 with the passage of legislation providing health services for sick and disabled U.S. seamen. Between 1799 and 1870 hospitals were established along the seacoast and interstate waterways. The Marine Hospital Service was established in 1870, followed by the Commission Corps in 1899. In the latter, the federal government paid private physicians to engage in public health activities. Under the Federal Quarantine Act of 1878, the Marine Hospital Service could provide quarantine laws and by-laws for ports or states where state and local regulations did not exist.

A federal research focus developed in 1887, when the Marine Hospital Service established its hygienic laboratories. In 1892 the service was renamed the Public Health and Marine Service (later the Public Health Service), and the Office of the Surgeon General was created as its administrative head. The Biologics and Control Act in the same year gave the Public Health Service licensing and regulating responsibilities for biologically derived health products.

Congress also provided some direct health care for soldiers wounded in wartime. This program began in earnest with the development of the Civil War soldiers' homes. In 1921 Congress established an independent service bureau to treat the medical needs of veterans returning from World War I. The Veterans Act of 1924 extended medical care to treatment of disabilities not associated with military service, if veterans could not afford private care. Congress created the Veterans' Administration (VA) as an independent agency in 1930. After World War I there were many veterans, and they were organized. By 1978, as a consequence, 4 percent of all money spent on health care in the United States was spent in hospitals set up by the VA. Further, one quarter of all the nation's doctors interned in VA hospitals from 1930 through the 1970s. VA hospitals were among the many goods that could be distributed to congressional districts for the electoral benefit of incumbents. Hospitals provided employment for workers serving professionals and paraprofessionals as well as services to veterans.

The Maternal Infancies Act of 1921 (Sheppard-Towner Act) provided grants to states for developing services for mothers and children. Many state and local governments strongly opposed these grants, as did the medical profession through its umbrella lobbying group, the American

Medical Association (AMA). Historically, the medical profession has opposed federal involvement in the provision of medical care and federal control over conditions of service. For example, it has successfully opposed the extension of VA services to out-patient activities; thus, services for aged and indigent veterans and others are delivered in more expensive institutional settings, increasing costs to the taxpayer.

The hygienic laboratory established in 1897 was renamed the National Institute of Health in 1930. In 1937 Congress created the National Cancer Institute. The 1935 Social Security Act included a health research component allocating up to $2 million annually to be spent by the National Institute of Health. In 1946 Congress created the National Institute of Mental Health (NIMH), followed by the National Heart Institute in 1948. The 1950 Omnibus Medical Research Act established numerous other research institutes. These institutes, collectively known as the National Institutes of Health, later became part of the Public Health Service, established under the 1944 Public Health Service Act. This act gathered all previous existing federal health care legislation into one statute. The Public Health Service conducted research and investigated diseases and health problems. It had no direct medical authority but could cooperate with state and local health agencies in preventing and controlling communicable diseases. Even with the subsequent passage of "medicaid," Congress has preserved the state component in federally funded service delivery.

Despite this long history of action, any national impetus for control of the practice of medicine or licensing facilities came initially from the medical profession itself. The oversupply of doctors in the middle and late nineteenth century contributed to this movement. In Kansas, in particular, where homeopaths competed with "regular" doctors, the number of doctors per thousand people was twice the ratio that was considered uneconomic (Bonner, 1959), which is twice the ratio existing today.

Direct power to license doctors and restrict the practice of medicine belongs to the states, not the federal government. Hence, the AMA persistently lobbied state legislatures to establish licensing procedures for doctors. At the same time, both the AMA and the American Association of Medical Colleges developed accrediting procedures for medical schools through the liason Committee on Medical Education and encouraged states to set up boards that would license only doctors who had been trained at an accredited school.

Between 1870 and 1910 the AMA and its allied state associations had succeeded in having laws passed to control the practice of medicine in every state. State law delegated to professional groups control over the construction of hospitals and medical education so long as Congress attached no conditional strings or obligatory service.

For the last decade the trend has been moving in the opposite direction, and states have directly legislated some fiscal and other restrictions. The New York State Board of Regents has recently developed what are, in effect its own medical school licensing procedures, independent of the norm set by the Liaison Committee on Medical Education. By 1980 seven states had enacted laws that imposed service obligations on students attending state-supported medical schools. California requires all applicants for medical certificates to have taken courses in nutrition, child-abuse detection, and sexuality. Now legislatures more often use their controls over licensing and accreditation to facilitate public policy directly rather than work through the medical associations. In addition, as will be seen, the federal government has not only increased its role in the building of hospitals, the training of professionals, and the actual provision of services, (e.g., through Medicaid), but has increasingly used its financial involvement as a lever to compel area planning of medical facilities and cost containment on fees for service.

The most important health care legislation passed in the immediate postwar period was the Hospital Survey and Construction Act, better known as the Hill-Burton Act of 1946. This act provided grants to assist states in inventorying their existing hospitals and health centers and surveying the need for construction. After states did the needed surveys and planning, the Congress provided construction grants for up to one-third of the total cost of any hospital. For the first time the planning boards had to include representatives of consumers of hospital services. For the first time also the act placed a ceiling on the bed-to-population ratio in areas served by Hill-Burton-supported hospitals. Congress used the Hill-Burton Act to pour large amounts of visible federal money into neighborhoods. Within three years most states took advantage of Hill-Burton funding. State health departments administered the law in each case. In 1949 the federal government increased its share of the funding of hospital construction to two-thirds of the total. In 1954 Congress added rehabilitation centers, nursing homes, and hospital out-patient departments to the list of capital facilities that Hill-Burton funds could support.

Any hospital receiving Hill-Burton construction funds had to provide some care to persons unable to pay and to make services available to all persons residing in its community. Hill-Burton hospitals based the amount of free, non-emergency care they provided on their operating budgets and the amount of federal assistance received. However, a hospital could turn no one away at the emergency room, whether it had already satisfied the free-care component of Hill-Burton or not.

This exchange of federal construction support for the promise of voluntary charity in a state-controlled program was consistent with Eisenhower's view that federal aid should be indirect. Another instance of indirect aid was the 1954 Public Health Service Act, which provided additional mortgage loan insurance directly to doctors, corporations, or public-sector entities desiring to build hospitals. Within the newly created HEW, the surgeon general directly administered this insurance program. Whatever capital funds the hospitals did not obtain from the federal government under Hill-Burton they could borrow from the private sector with federally guaranteed loan insurance.

Federal activity in this area remained steady in the eight years of the Eisenhower administration. Many, but not all, health programs were brought under the umbrella of HEW (see Chapter 2). However, all the health programs passed during the Eisenhower era reflected the continual bias of both the executive and Congress in favor of support for professional training, capital construction, and state health programs. For example, the 1956 Health Amendment Act provided funds to the states to support their mental health hospitals and establish training programs for advanced nursing. The 1958 Health Amendments provided formula grants for public health schools, one of which exists in almost every state. In these instances indirect aid through state governments benefits service providers in almost every constituency.

From 1936 and continuing under the Public Health Service Act of 1944, Congress made general grants to states to help support their public health commitments. In the 1950s, they became, in effect, block grants. (see Reading 5-1). By the middle to late 1950s, however, general health grants accounted for only a small fraction of the funds appropriated through the Public Health Service. Congress established programs for maternal and child health services, crippled children's services; tuberculosis, cancer, and heart disease control, mental health; and others. These programs were a response to the claims of organized service providers and beneficiaries. However, state-level health authorities resisted federal categorical programs because they lacked flexibility. In 1954 the House of Representatives passed legislation eliminating all special programs except those for mental health. The professional groups that provided services in each of the categorical areas successfully resisted this legislation, and the Senate Committee on Labor and Public Welfare did not report the bill out of hearings. A report by the Joint Federal State Action Committee made it clear that although it favored consolidation of medical programs into a block grant, such a proposal was unrealistic given congressional and professional opposition (ACIR, 1977).

Since the middle of the nineteenth century, Congress had helped fund state institutions for the mentally ill. The Mental Health Act of 1946 established NIMH, and the Mental Health Study Act of 1955 provided grants for research into methods of caring for the mentally ill. To this point federal activity resembles that in other health-related areas: the focus was on research and indirect capital aid to states. Yet mental health was excluded from the House's consolidating legislation in 1954 because mental health professionals and the families of the mentally ill had indicated that planning agencies that deal with both health and mental health issues are typically ignorant of the latter (Rich and Kelley, 1983). Mental health programming thus benefits from the separation of mental health funding at both the federal and the state level from general health care appropriations.

The last significant legislation of the Eisenhower era—the Social Security Amendments of 1960, better known as the Kerr-Mills Act—was passed in response to constituency pressure for federal health care programs that would benefit the elderly whose major or only source of income was Social Security. Both the Eisenhower administration and much of Congress resisted direct contractual relationships between such individuals and the federal government. Instead, they followed a time-honored formula for providing payments to states, which would then organize their medical aid for the indigent elderly. This model (see Reading 5-1) made state participation optional. Only twenty-five states chose to participate. As in the case of federal programs for education and highways (see Chapters 3 and 4), the federal government provided matching grants. The match depended upon income levels within the state and the number of indigent elderly. One can view Kerr-Mills as a compromise. It was one of the last major pieces of legislation providing federal funds only through state-level distribution. It was also the first federal program in the health area to provide funds for medical benefits for the indigent elderly, in contrast to the "voluntary charity" provided by hospitals under the Hill-Burton Act from 1946 on.

Agenda

A rapidly growing economy can make the agenda for almost all government services one of expansion in size and scope. This was equally true of federal funding of education (Chapter 3), transportation (Chapter 4), and health care. Federal support for health-professional training increased rapidly in the 1960s with the passage of the Health Professional Education Assistance Act of 1963 and the Nurse Training Act of 1964. The latter provided the first set of categorical grants to support construction of nursing schools as well as scholarships and loans for student nurses. The Health Professional Assistance Amendments of 1965 provided scholarships to medical schools, which they in turn dispersed to eligible but needy students. Congress designed this assistance both to increase the number of professionals in training and to encourage medical schools to change the racial and gender mix of their students. More pressure to change the system came from organized minority constituencies, predominantly in urban areas. Although the federal government could not tell medical schools which students to accept, it could make it easier financially for them to accept more minority students. Because schools served as the financial and program intermediaries between government and student, and because the choice of students and programs remained in the hands of professionals, the AMA and state medical societies were supportive of this legislation. The 1966 Allied Health Professions Personnel Training Act extended the construction and improvement grants previously used in the training of doctors. The bill also revised the student loan program to make loans more available to students in health-related areas.

Meanwhile the Health Services Act of 1962 had established a program of direct grants for family clinics and other health services for migrant workers. It foreshadowed some features of the Mental Retardation Facilities and Community Mental Health Centers Construction (CMHC) Act of 1963. Amendments to the latter act provided personnel staffing grants to community mental health centers in 1965 and to alcohol programs in 1968. Oddly enough, the legislation that commenced in

1963 was at odds with a report that the Joint Commission on Mental Illness and Health had taken five years to prepare. This study suggested innovations in service delivery, but these would come about within existing health and mental health treatment facilities. Within this context, the report recommended establishing one clinic per 50,000 people to provide a first line of defense in reducing the need for long or repeated hospitalizations for people with mental illness.

The Kennedy administration instead proposed to start a new program with new monies to facilitate the comprehensive treatment of mental health. This was a clear symbolic response to the program needs of organized constituencies. In the 1960s, moreover, money to create new programs was available from increasing tax revenues.

Before 1955 mental health monies granted to states could not be spent on state hospital systems; the federal government had already provided ample support for these systems within the Public Health Service. However, states could use money allocated under the 1955 Mental Health Study Act in almost any way they desired. Going one step further, the 1963 CMHC Act allowed the government to contract directly with the service provider, in effect bypassing the state.

The CMHC Act was the result of a successful attempt by pressure groups and health professsionals *within* the federal government to use federal money to support the provision of comprehensive community-based mental health care. The presumption was that states would eventually emulate the better model established by the federal government. Some states (e.g., New York, Massachusetts) already had such programs; others did not follow for many years. Overall the community mental health experience indicates that the federal government cannot use a carrot combined with large amounts of funding to prompt states to organize and deliver services for which they are neither fiscally, politically, nor professionally prepared. When states have passed laws requiring least restrictive treatments of mental health or mental retardation patients and have then not provided sufficient care, they have gotten into legal and financial troubles in both state and federal courts. However, the federal government has no tool available to force states to provide treatments based upon models developed by professionals within the federal bureaucracy. Interestingly, 90 percent matching money works far better as a carrot to prompt states to redirect their own spending especially when the matching funds are for employment-inducing activities like road construction. States resisted following the model of the federally supported community-based mental health centers because they take work away from already organized state professionals and union members operating state mental health and retardation hospitals (Rich and Kelley, 1983).

In 1965 Congress passed over twenty measures involving public health and doubled federal appropriations for health programs. The form of aid changed from direct help to state governments and their health-related activities to support for programs that could benefit smaller, identifiable groups and, as a consequence, benefit congressional incumbency. The general grants to states provided under the Public Health Service Act of 1944 had become an insignificant 6 percent of federal aid. State flexibility in spending federal funds was minimal. I reaction and to increase budgetary efficiency, President Johnson proposed yet another reorganization of the Public Health Service and urged Congress consolidated many of the specific categorical grants passed over the preceding several decades into a block grant. Congressional committees, or at least their staffs, recognized the desirability of simplifying the process of appropriating monies for federally sponsored health programs. The 1966 enactment of the Comprehensive Health Planning and Public Health Services Amendments consolidated almost all public health programs into state-based block grants. Congress was most intensely involved with the distributional formula that determined the monies states could get. As was often the case (see, e.g., Title I of the 1965 ESEA; discussed in Chapter 3), the factors to be used in the allocation of funds were given in the legislation so that each congressperson would still know approximately how much funding was going to his or her district. The exact weighting of the factors was not described and was the subject of much bargaining between congressional committees and health bureaucrats. In this way congresspeople could avoid internal institutional conflict over the distribution of the money within states but had access to those determining distributions if incumbency needs so required.

The most important expansion of the federal role in providing health care in the 1960s came under the Health Insurance for the Aged Act of 1965 (Title XVIII of the Social Security Act—Medicare) and the same year's grants to states for medical assistance programs (Title XIX of the Social Security Act—Medicaid). Congress designed these two acts in part to replace the Kerr-Mills program. Kerr-Mills had passed in 1960 as a hybrid or compromise measure: health benefits were provided to the elderly and the indigent elderly, but only through the states that voluntarily joined the program. Title XVIII eliminated the states entirely. Part A of Medicare provided basic protection against hospital costs and some posthospital services. Part B provided supplemental mental health and medical insurance benefits. It was a voluntary program financed partly by payments from those eligible for social security and partly through federal revenues. In effect, then, Title XVIII of the Social Security Act became a contract between citizens and government for the prepayment of some medical care (in Part A) and a subsidized insurance contract between citizens and government for extended major medical coverage (in Part B). The legislation effectively eliminated states, hospitals, and service providers from the equation, except insofar as the federal government initiates cost-containment measures.

Title XIX (Medicaid) created federal matching health care programs for the poor. State participation was voluntary. To participate, states had to provide five basic services: in-patient, out-patient, laboratory, X-ray, and skilled nursing home services. A number of other, optional categories were included under federal matching formulas. These formulas ranged from 50 to 83 percent, as in Kerr-Mill. Although not compulsory (Arizona never accepted), Title XIX's generous matching formulas and the eventual extension of the definition of medical indigence to almost all categories of state or federal welfare recipients made picking up the optional categories very tempting. At the same time, the open-ended nature of the optional provisions allowed the states, in effect, to determine the amount of federal expenditures in the program once the state matching formulas had been set. Such open-ended funding frequently results in payments out of the federal exchequer to states even when Congress had not appropriated funds for such purposes.

The 1967 amendments to the Social Security Act provided for the purchase of services by public welfare agencies from private providers. In addition, the amendments added the operation of Job Welfare Services within the Social Security Act to the already existing Aid to Dependent Children (ADC), with the proviso that the two should be administered together. The delivery of health and social services to families with children provided a context for rapidly increasing federal expenditures.

The 1960s saw drastically increased attention to direct and indirect federal funding for health care. One motive was to encourage states to do the same. Sometimes the legislation simply increased support for programs passed earlier that partially funded planned and delivered services. The federal government gave up its control of part of the cost of some of these programs once the state had selected the optional programs. Such legislation induced demand for services from individuals who might not otherwise have been able to afford needed or unneeded medical care. Because Medicare and Medicaid were new programs, however, cost increases during the 1960s were not excessive.

A combination of political factors permitted the passage of Medicare and Medicaid, typically hybrid programs. Previous federal programs (e.g., Kerr-Mills) had referred to the right of all citizens to adequate and needed medical care, yet allowed states to decide whether and how to do this. Generous federal funding encouraged state participation by covering some of the medical-welfare monies already spent by states. Additionally, states could adjust program supply and finance to the realities of state and local electoral politics. All this was done at a time when federal revenues to support such programs were increasing, and urban and retirement-area congresspeople had organized sufficiently to pass such legislation. However, Medicaid (and Medicare) represented a major break with the reliance on either states or the private sector as the only insurers of health. Although the private sector provided health care, the principal payers under Medicaid were federal and state government.

Like Medicaid, Medicare represented a one-step extension of an insurance scheme at a time of ample federal revenues (see Reading 5-2). Under Title XIX, part A, citizens now self-insure against unforeseen medical needs in old age. Part B is a distribution to the elderly. If one combines this with the benefits to industrialized states and large cities under Medicaid, it is clear that a large number of congresspeople received electoral benefit from the passage of Medicare and Medicaid together.

Professional health care providers and hospitals also benefited. Medicare and Medicaid paid for a number of services that would formerly have been provided as "voluntary charity" under the provisions of Hill-Burton. Professionals were paid on a fee-for-service basis at or close to private-sector rates. Although medical societies opposed Medicare and Medicaid, largely because of the programs' recordkeeping and reporting requirements, the legislation actually guaranteed many doctors an income.

Federal attention to the expansion of medical facilities and personnel increased in the 1970s. Concerned with the continuing lack of adequately trained medical personnel, Congress enacted the Emergency

Health Care Personnel Act of 1970. This created a national health service corp composed of doctors in the Public Health Service, who would take assignments in areas of the country where medical personnel were underrepresented. The act set no numerical goals or time tables. One could not consider the National Health Service Corporation a program for compelling doctors to move to underserved areas, since doctors could always resign from the health service and still practice medicine.

Two other innovations in federal support for medical training were the Comprehensive Health and Manpower Training Act of 1971, which for the first time gave medical schools capitation rather than program grants, and the Ford administration's 1976 success in tying capitation grants to training and internship in primary care. The goal was to have 35 percent of all on-site medical training occur in the area of primary care. Linking public support for training with the distribution of medical skills is more likely to work than the use of financial incentives to move into particular health care or geographic areas. Even in Britain, where the government controls the supply of doctors much more closely and doctors are paid relatively less, financial incentives to practice in geriatric hospitals or underserved areas of the country do not work. Instead, the government has effectively used an increase in the required period of internship to remedy understaffing.

Support for ancillary manpower also continued through the 1970s. The states could draw upon open-ended funds under the 1967 amendments of the Social Security Act to help support nursing home staffs and the nonprofessional aspects of community care for the mentally ill or retarded and children receiving AFDC cash assistance. In 1972 the Congress capped the funds available under the 1967 amendments at $2.5 billion. Finally, in 1975 Title XX of the Social Security Act, "grants to states for services," redefined the relationship between the states and the federal government. The new act gave the states a primary role in operating social service programs, but required them to account to HEW for the funds they received.

Although Congress passed three health related block grants (esp. Title XX of the Social Security Act) between the 1966 Partnership for Health Act (Comprehensive Health Planning and Public Health Service Amendments) and 1980. Congress clearly preferred categorical programs, they allowed easier tracing of money and services to constituents. Between 1969 and 1976 Congress established more than a hundred new categorical programs within the general area of health. In 1976 the

Ford administration proposed replacing fifty-nine categorical programs with four block grants in areas of health, education, child nutrition, and community services. Congress supported these consolidations, which were possibly as significant as some of the block grants passed under the Omnibus Budget Reconciliation Act of 1981. Pressure for consolidation came from state and local service providers who were incapacitated by the sometimes conflicting reporting and program requirements of the fifty-nine programs.

Over a decade of federal expansion of direct and indirect support for medical care had drastically increased the demand component of such services. The Medicare or Medicaid patient, not the service provider, hospital, clinic, or payer (i.e., federal and state governments or private insurance plans), determined the amount of services received. In contrast to the British National Health Service, scarcity and queuing were not used to ration services. Hence, the pressure for planning and the costs of facilities and services continually increased. Professionals were paid at or close to market rates. As a consequence, private insurance rates and the insurance component of employee benefits expanded alarmingly. Almost every user had ample incentive to seek any level of medical care desired: the insurance company or the public purse paid most of the bill. Medical costs skyrocketed.

Process

The Nixon administration made two attempts to control the increasing costs of medical care. First, it attempted to use health maintenance organizations (HMOs) as a vehicle for increasing competition in the supply of medical services. HEW officials publicly supported the creation of HMOs from 1970 onwards, and from fiscal year 1971 to 1973, the government spent $28 million on grants and contracts related to HMO development (Schlenker, 1973). State laws against prepaid medical plans thwarted the development of HMOs and the AMA insisted on the fee-for-service system as a cornerstone of the individualized doctor-patient relationship. By 1973 seventeen states had passed laws permitting the development of HMOs. In the aggregate, however, states continued to resist them. States often required HMOs to obtain from state regulatory agencies the same "certificates of need" demanded of other health facilities prior to construction or the purchase of major equipment. Given that HMOs were intended to create competition on the supply side, the requirement of certificates of need seems hardly justified, but state and federal law allows professionals to dominate the state planning process. This is another instance of the legislated domination of professional service providers, whose interests may conflict with cost-control measures that would benefit less well organized constituencies like service recipients and taxpayers.

The 1969 Social Security Act Amendments allow the use of Medicaid funds for prepaid health plans. However, requirements that all Medicaid eligibles receive the same scope of services and that the same services be available throughout the state made use of Medicaid money by HMOs difficult until the organizations were widespread. Social Security Act Amendments of 1972 allowed states to waive these requirements, but regulations for implementing this waiver were not published in the Federal Register until 1974. Only Florida and California had a large number of Medicaid recipients enrolled in HMOs until 1986. The use of Medicare funding for HMO services is similarly low. In 1974 only about 5 percent of all HMO members received Medicare benefits.

Some clear policies at the federal level encourage the development of HMOs, however. The Health Maintenance Organization Act of 1973 made almost $2 billion available for grants, contracts, loans, and loan guarantees for the establishment of HMOs. Certified HMOs must provide a wide range of services (wider than that typically offered), are subject to permanent regulation by the secretary of HEW, (now Health and Human Services) and must have open-enrollment periods for at least thirty days a year, during which time they must accept individuals without regard to health conditions. All of these features will increase the price of health care and, hence, the premium HMOs must charge members.

At about the same time, in response to pressure from insurance companies and other large payers of medical benefits, Congress attempted to control the cost of health care through planning. The National Health Planning and Resource Development Act (HSA Act) of 1974 replaced the regulatory component of regional medical programs and the Hill-Burton restrictions. The act required the establishment of Health Systems Agencies (HSAs), of which there were 203 in 1986. These are either private nonprofit agencies or public regional planning bodies. A majority of members are health care consumers rather than providers. In order to restrain the costs and increase the accessibility of health services, each HSA must develop a plan against which any new medical facility or program within the HSA is reviewed. HSAs must also approve or reject any proposed use of federal funds for construction and equipment and federal loan guarantees, although most large funding programs like Medicare and Medicaid are excluded from review. Further, the secretary of HEW (now HHS) can override HSA decisions. An investigation of twenty-one states over four years showed that local political support for programs almost invariably prompted the secretary to overrule a dissenting HSA (Rich and Kelley, 1983). This very much parallels the role of the secretary of state for health in Britain: on appeal, no small facility is ever closed in a highly competitive electoral district.

Congress designed the HSA Act to help allocate medical equipment, programs, and facilities in an efficient manner. However, aside from the use of certificates of need for capital construction and equipment purchases, health planning probably has done little to reduce the total cost of health care. Planning itself costs money. The activities of HSAs do not themselves limit access to medical care, the development of new professional programs, or professional costs, and they do not affect the flow of Medicaid or private insurance money. The HSA Act merely translated the vague, generalized concerns of consumer groups and insurance companies into legislation involving planning by even more professionals.

In extending the Partnership for Health Act in 1974, Congress was concerned with the closer monitoring of where the money was spent in states. At the same time, it increased the monies block-granted to states and the number of ways states could use them. Ford, understanding that one way to spend less money on health care is to veto health care legislation, vetoed the 1974 extension. In 1975 Congress passed a Special Health Revenue Sharing Act over Ford's veto. HEW viewed the block grant as a largely unrestricted grant of federal money to the states, and it remained neutral with respect to the content of state programs. Hence, Congress passed legislation increasing the funds spent on health care and its own capacity to see that the monies are spent in electorally as well as medically relevant ways. The executive, however, having failed to sustain its cost-controlling veto, administered the program in a manner that makes it much less beneficial to congressional incumbency.

Although the Nixon administration continued the expansion of federal support for health care and only toward the end promoted measures designed to contain costs, Ford attempted to use vetoes, block grants, and administrative procedures to limit health care costs to the federal government and maximize states' ability to use federal money effectively. The

Ford administration also attempted administrative changes to lower costs: Medicare and Medicaid reimbursement for hospital care and other services was to be indexed so that medical costs would rise no more rapidly than other costs (see Reading 5-3). Ford also proposed cost-cutting legislation to affect Medicare in 1976 (see Reading 5-4). Carter continued Ford's emphasis on cost cutting. In March 1977 he shifted the Medicare and Medicaid programs from the Social Rehabilitation Service to the Health Care Financing Administration, in part because the new agency, devoted primarily to managing Medicare and Medicaid, could better control costs.

Both the Ford and the Carter administrations felt that introducing competition could augment budget reductions and block grants in lowering public-sector costs. In 1978 the capacity of state medical associations and the AMA to restrict competition through the AMA code of ethics was successfully attacked. The Federal Trade Commission ruled that the codes of ethics, when incorporated into state or professional regulations, violate antitrust laws. Consider the Michigan Optometric Association in 1969 (Goodman, 1980, p. 26). To be licensed, an optomologist needed 80 points. One gets points for not advertising in any media including telephone book listings or window displays (30 points); location in a professional or office building (25 points); limiting office identification to the approved size and content (15 points); educational activities (14 points); fiscal capacity (8 points); and adequate equipment (8 points).

In 1978 Carter sent Congress proposals to recover tax losses on the financing of private health insurance. Health expenditures can also be tax expenditures. When citizens spent beyond 3 percent of their gross income on health-related activities, the federal government paid a part of all subsequent medical bills through an itemized tax deduction. Carter claimed that this provision created an artificial demand for services that did not have to be paid for in full. As a result of the Health Cost Restraint Act of 1979, medical costs must exceed 5 percent of gross income in order to be deducted (see Reading 5-5).

A final Carter attempt to control health care costs was his unsuccessful proposal on hospital cost containment. States and hospitals were voluntarily to hold rates to those calculated for each state and each hospital by the surgeon general, or he would apply compulsory controls based on a formula included in the legislation. If the hospital ignored these controls, it would not be eligible for Medicare, Medicaid, and other forms of federal reimbursement (see Reading 5-6). In other words the Carter administration proposed to apply negative regulation to the activities of private-sector individuals and hospitals providing health care. Such a proposal can be effective only when the federal government has already committed large sums of money to support individual health care. In this case, the stick was withdrawal of the federal government as paying sponsor of health care services for the elderly or the indigent that hospitals would still have to provide under the conditions of Hill-Burton and other legislation.

In the 1970s the federal government shifted from an initial emphasis on extending the many programs developed in the 1960s to a concern for both fiscal and program accountability. By 1974–75 congresspeople were more concerned with the fiscal authority for monies spent under block grants and more eager to ensure that grants for community mental health and other service providers were actually serving the intended organized beneficiary groups. Professionals within agencies like HEW and HHS agreed on the need for detailed accounting, but were more concerned with specifying treatment modalities particularly in the case of community mental health (compare the concern of nationally organized education professionals that all bilingual education monies be spent on a single method: transitional bilingual education; see Chapter 3). In contrast, top-level federal bureaucrats, particularly political appointees, wanted to give maximum program discretion to state and local authorities so that federal funds would be used efficiently and in response to local needs.

By the end of the decade, Carter and Congress had used changes in the tax schedule and administrative adjustments to reduce the demand for health care and create greater efficiency. When negative regulation was directed squarely at controlling the monies going to professionals and hospitals, however, it never passed Congress. It was not until 1982 that some limits were successfully placed on hospital cost increases.

Consequences

Ford offered changes in Medicaid regulations that would lower the cost to government and vetoed new programs; Carter tried to use negative regulation and tax and administrative changes to lower the costs of medical care to both government and citizens. Reagan proposed the next step: simply cut. In 1981 Congress cut the National Health Services Corps to a small fraction of its former size. In the same year Congress eliminated capitation grants for nurse training institutions and in 1982 medical school capitation grants. The federal government stopped supporting the establishment of HMOs and cut medical student loan programs by one half.

In 1981 the Omnibus Budget Reconciliation Act established block grants in a number of areas. Mental health and alcohol and drug abuse programs were soon under one block grant totaling 26 percent less than the sum originally allocated to the individual programs. Congress likewise combined eight other health programs within a preventive health block grant. The federal government reduced its matching reimbursement for Medicaid by 3.0 percent in 1981, 4.0 percent in 1982, and 4.5 percent in 1983. Exceptions were made for states with an unemployment rate of 15 percent over the national average, but such states had to have fraud-detection systems fully in place. Congress anticipated that states could make up for the loss of federal reimbursements by improving fraud and error detection; hence, no real cuts in benefits were to occur. In effect, this was a case of negative regulation before the fact: money was taken away from states, but the federal government told them that they could get it back by pursuing the antifraud programs both the administration and Congress wanted.

Congress attempted to control the public cost of medical care by putting ceilings on hospital reimbursements: hospitals that charged more than peer institutions would only be paid 108 percent of average costs across such institutions; change in reimburseable rates were limited. Congress avoided repeating Carter's mistake of 1978. Instead of trying to limit what hospitals charged, Congress limited what it would pay.

The Tax Equity and Fiscal Responsibility Act of 1982 lowered personal income taxes progressively over two and a half years (see Chapter 7). However, the act also required lower error rates and less overpayment of claims in state-administered Medicaid programs. Again, the stick was the withdrawal of federal matching funds. In addition, the act stipulated that part B, the voluntary insurance part of Medicare, would charge fees that would recover 25 percent of the cost of the program. In effect, then, the cost to senior citizens of the voluntary insurance component of Medicare became indexed to the cost of medical care and administration. Finally, Medicare reimbursements were not to be paid to hospitals on a negotiated cost reimbursement basis. Instead, HHS set rates in each of the large number of diagnostically related groupings. It took over a year to produce regulations and associated costs to implement this part of the act. Once such a reimbursement scheme was in effect, however, the inequities it produced were great (see Reading 5-7).

So far increased competition has not lowered the cost of health care generally; cuts in federal spending on health affect people who do not have adequate funds to pay for access to the service itself (see Reading 5-8). As a consequence of these cuts, some congresspeople are concerned about the access of differently situated groups and individuals to health service to ensure adequate health care for all. Yet wider knowledge about the British National Health Service's rationing of service through waiting might qualify one's belief about the adequacy of such a system in the United States. In any event, such a system would only serve those who have less access to health care in the United States if lack of access were due to lack of money, rather than to distance from doctors or lack of information about medical services.

In spite of all cost-containment measures, the basic reference point for health care service payments is the private-sector fee. Price competition is not part of medical practice here, although recent FDC and court antitrust decisions have opened up the possibility that it might become more important. The government cannot control the costs and conditions of the practice of health care unless it supports and controls entry into the profession itself (as occurs in Britain through the government's partial subsidy of undergraduate medical training and control over entry into such training). Hence, any national health model would become a further income subsidy or, at least, an income floor for medical practitioners, regardless of the extent to which it serves needy citizens.

In 1979 Carter proposed a less encompassing national health plan. Another option, offered by Sens. Robert Dole, John Danforth, and Pete Domenici, provided for a still more limited national catastrophic health insurance plan. These proposals responded to the inequities in access to health care that existed even before the federal cuts of the early 1980s. The emphasis since 1980 has been on competition and cost-effectiveness rather than on providing benefits for somewhat unorganized and even undefined people. In a time of large public-sector deficits, new money is not spent on electorally marginal people.

The evolution of federal health policy parallels that of education and capital construction policy (see Chapters 3 and 4). First, federal help went to the construction of capital facilities, loan guarantees, and professional training. Service to individuals, even when funded by the federal government, occurred first through state and professional intermediaries. Often states had to provide matching funding to receive federal money. Only from the mid-1960s on did the federal government target benefits directly to individuals through Medicare and Medicaid.

The rates at which the government reimburses service providers are close to prevailing market rates. In this sense direct aid to citizens also becomes direct aid to the professionals providing services and charging the rates to which they are accustomed.

Congress used administrative reorganization and co-payment in an attempt to lower the demand for health care and increase the efficiency of programs. It changed the tax structure so that upper-income people do not obtain huge federal subsidies for open-ended expenditures on health care and used negative regulation to force hospitals and nursing homes to demonstrate a need for new facilities and equipment. Carter proposed a similar effort to control the costs of hospital care, but the plan was too extreme to pass. Moreover, negative regulation does not work well when directed toward professionals whose powers have been delegated by state legislatures, rather than by Congress. Instead, Congress settled for capping what it would pay for services, and then had to base its ceiling on private-sector charges. Ford proposed and Reagan actually secured legislation that cut or limited the federal monies to be spent on health programs. To the extent this is successful, those people who lose benefits would be the poor and less well organized—those most recently brought into the system of congressionally funded benefits. So far, however, cuts have been minimal.

What is the future of federal involvement in health care? One possibility is that it will keep some degree of co-payment to control demand but will encourage prepayment, even through public and private insurance plans, to help average out and control costs. Further public sector advances are unlikely so long as a locally elected Congress needs to provide identifiable benefits to constituents but, at the same time, lacks the power to control costs or distribution of the components of health care on the supply side.

Readings

5-1. THE ORIGINAL HEALTH BLOCK GRANT*

This 1954 bill (H.R. 7397) reauthorizes a block grant to states to promote public health services. It was also the funding model for later

*From hearing on the Public Health Service Act A.R. 7397 Committee on Interstate and Foreign Commerce. March 4, 5, 12, 1959. Washington D.C. U.S. Government Printing Office.

legislation, like Kerr-Mills, that uses states as both fiscal and program intermediaries. Over the next decade funding would decline relative to other constituency-specific legislation favored by congressional incumbents. As a consequence, state governments would become less important as intermediaries in channeling federal health funding until the advent of Medicaid.

A bill to amend the Public Health Service Act to promote and assist in the extension and improvement of public health services, to provide for a more effective use of available Federal funds, and for other purposes.

Be it enacted by the Senate and House of Representatives of the United States of America in Congress assembled, That this Act may be cited as the "Public Health Grant-in-Aid Amendments of 1954." . . .

Sec. 314 (a) There are hereby authorized to be appropriated for each fiscal year, beginning with the fiscal year ending June 30, 1956, such sums for grants to carry out the purposes of this section as the Congress may determine. The sums so appropriated for any fiscal year shall be available for—

(1) grants to States to assist them in meeting the costs of public health services;

(2) grants to States to assist them in initiating projects for the extension and improvement of their public health services; and

(3) grants to States and to the public and other nonprofit organizations and agencies to assist in combating unusually severe public health problems in specific geographical areas, in the carrying out of special projects which hold unique promise of making a substantial contribution to the solution of public health problems common to a number of States, and in meeting problems of special national significance or concern.

The portion of such sums which shall be available for each of such three types of grants shall be specified in the Act appropriating such sums.

(b) (1) From the sums available from any fiscal year for grants to States to assist them in meeting the costs of their public health services, each State shall be entitled to an allotment of an amount which bears the same ratio to such sums as the product of (1) the population of the State and (2) the square of its allotment percentage (as determined under subsection (h)) bears to the sum of the corresponding products for all the States. The allotment to any State under the preceding sentence for any fiscal year which is less than $55,000 (or such other amount as may be specified as a minimum allotment in the Act appropriating such sums for such year) shall be increased to that amount, the total of the increases thereby required being derived by proportionately reducing the allotments to each of the remaining States under the preceding sentence, but with such adjustments as may be necessary to prevent the allotment of any such remaining States from being thereby reduced to less than that amount.

(2) From each State's allotment under this subsection for this fiscal year, the Surgeon General shall pay to such State an amount equal to its Federal share (as determined under subsection (j)) of the cost of public health services under the plan of such State, approved under subsection (e), including the cost of training of personnel for State and local health work and including the cost of administration of the State plan.

(c) (1) From the sums available for any fiscal year for grants to States to assist them in initiating projects for the extension and improvement of their public health services, each State shall be entitled to an allotment of an amount bearing the same ratio to such sums as the population of such State bears to the population of all States. The allotment to any State under the preceding sentence for a fiscal year which is less than $25,000 (or such other amount as may be specified as a minimum allotment in the Act appropriating such sums for such year) shall be increased to that amount, the total of the increases thereby required being derived by proportionately reducing the allotments to each of the remaining States . . .

(2) From each State's allotment under this subsection for any fiscal year the Surgeon General shall pay to such State a portion of the cost of approved projects for the extension and improvement of public health services (including their administration and the training of personnel for State and local health work) under the State plan. The Surgeon General shall approve any project for purposes of this subsection (e) which constitutes an extension or improvement of public health services under the State plan or will contribute materially to such an extension or improvement.

5-2. THE BEGINNINGS OF MEDICARE

Following is part of the text of the bill enacting Medicare, Title XVIII of H.R. 6675. Notice the provision preventing any federal influence on patient choice or doctor-patient relations. This is similar to the boiler-

plate provision in education legislation that asserts that federal officials cannot become involved in curricula (see Chapter 3). Of course, dollars often influence emphases in both medical and educational practice. In the adjoining testimony, notice the response of doctors to any proposal to move the insurance scheme out of the doctor-controlled private sector. Notice also that Alabama opposes "centralization."

Title XVIII—Health Insurance for the Aged

Prohibition Against Any Federal Interference

Sec. 1801 Nothing in this title shall be construed to authorize any Federal officer or employee to exercise any supervision or control over the practice of medicine or the manner in which medical services are provided, or over the selection, tenure, or compensation of any officer or employee of any institution, agency, or person providing health services; or to exercise any supervision or control over the administration or operation of any such institution, agency, or person.

Free Choice by Patient Guaranteed

Sec. 1802 Any individual entitled to insurance benefits under this title may obtain health services from any institution, agency, or person qualified to participate under this title if such institution, agency, or person undertakes to provide him such services.

Option to Individuals to Obtain Other Health Insurance Protection

Sec. 1803 Nothing contained in this article shall be construed to preclude any State from providing, or any individual from purchasing or otherwise securing, protection against the cost of any health services. . . .

Part A—Hospital Insurance Benefits for the Aged

Description of Program. Sec. 1811 The insurance program for which entitlement is established by section 226 provides basic protection against costs of hospital and related post-hospital services in accordance with this part for individuals who are age 65 or over and are entitled to retirement benefits under title II of this Act or under the railroad retirement system.

Scope of Benefits. Sec. 1812 (a) The benefits provided to an individual by the insurance program under this part shall consist of entitlement to have payment made on his behalf (subject to the provisions of this part) for—

(1) inpatient hospital services for up to 60 days during any spell of illness;
(2) post-hospital extended care services for up to 20 days (or up to 100 days in certain circumstances) during any spell of illness;
(3) post-hospital home health services for up to 100 visits (during the one-year period described in section 1861 (n)) after the beginning of one spell of illness and before the beginning of the next; and
(4) outpatient hospital diagnostic services.

(b) Payment under this part for services furnished an individual during a spell of illness may not (subject to subsections (c) and (d)) be made for—

(1) inpatient hospital services furnished to him during such spell after such services have been furnished to him for 60 days during such spell; or
(2) post-hospital extended care services furnished to him during such spell after such services have been furnished to him for 20 days during such spell.

Testimony before the House Committee on Finance*

Statement of Hon. Anthony J. Celebrezze, Secretary of HEW . . .

The major purposes of H.R. 6675 are to provide protection for the nation's workers and their families against the high cost of health care in old age, to increase cash benefits under social security and to make other substantial improvements in the old-age, survivors, and disability insurance program, to provide for more adequate medical and monetary assistance for the needy, and to improve health care for handicapped children.

No other social security amendments have approached the scope of these proposed amendments. For older people, for widows and orphans,

*Hearings on Health Insurance for the Aged before the Committee on Finance, U.S. House of Representatives, 89th Congress, 1965.

and for the disabled and their families, the payment of benefits where none are now available would turn despair into hope. Every community in our nation would share in the good that the bill would do.

This proposed legislation will lift from the shoulders of our senior citizens a heavy burden of fear—fear that their lifetime savings will be wiped out by the heavy costs of major illness or that they will have to turn to welfare or private charity or sons and daughters for help in meeting these costs. It is my view that this bill, if enacted, will make the most important contribution to security in old age since the social security program was enacted 30 years ago.

It is one of unfortunate facts of life that in old age, when people are living on substantially reduced incomes, health costs are much higher than in younger years. And since, as a general rule, old people have relatively little in the way of resources that can be readily converted into cash and little or no possibility of gaining new income or assets, many find that their higher health costs are too much for them. The years of security and independence that they had hoped for and planned for are spent in a losing battle against dependency.

Despite commendable efforts by private insurance industry, the voluntary health insurance effort has not proved adaptable to the almost universal need of the aged for adequate health insurance; few of the aged can afford to pay the premiums which older people must be charged for broad health insurance protection. Nor does the solution to the problem lie in public assistance.

Though necessary and desirable, public assistance is not acceptable as the first line of defense against insecurity, whether that insecurity is caused by high health costs or other factors. Unlike social insurance, the public assistance program—even though strengthened and approved as proposed in H.R. 6675—cannot prevent dependency; it can only provide for relief after the dependency has occurred. A key to the solution to the problem lies in the approach taken by our well-established contributory social security program.

I would like to emphasize, though, that the health benefit provisions in the bill are built around the idea of using the several resources that can contribute the most, each in its own way, to fortifying ourselves against the insecurity that stems from illness in old age.

A system financed by earmarked employee, employer, and self-employed contributions would serve as the foundation. It would assure that everybody has basic hospital insurance in old age. Only such a system can provide this assurance. Under this method, people can contribute during their productive years toward the hospital insurance that they will need in their later years when their incomes will generally be reduced. After they retire, they need make no further contributions.

The bill would also make provision for those relatively few people who are already in advanced years and not eligible for social security benefits.

Statement of Nelson H. Cruikshank, Director, Department of Social Security, AFL-CIO

I am appearing this morning representing the AFL-CIO in support of H.R. 6675, the Social Security Amendments of 1965.

We appreciate always the opportunity to appear before this committee to present our views, particularly in this case on a series of amendments to the Social Security Act which are some of the most far-reaching, we believe, since the social security program went into affect some 30 years ago.

I am not going to attempt to analyze in detail all the complicated and interrelated provisions of this comprehensive measure.

My purpose is rather to give you, in the brief time available, the major reasons why the AFL-CIO, representing some thirteen and a half million wage earners and their families, and reflecting, we believe, the views of millions more, wholeheartedly supports H.R. 6675 and why we urge this committee and the Senate to grant it speedy and favorable consideration.

There are six main reasons why we support this bill.

1. It provides basic health benefits for the aged, financed through contributory social insurance.
2. It provides for contributions from general revenues toward health insurance coverage, without the imposition of a means test.
3. It provides substantial increases in cash benefits to social security recipients.
4. It increases the amounts of earnings insured under the system—
   (a) By raising the wage base; and
   (b) By including earnings received in the form of tips.
5. In provides adequate and equitable financing for both the broadening of existing social insurance programs and for the newly inaugurated ones.

6. It provides improved standards and broadened coverage for the State programs of medical assistance for needy persons.

The first two of these stated reasons are especially important to us, not only because of the immediate protection afforded nearly 19 million people, but because of the acceptance of the basic principles they reflect. The extension of the proven principle of contributory social insurance to meet major health costs is of far-reaching and historic significance. Nearly every other industrial country in the world took this step years ago.

Of almost equal significance is the recognition that it is appropriate to use funds from general revenues to help pay the costs of health insurance without the application of a means test. This bill takes this important step in two areas:

(a) By meeting during the early years of the program the costs of benefits under the basic plan for those not covered by social security or railroad retirement; and

(b) By matching . . . the $3 monthly premium for each individual enrolling in the supplementary plan.

If this bill did nothing more than establish these two principles, while at the same time translating them into concrete benefits, as it does, it would merit our wholehearted support.

Statement of Dr. Russell B. Carson, Chairman, Board of the National Association of Blue Shield Plans . . .

You have before you the testimony, together with several exhibits.

Our comments and recommendations will relate principally to the voluntary supplemental health benefits program, so designated in part B of title XVIII of H.R. 6675.

I. We are here to testify that the best interests of the aged population will be served by granting a choice of programs, one of which should be the traditional Blue Shield pattern.

II. To testify that the aged citizen should be offered the opportunity to continue the pattern of prepayment to which he is accustomed.

III. To testify that Blue Shield can make its maximum contribution to this program in a full carrier role.

IV. To testify that our services can be most effectively used on a nationwide, rather than a regional or other geographical basis.

V. Finally, to testify that under these conditions Blue Shield can contribute in a major capacity in carrying out the purposes of this legislation.

The National Association of Blue Shield Plans believes that the Senate has an opportunity greatly to improve the impending Social Security Amendments of 1965, specifically by amending part B of the new title XVIII, relating to the proposed voluntary supplemental health insurance plan, in such a way as to afford the beneficiary a free choice among the patterns under which the entire voluntary health insurance movement has grown in the United States.

We submit that it would be consistent with repeated congressional declarations against the establishment of "socialized medicine" in the United States, for the Government not only to purchase medical prepayment from the major private carriers, but to offer the voluntary beneficiaries a reasonable degree of choice among the major patterns of prepaid care already available to the people.

The Federal employee health benefit program, enacted by Congress in 1959, took cognizance of the major forms of voluntary health insurance which have grown competitively in the United States, and whose competition has produced the most phenomenal insurance development in our history.

As presently proposed in H.R. 6675, the supplemental program offers a single pattern of medical and health benefits, all subject to an annual calendar year deductible of $50 and thereafter to a coinsurance factor of 20 percent.

The single pattern of benefits provided in part B of H.R. 6675 is virtually identical to the Government-wide indemnity program, one of the two Government-wide plans offered under the Federal employee health benefits program—the other principal alternative being the Government-wide service benefit program, offered through Blue Shield and Blue Cross.

At present, 56.2 percent of all enrolled Federal employees have chosen the Blue Shield program, and 20.5 percent are enrolled in one or another of the 36 qualified local plans, many of which, like Blue Shield, are "service benefit" plans. The remaining 23.3 percent have chosen the "Government-wide indemnity program," which is essentially the same as the program now specified in part B. Thus a substantial majority of the Federal employees have chosen a pattern of benefits other than the only one offered the aged under H.R. 6675 (exhibit A).

Should the Federal Government now choose for its aged citizens a program that is preferred by less than one-fourth of the Government's own employees?

This is a voluntary program, and it would seem only reasonable that its beneficiaries should be able to choose among the major patterns that are available to other citizens. The aged citizens should have the same privilege of choice, which they have exercised in their earlier years and which is still available to their younger fellow citizens.

Statement of W. B. Hicks, Jr., Executive Secretary, Liberty Lobby

Mr. Chairman and members of the committee, I am W. B. Hicks, Jr., executive secretary of Liberty Lobby. Liberty Lobby represents over 130,000 Americans including a significant percentage who are elderly people—people who must live on very low incomes in many cases—people on social security and others who are not covered by social security benefits.

It is our function to represent the interests of these patriotic Americans in preserving the Constitution and freedom of the United States. At the same time, we recognize that there is a problem of serious dimensions in the high cost of medical care for the aged who must live on fixed incomes.

The members of this committee are quite familiar with the reasons for this problem. Basically, it is a problem created by the very government that now seeks to solve it, because the Government has followed a policy of ever increasing the false expansion of the economy—otherwise known as inflation. Inflation is the real villain of the case. It is one threat against which the elderly are most helpless.

Liberty Lobby desires the best medical care, for the most people, at the lowest cost, just as much as any witness who has appeared before this committee. The question before us is: Does H.R. 6675 accomplish the purpose? We feel that it does not. Further, we see in this bill a threat to the future of the Nation far more serious, even, than the problem it seeks to solve.

The major fault of this bill is that it is irrevocable. Does any member of this committee imagine for a moment that, once enacted into law, this bill can ever be repealed? It is not true, that no matter what serious error it may contain; no matter what future development might demonstrate that the bill was not necessary; or that it went too far in promising too much to too many—is it not true that it can never be revoked?

The bill, we believe, is a proposal to sell insurance to the American people. In effect, it offers a contract that, once signed by the President, will, for all time, bind the taxpayers of the nation to the principle of socialized medicine—a contract that, no matter how regrettable its consequences, cannot in good conscience be broken.

For, once this bill becomes law, I can assure you from my own correspondence that millions of elderly citizens and millions of younger people are going to believe that the Government has promised to care for their medical needs. Those workers who must take home less pay as a result of the new medicare tax are going to expect the Government to keep its end of the bargain, and rightfully so. The elderly, who have believed the promises implied and explicit in the arguments of the proponents of medicare, will cancel their hospitalization policies immediately and, once those policies are canceled, they will never be reinstated.

Statement of Dr. John M. Chenault, Medical Association of the State of Alabama . . .

The general provisions relating to the health insurance programs are, for the most part, unwieldly, and we believe unnecessary in our State. In Alabama, the State board of health has the responsibility for licensing and inspecting health care facilities, including hospitals and nursing homes. Our established procedure is efficient, adequate and appropriate for our needs.

We oppose many of the provisions of this bill, especially part 1-A of title I—proposed new title XVIII—which provides financing of hospital care through social security. This legislation would centralize control over many aspects of the care of the sick. We feel strongly that there is a basic error in the concept of our Federal Government providing a service of this nature to the aged segment of the population.

It appears to us that, of necessity, the administration of the proposed program will result in control of both the vendor and the recipient of the services. We sincerely believe that such a step would be dangerous to the physical health of our people, not in the public interest, and an improper function of the Federal Government. The practice of medicine—art and science—is a highly individualized endeavor, fitting particular needs with best available remedies, and does not lend itself to rigid rules or regimentation.

The propoasl is a radical departure from present procedure in that the Government undertakes the provision of services rather than funds for the needy.

As it is now written, H.R. 6675 excludes coverage of the services of pathologists, radiologists, physiatrists, and anesthesiologists as a part of inpatient hospital services. We urge that this feature be retained as it now stands. The practice of pathology, radiology, anesthesiology, and physical medicine are branches of the practice of medicine just as are surgery, general practice, and internal medicine. The services of these physicians are not hospital services and do not belong in that portion of the bill solely designed to offer hospital benefits. The approval of any amendment classifying these four specialties as "hospital services" would force approximately 15 percent of this country's physicians to become salaried employees rather than independent practitioners.

The use of a regressive tax to fund this proposal of health care, we feel, is another basic error. While we make no claim as financial or fiscal experts, we understand some of the errors of a regressive tax. We consider it to be unjust to tax the working people of this country to provide health care for everyone 65 years of age, regardless of their financial need. It seems unrealistic to expect a young couple with children, and multiple costs-of-living payments, to be saddled with an additional tax for the care of all the elderly.

In Alabama, according to our latest available figures, 8 percent of the total population is 65 or over; 52 percent of our State's population is between the ages of 18 and 64; 50 percent of all the families in Alabama have an annual income under $4,000 and 71 percent have an annual income under $6,000. In Alabama, 50 percent of the nonwhite families have an income of less than $2,000 and 80 percent of these families are under $4,000. A large percentage of this group are the so-called disadvantaged. The point is that the lower income families would pay a tax disproportionately high. We consider this to be unwise, unfair, and discriminatory against these very people whom we are all desperately trying to help, at both the State and Federal levels.

Statement of Dr. William E. Flannery, Past President, Pennsylvania Medical Society

There are aspects of H.R. 6675 which we favor, such as that portion which would increase the cash benefits to social security recipients and the concept of voluntary participation in medical insurance subsidized by general fund revenues. Our position on the measure as a whole, however, must be one of opposition. This is why:

The departure from cash benefits to service benefits removes from the recipient the freedom to purchase that which most adequately meets his individual needs.

In the departure from cash benefits, there is no provision for higher hospital costs which have been increasing at a 7 percent annual rate for some years. Thus, the Department of Health, Education, and Welfare will have to purchase those services at "market prices" or it must control the vendors.

There is widespread misunderstanding among persons of all ages as to what services H.R. 6675 would provide. Should the bill pass in its present form, the disillusioned age 65 and over recipients who expect considerably more benefits than the bill provides would exert massive pressures for expansion of the benefits, pressures that could not be resisted.

The service proposals make a further departure in that they are not even subject to the same earned-income limitations as are the cash benefits.

The administration of medical matters should rest in the hands of those with the highest medical training and should take place at the lowest practical governmental level.

Administration at the lowest level is the most economical administration.

The Pennsylvania Department of Public Welfare administers our medical assistance for the aged program and does it well, but welfare departments in general certainly are not as well qualified as are health departments to administer health services. These are numerous references in H.R. 6675 to the establishment of advisory and regulatory bodies and of authority, without guarantees that there would be adequate representations of medical doctors, and without specifying that medical decisions would be made by persons medically trained.

The public should be spared the lower quality of medical care resulting from over and/or poor utilization of health care facilities, but such control is limited by human pressures to which there is a practical limit. The increased demands on facilities that the passage of H.R. 6675 would bring would result in deterioration of the hospitalization and medical care provided to the entire public.

Hospitals do not provide the highest medical skills and arts; the physicians do, and may they continue to do so if the high quality of medical care in this Nation is to continue to advance.

We don't feel the hospital benefits portion of the bill should be expanded. We are suggesting that the hospital benefits portion is the wrong way to solve any existing problem. It does not differentiate between the needy aged and the affluent aged in the degree of help it provides.

We believe the direction of H.R. 6675 would be impossible to reverse when it proves to be unsatisfactory, and expansion to a complete system of Government medical care would be inevitable.

5-3. CONGRESSIONAL RESPONSE TO MEDICARE COST-CUTTING PROPOSALS*

The following remarks of Chairman Dan Rostenkowski of the Subcommittee on Health indicate congressional concern about a number of cost-cutting regulations, one of which is the indexing of charge increases. Such hearings enable congresspeople to try to influence the administration of policy. It is often easier for both members of Congress and administrators to use hearings as signals of disapproval than to have Congress legislate anew in the area and, in the process, possibly limit other elements of bureaucratic discretion as well.

The purpose of today's oversight hearing is to receive testimony from representatives of the professional community and the Department of Health, Education, and Welfare on four recently promulgated regulations relating to the medicare program. Each of these four regulations— to impose new utilization review requirements, to terminate the inpatient routine nursing salary cost differential, to revise the limit on reasonable costs for inpatient routine services, and to tie recognition of reasonable charge increases to an economic index—has given rise to substantial controversy and widespread adverse criticism from hospital and medical associations. The significance of the issues raised by these regulations is such as to warrant careful appraisal by the Subcommittee of their policy and administrative implications in the light of congressional intent relative to the conduct of the medicare program.

While much of the discussion has revolved around the objections raised by segments of the professional community—and these views and interests are certainly of major importance—the Subcommittee is very much concerned about the impact and consequences of these regulations for medicare beneficiaries. Central to any consideration of regulatory changes in the program must be an evaluation of the likely ef-

*Hearings on Selected Issues in Medicare Program Policy before the Subcommittee on Health, U.S. House of Representatives, 94th Congress, 1st sess., June 12, 1975. Washington, D.C., U.S. Government Printing Office, 1975.

fects on the availability, quality and cost of services furnished to beneficiaries. The Subcommittee wants to be sure that the interest of the beneficiaries is not lost sight of and that the discussion remains firmly focused on their status and needs.

Clearly the issues raised by these regulations have sweeping implications. The utilization review regulations would introduce substantial changes in the scope and conduct of hospital and physician review activities. The Department has indicated, in promulgating these requirements, that they are intended to bring about a single, uniform review system for both medicare and medicaid and to bring utilization review activities more closely into line with PSRO (1970) program. It is also asserted that these requirements are consistent with and implement the provisions enacted in the 1972 Social Security Amendments. Hospital and medical spokesmen have argued, however, that the utilization review regulations not only exceed the authority granted to the Secretary to issue regulations but introduce requirements that many hospitals, particularly rural hospitals, will not be able to meet, with potentially dire consequences for those hospitals and medicare beneficiaries.

The regulations relating to hospital cost reimbursement have similarly been justified by the Department as appropriate modifications of existing reimbursement methods warranted, in the case of nursing cost differential, by several factors including changes in the composition of the medicare population, the increasing number of special care beds and other changes in medicare cost allocation methods. In the case of cost limits on routine service cost, the Department has stated that the new hospital classification system adequately accounts for variations in routine service costs. Hospital spokesmen have held, on the other hand, that both of these reimbursement regulations violate congressional intent in that they will result in a failure of medicare to adequately recognize and reimburse all of a hospital's legitimate costs in providing inpatient services to medicare beneficiaries.

Finally, complaints have been made about the economic index to be used in determining what medicare will recognize as reasonable charges for physicians' services. Although the use of an economic index was authorized in the 1972 Amendments, it is held that the specific index provided for in the regulation has serious technical deficiencies, is not fully consistent with the congressional intent, and is unfair to physicians.

It is important also to take note of several recurring themes which have appeared in the controversy surrounding these regulations. First, it has been argued that despite the complexity and significance of these regulations the Department has promulgated them without due regard for the need to provide reasonable opportunity to thoroughly study and comment on the specific provisions. Thus, it is held that in several cases requests for additional time to evaluate and comment on the regulations were rejected by the Department.

Second, it has been argued that the utilization review and cost reimbursement regulations will have particularly damaging effects upon rural hospitals and that the consequences will be a diminution of hospital resources and services available to medicare beneficiaries residing in rural areas.

Third, serious charges have been made to the effect that the regulations either violate congressional intent or a specific provision of the Social Security Act. As a result of such views, two of the regulations have already resulted in legal action—suits to restrain the Secretary from implementing the utilization and revised cost limit regulations—and indications are that the other two regulations may also be taken to court. While recourse to the courts is certainly an appropriate and legitimate step for those genuinely in doubt about the legality of a regulation, it should be a matter of some concern to the Congress when so many recent regulations under a program as vital and as widely accepted as medicare law are challenged.

The Subcommittee's interest, therefore, is in obtaining a full accounting of the statutory basis, rationale, supporting evidence for and objections to these several regulations, not only to ascertain whether there has been compliance in specific cases with the congressional intent but also to assure that the medicare law continues to be properly administered.

We are not now concerned with the question of the wisdom of the statutory provisions on the basis of which these regulations were issued. The utilization review provisions of law, for example, were designed to serve as a mechanism for assuring appropriate use of services and facilities; the concept of such a mechanism remains valid whether or not the specific features of the current mechanism are fully effective. The Subcommittee does not, therefore, consider proposals to eliminate the provision or to markedly alter it as an appropriate part of this hearing. Similarly, the underlying statutory concepts of "reasonable cost" and "reasonable charges" are not here in question; what is under consideration is whether these concepts are being applied in accordance with the congressional purpose without creating unwarranted or unreasonable burdens on the providers of health care services or on beneficiaries.

5-4. INTEREST GROUP RESPONSE TO MEDICARE COST-CUTTING PROPOSALS*

Following are the comments of a representative of labor, a major future beneficiary of Medicare, on the co-payment and other cost-limiting provisions that Ford submitted to Congress in 1976. The connection between program beneficiaries and voters is explicitly made by Bert Seidman, director of the Social Security Department, AFL–CIO.

Thank you, Mr. Chairman.

Mr. Chairman, on behalf of the AFL-CIO, I wish to thank you for the opportunity to present our views with respect to the administration's proposals for the medicare program.

Let me interject, however, that nobody from the administration has been in touch with us regarding any change in their proposal. Therefore, we have heard, only for the first time this morning from you, Mr. Chairman, what these proposed changes are. Of course, we have not been able to give them proper consideration.

AFL-CIO president, George Meany, recently sent out a letter to AFL-CIO affiliates and central bodies on the President's proposal for catastrophic health insurance for medicare beneficiaries. A copy of that letter is attached to my statement and I respectfully request that it be included in the record of the hearings.

Mr. Chairman, the AFL-CIO was dismayed at President Ford's budget message. We were shocked to find out that the President, under the guise of providing a new catastrophic health program for medicare beneficiaries, was actually proposing major cutbacks in the existing program.

After analyzing the President's proposal, and indeed after hearing the changes which you just indicated, it still appears to us to be an obvious, polite maneuver to win favor with the high income elderly in presidential primaries at the expense of the Nation's elderly poor and sick.

President Meany described the President's proposal as "Robin Hood

*Hearings on the President's Medicare Proposals before the Subcommittee on Health, Congress, sess., Feb. 9, 10, 11, 1976.

in reverse, taking from the aged poor to reduce the Federal budget deficit."

The President proposes a new coinsurance payment of 10 percent on charges for all inpatient hospital and extended care after the first day. The existing deductible provision for the first day in the hospital is maintained. So far as I can tell, this proposal remains in the current version of the President's proposals.

Currently, the existing deductible is $104. It is expected to be $124 in 1977.

In contrast, there is no additional charge currently under medicare for the first 60 days. There is coinsurance equal to one-fourth of the first day deductible, now $24 for days 61 to 90, and one-half of the first day deductible, now $52 for lifetime reserve days 91 to 150.

Under present medicare provisions, a medicare patient who is hospitalized would not incur $500 in hospital charges until about the 76th day of his or her stay. Only 35 out of every 1,000 medicare patients had hospital stays that long in fiscal year 1974. This means that under the President's proposals, 299 out of every 300 hospitalized beneficiaries will pay more during a year as a result of the President's proposal. Only one will gain. Perhaps this number would be slightly reduced under these revised proposals, but the principle would still remain that the overwhelming proportion of the hospitalized beneficiaries will pay more if the President's proposals are adopted than they would pay under the present law.

Under the original proposal, the out-of-pocket costs would have totaled at least $1.8 billion for the first fiscal year or more than three times the total cost of the proposed catastrophic program.

It is quite clear that even under the new proposals, the new costs that the elderly and medicare beneficiaries will have to pay for will be greater than anything that they will get out of the proposed program.

The longer run impact of the President's proposal would be even more serious. Under the original proposal, in fiscal 1977, the outlays for medicare part A would be $15 billion under present law, but $13.3 billion under the proposal—over $2 billion less and that $2 billion would largely come out of the pockets of the elderly.

By fiscal 1981, the figures would be $27.6 billion and $18.8 billion, a reduction of nearly $9 billion a year coming out of the pockets of the elderly.

During the 5-year period 1977 to 1981, Federal expenditures for the medicare program would be reduced by more than $26 billion. Medicare beneficiaries, among the most poverty-stricken groups in the country, would be forced to absorb most of these cutbacks out of their meager resources.

5-5. USING TAXES TO LOWER THE COSTS OF MEDICAL CARE*

Following are two explanations of the way in which tax credits alter the demand for medical services. Such credits cost Congress tax revenues and increase the cost of health care by artificially increasing demand. The proposed legislation (H.R. 5740) also attempts to introduce more competition into the field of health care.

Statement of Emil M. Sunley, Deputy Assistant Secretary of the Treasury for Tax Analysis

I believe that this subcommittee is especially interested in the effect of the tax expenditures for health on the demand and price of medical care.

Exclusions for medical care, like many other tax expenditures, are mostly open-ended. That is, there are few, if any, budget limits on the amount of the expenditure that can occur. Earners have a substantial and fairly open-ended incentive to convert wage compensation into nontaxable compensation in order to minimize their taxes. For instance, for a taxpayer with a 20 percent marginal tax rate from all sources, $1 in cash compensation is equal to only $0.80 in nontaxable compensation. The tax incentive lowers the price of the nontaxable fringe benefit—far beyond the demand that would exist in absence of the incentive.

Over the last three decades, these demands have increased enormously, and noncash compensation has become a large part of the compensation package of most workers. As a result, the income tax base has been eroded. To compensate for this, the rate of tax on cash wages effectively must be increased if a given amount of revenue is to be raised; thus, marginal rates of tax on cash wages must go up even if average rates of tax on all compensation remain steady. Workers who

*Hearings on the Proposal to Restructure the Financing of Private Health Insurance before the Subcommittee on Health, Ninety Sixth Congress, 2 sess., Feb. 25, 1980. Washington D.C. U.S. Government Printing Office, 1980.

receive larger proportions of their compensation in cash—often workers in weak firms or secondary workers—suffer the most from this shift in tax liabilities. Also, the social security tax base has been eroded, slowly forcing other changes in that system of taxation. Moreover, some inflationary pressures can be traced in part to demands of employees for greater increases in payments to nontaxable benefit plans than for increases in cash compensation. It should also be noted that policies to grant equal pay to employees of both sexes are often hindered by the inability of the secondary worker to receive equal value of pay in fringe benefits.

These problems are present with all exclusions of fringe benefits, which in turn weaken the effect of policies which are based on cash compensation.

In the case of health benefits, income in the form of employer-paid health insurance premiums is exempt from Federal income tax, State income tax and social security tax. Thus employees may be inclined to accept a larger share of their compensation in the form of health insurance than they would if the income-in-kind was taxable. This has contributed to the growth in employer payments to group health plans from 0.8 percent of wages and salaries in 1955 to about 4 percent in 1980.

Since the exclusion provision reduces the price employees must pay for health insurance, it is also likely to increase the demand for coverage under health insurance. Increased coverage may be reflected in a reduction of the deductible amount or the copayment rate, or inclusion of previously uncovered services. Since tax rates are higher in higher income brackets, the price reduction—and the price incentive to increase the quantity of services demanded—increases with income.

The effect of allowing itemized deductions for health care expenses must be analyzed along the same lines. The deduction for health insurance premiums has much the same effect as the exclusion: it reduces the after-tax price of health insurance or health care, and the reduction is of greater value at higher income levels. The major difference is that the exclusion is available regardless of whether the taxpayer itemizes deductions or takes the standard deduction, whereas the personal deduction for health insurance premiums must be itemized. For the majority of taxpayers who do not itemize, there is no price reduction.

The requirement that medical expenses exceed 3 percent of AGI [adjusted gross income] before qualifying as a deduction (except for 50 percent of health insurance premiums up to $150) is somewhat similar to a deductible clause in an insurance policy. Although the evidence is not conclusive, some researchers have found that a small deductible has little effect on the demand for hospitalization, while, for ambulatory and other nonhospital services, a moderate size deductible is likely to influence demand markedly.

While the 3 percent floor is roughly analogous to a deductible in an insurance policy, the exclusion of the employer premiums and the deduction of all expenses above the 3 percent floor are both analogous to a copayment rate. For employers in group health plans and for itemizers above the 3 percent floor, then, the marginal tax rate determines the proportion of the last dollar of medical expense or medical insurance paid by the Government; thus, the copayment rate equals one minus the taxpayer's marginal tax rate. Again, the tax incentive for increased use for medical services is greater the higher the taxpayer's taxable income.

Because tax subsidies tend to increase the demand for medical care, they also tend to increase its market price. A subsidy creates a wedge between the market price received by the seller and the net cost to the buyer. Increases in price result in the tax subsidy (or the wedge) being shared with the providers of medical care; thus, the greater the increase in market price, the less the tax subsidy reduces the net cost of medical care to taxpayers.

To make matters worse, market price increases probably apply fairly uniformly to many types of purchases of medical care, while the value of the tax subsidy increases with the taxpayer's income. Thus, even if the tax subsidy results in a net price (after subsidy) decrease to the average taxpayer, it may still result in a net price increase for low- and moderate-income taxpayers who receive only a small price subsidy. For those who do not receive any subsidy, a net price increase is almost certain.

Chairman Ullman's proposal would enhance competition among types of medical care delivery systems by granting favorable tax treatment to employer contributions only if employers offer a low-cost option or an HMO; "nearly" equal contributions—90 percent of the difference between the high cost plan and the option selected by the employee must be "rebated"; and provide a "comprehensive" benefit package (including catastrophic, hospital, x-ray, diagnostic, and inpatient drugs).

**Statement of Karen Davis, Deputy Assistant Secretary for
Planning and Evaluation/HEW**

We are very pleased with this committee's interest and support of
health maintenance organizations—one of the more efficient methods of
financing and providing health care. We are also pleased with your
positive action on the administration's Medicare HMO Reimbursement
Reform Act, and note that similar provisions are included in the bill you
are considering today—The Health Cost Restraint Tax Act of 1979
(H.R. 5740).

Despite its many strengths, our health care system has serious flaws.
Today we face three pressing—and immediate—challenges:

First, we must find ways to control rapidly escalating health care
costs. During the ten years between 1968 and 1978, expenditures for
health-care services have risen at an average rate of 12 percent per year.
If current trends continue, national health spending will be close to $400
billion by 1984—over 10 percent of our gross national product.

Second, we must protect our citizens from financial hardship imposed
by medical bills. Today 22 million Americans have no health insurance
coverage. Seven million of the uninsured have incomes below the
Federal poverty level—an income of $7,500 for a family of four in
1980. For these individuals, any medical expense is virtually a catastro-
phe.

Third, we must improve access to health care services and assure
provision of more appropriate types of care. More than half of our citizens who have incomes below the poverty level are not eligible for
medicaid and encounter financial barriers in seeking health services.
Millions more poor Americans live in medically underserved areas with
few providers, and they may not have easy access to a health care
provider.

Alternative health delivery systems—such as health maintenance organizations or community health centers—are not present in most parts
of the country. Finally, our current financing and delivery systems tend
to stress provision of expensive acute care services rather than primary
and preventive services.

As I am sure you are aware, the health care sector has many unique
features which either prevent competition or inhibit the ability of competitive forces to exercise restraint on rising costs:

First, providers dominate the decisionmaking process. Overall, 70 percent of the health care expenditures are generated by physician decisions. Physicians determine which tests to order and whether a patient needs hospitalization or surgery. The central role of providers in health care means that physicians can- and do—create demand for their own services.

Second, patients generally have limited ability to question physician judgements because consumers tend to be unaware of the costs of coverage or care. But it is also because medical care is not like other commodities that consumers purchase. Consumers generally do not have sufficient knowledge to judge the specific types of services they require or the quality of care they receive. The decision to seek medical care is often made at a time of stress, when any consumer is loath to question a physician's recommendation.

Third, current forms of insurance coverage exacerbate the inherently noncompetitive features of the health care market. Insurance insulates both providers and patients from the immediate impact of health care costs—and makes them less concerned about the costs of services they use. Most workers receive coverage through employer-related plans—a system which incorporates tax incentives encouraging purchase of comprehensive, first dollar coverage.

There are numerous ways we could attempt to promote competition in the health care sector. We could provide more information to consumers, encourage providers to participate in cost-efficient prepaid practices, encourage certain alternative modes of delivery such as expanded use of nurse practitioners, and increase review activities to make providers more conscious of the costs associated with the services they provide.

H.R. 5740 addresses itself to increasing competition in the health insurance selection process. The administration's NHP [National Health Plan] includes competitive elements as a part of a comprehensive strategy for reforming the health system.

5-6. THE FAILURE OF FEDERAL ATTEMPTS TO CONTROL HOSPITAL COSTS

Following is Carter's message to Congress (H. Doc. 96-98) accompanying a proposal to control hospital costs—H.R. 2626, parts of which are also included. The bill would allow the secretary of HHS to determine professional and other fees if hospitals and the administra-

tion did not reach agreement. The language of the act implies that doctor costs per se would not be controlled. The negative sanction available to the government to force compliance is the withholding of Medicare/Medicaid reimbursements. The bill did not pass because it too directly attacked professional and private-sector prerogatives.

Hospital Cost-Containment Message from the President of the United States

To the Congress of the United States:

Inflation is America's most serious domestic problem. It affects every individual and every institution in the country, and it damages the health not only of our economy but of our society. The American people are demanding prompt action against inflation from their elected representatives—action that is strong, prompt and effective.

One of the most important components of inflation is the soaring cost of hospital care, which continues to outpace inflation in the rest of the economy. A decade ago, the average cost of a hospital stay was $533. In just the past two years, the average cost of a hospital stay has increased by $317 to $1634 a day—an increase of almost 24 percent.

Hospital cost inflation is uniquely severe. It is also uniquely controllable. It offers us one of our best opportunities to bring down the rate of overall inflation. This year, once again, I ask the Congress to join me in grasping that opportunity by enacting a tough program of hospital cost containment.

The Senate passed a Hospital Cost Containment bill last year, but the House did not complete action on it. The legislation I am transmitting to the Congress today is similar to the bill that passed the Senate last year. It responds to Congressional concerns that were raised during consideration of last year's bill, and it is strong enough to do the job.

The Hospital Cost Containment Act of 1979 will be one of the clearest tests of Congress' seriousness in dealing with the problem of inflation. Through this one piece of legislation, we can, at a stroke, reduce inflation, cut the Federal budget, and save billions of dollars of unnecessary public and private spending.

The legislation I am transmitting today will save $3.7 billion in fiscal year 1980. It will save $1.4 billion in the Federal budget, over $420 million in state and local budgets, and almost $1.9 billion in private health insurance and payments by individuals. Altogether, the potential savings that could result from this measure amount to some $53 billion over the next five years.

Because most hospital bills are paid by public or private health insurance programs, the impact of hospital inflation is sometimes disguised. But that impact is painfully real for every American.

The inflationary rise in hospital costs is not inevitable. While there have been dramatic and desirable improvements in the quality of hospital services, much of the increase in hospital expenses has been unnecessary. No one's health is improved by the existence of thousands of unfilled hospital beds, by hospital stays that are unnecessarily long, by surgery and X-ray tests that are unneeded and sometimes harmful, by wasteful supply purchasing practices, by inefficient energy use, or by pointless duplication of expensive facilities and equipment. But these wasteful practices cost billions.

In the past, hospitals have had little incentive to be efficient. The hospital sector is fundamentally different than any other sector in our economy. Normal buyer-seller relationships and normal market forces do not exist. The consumer of services—the patient—rarely pays the bill directly. Nor does the patient decide what services he or she will receive in the hospital. The person who makes the decisions—the physician—does not pay the bill either, and therefore has little or no incentive to see that services are provided in an efficient manner. Often, doctors do not even know the costs of the tests and X-rays they order.

There is growing determination throughout the country to make hospitals efficient. Nine states—Colorado, Connecticut, Maryland, Massachusetts, New Jersey, New York, Rhode Island, Washington, and Wisconsin—have enacted mandatory cost containment programs. Hospitals in these states, which include many of the most renowned medical institutions in the world, have reduced cost increases substantially while continuing to provide care of high quality.

The Hospital Cost Containment Act of 1979 is reasonable and realistic. It permits a period of time for voluntary action, with mandatory limits only if voluntary action fails to meet the reasonable goals established in the bill. Under current assumptions the goal will be 9.7 percent in 1979; it will be adjusted to reflect the actual increases in the price of goods and services hospitals use. In 1977, one-third of the nation's hospitals—from all regions and of all types—had cost increases of 9.7 percent or less.

Congress had debated hospital cost containment for almost two years.

There is now no reason for delay. I call upon the Congress to demonstrate its commitment to the fight against inflation by promptly enacting the Hospital Cost Containment Act of 1979.

Jimmy Carter
The White House
March 6, 1979

A bill

To establish voluntary limits on the annual increases in total hospital expenses, and to provide for mandatory limits on the annual increases in hospital inpatient revenues to the extent that the voluntary limits are not effective.

Be it enacted by the Senate and House of Representatives of the United States of America in Congress assembled.

Short Title

Section 1. This Act may be cited as the "Hospital Cost Containment Act of 1979."

Establishment of Voluntary Limits

Sec 2 (a) The Secretary, during January of 1980, and during January of each succeeding year, shall promulgate a national voluntary percentage limit. That limit shall consist of the sum of the following amounts (as determined or estimated by the Secretary):

(1) the average percentage increases in wages paid in the preceding year over wages paid in the second preceding year per employee per hour to employees (other than to doctors of medicine or osteopathy and to supervisors) of hospitals in the United States, multiplied by the average fraction (as determined or estimated by the Secretary from time to time) of the expenses of hospitals in the United States attributable to such wages.

(2) the greater of—

(A) the sum of the products of the average percentage increase in the United States in the price of each appropriate class (as determined by the Secretary) of goods or services (other than those covered by paragraph (1)) in the preceding year over the price in the second preceding year per unit of the class and the average fraction (as determined or estimated by the Secretary from time to time) of the expenses in hospitals in the United States attributable to that class, and

(B)(i) in 1980, 5.12 per centum, or

  (ii) in any succeeding year, the amount determined in the previous year under subsection (d)(2),

(3) the percentage increase in the population in the United States in the preceding year over the population in the second preceding year, and

(4) 1 per centum (as an allowance for the net increase in service intensity in hospitals).

(b) The Secretary, during January of 1980, and during January of each succeeding year, shall promulgate a voluntary percentage limit for each hospital for the hospital's accounting period ending in 1979. . . .

Applicability of Mandatory Limits

Sec. 3 (a)(1) The Secretary, before July 1, 1980, and before July 1 of each succeeding year, shall determine or estimate the dollar amount by which the percentage increase in the expenses of each relevant hospital in the accounting period of the hospital ending in the preceding year over its expenses in the preceding accounting period exceeded (or was less than) the voluntary percentage limit for the hospital for the accounting period (as promulgated under section 2(c)).

(2) For purposes of paragraph (1), a "relevant hospital" means a hospital not subject to mandatory limit under subsection (d) for the hospital's accounting period ending in the year preceding the year in which the Secretary is making the determinations or estimates under this subsection.

(b)(1) The Secretary, before July 1, 1980, and before July 1 of each succeeding relevant year, shall determine the sum of the differences determined or estimated under subsection (a). If the Secretary determines that the sum is equal to or less than zero, no hospital shall be subject to a mandatory limit under this Act for its accounting period ending in the year.

(c)(1) The Secretary, before July 1, 1980, and before July 1 of each succeeding year, shall, if he has determined under subsection (b) that the sum of the differences is greater than zero, determine the sum of the differences determined or estimated under subsection (a) for hospitals in each relevant State. If the Secretary determines for a particular State that the sum is equal to or less than zero, no hospital in that State shall be subject to a mandatory limit under this Act for its accounting period ending in the year.

Conformance by Certain Federal and State Programs

Sec. 8 (a) Notwithstanding any provision of title XVIII of the Social Security Act, reimbursement for inpatient hospital services under the program established by that title shall not be payable, on an interim basis or in final settlement, to the extent that it exceeds the applicable mandatory limits established under this Act or under a State mandatory hospital cost containment program of a State whose hospitals have been excluded under section 4 from the application of the mandatory limits established under this Act.

(b) Notwithstanding any provision of title V or XIX of that Act, payment shall not be required to be made by any State under either of those titles with respect to any amount paid for inpatient hospital services in excess of the applicable mandatory limits established under this Act; nor shall payment be made to any State under either of those titles with respect to any amount paid for inpatient hospital services in excess of those limits.

5-7. THE UNEVEN COSTS OF FEDERALLY FUNDED MEDICAL CARE*

The following article illustrates the consequences of fiscal controls and cutbacks on fiscal distribution. Neediest areas are hurt first. To undo the damage, the intermediate service providers (hospitals) must petition Congress and use the federal courts. Even then, progress is slow.

Under pressure from Congress and a Federal judge, the Reagan Administration authorized higher Medicare payments today for hospitals serving large numbers of poor people.

Three times since 1982, Congress has directed the Secretary of Health and Human Services to make appropriate adjustments in Medi-

*Robert Paer, "Medicare Payments Raised for Hospitals Serving Poor," *New York Times,* July 2, 1985.

care payment rates for hospitals that serve "a significantly dispropor- tionate number of patients who have low income." Until today the Ad- ministration resisted, saying there were no valid statistics to prove that such hospitals had higher costs that would justify higher reimburse- ments.

Medicare is serving 30 million elderly and disabled people this year, at a total cost of $71 billion. About two-thirds of the money is paid to hospitals for the care of inpatients.

Hospitals Must Apply

In rules issued today the Department of Health and Human Services said it "may adjust" Medicare payment amounts to "take into account the increased costs incurred by hospitals that serve a significantly dis- proportionate number" of low-income people. To obtain the extra amounts, hospitals must file applications with the Government and must demonstrate that their Medicare costs are higher because of the "special needs" of indigent patients.

Numerous studies by health economists and physicians have con- cluded that the average cost of a Medicare case is higher in hospitals with a "disproportionate number" of indigent patients. These patients, according to the studies, have less access to preventive care and are more severely ill than the average patient when they enter the hospital. In addition, the studies say, the indigent often stay in the hospital longer because they have no permanent home, live in substandard housing or have no one to help them with personal hygiene, medication or special dietary needs.

Margaret M. Heckler, the Secretary of Health and Human Services, said she "strongly disagrees with the appropriateness" of the new rules, but was issuing them because she had been ordered to do so by a Federal district judge, Marilyn Hall Patel, in San Francisco. "Failure to promul- gate these rules," Mrs. Heckler said, "could result in contempt pro- ceedings against the department."

Process Called Cumbersome

Representative Fortney H. (Pete) Stark of California and Charles B. Rangel of Manhattan, both Democrats, have prodded the Administra- tion to issue such rules. Mr. Stark, who is chairman of the House Ways and Means Subcommittee on Health, said at a recent hearing that the effect of the delay was to "cheat poor elderly people out of medical care."

Larry S. Gage, president of the National Association of Public Hospitals, which represents about 70 hospitals across the country, welcomed the new rules as "a tremendous step forward." But he said the procedure adopted by the Administration, requiring hospitals to apply for the extra payments, would be "much more cumbersome" than providing an automatic adjustment to hospitals that met criteria set by the Government.

Edmund B. Rice, vice president of the American Hospital Association, said his organization was still trying to persuade Congress to adopt an automatic adjustment through legislation. It would be feasible, he said, to provide such an adjustment for 500 to 600 hospitals, representing about 10 percent of the 5,405 hospitals operating under the new Medicare payment system. . . .

The system gives hospitals a strong incentive to economize because it pays a fixed amount, set in advance, for each type of ailment or illness, regardless of how long the patient stays in the hospital.

The new rules, published today in the Federal Register, are scheduled to take effect Aug. 1, as Judge Patel ordered. The Administration said that it did not know how much the additional Medicare payments would cost the Government, but was preparing an estimate.

The new rules also permit extra payments to hospitals that incur "extraordinary and unusual costs" and those that are the only source of inpatient care in a particular community. Until now, the Administration had refused to make such payments, although they were authorized by Congress.

Judge Patel's order was issued in a lawsuit filed by Redbud Community Hospital, a 40-bed public facility in Clearlake, Calif. The Federal Government is appealing her decision to the United States Court of Appeals for the Ninth Circuit. The appeals court has denied the Government's request to delay the effect of her order.

5-8. THE UNEVEN BURDEN OF HEALTH COST CONTROL*

The following New York Times *article describes the new Medicare reimbursement system and the inequities it produces. Under this system the amount of service offered appears to be more closely tied to the wealth of a geographic area than previously.*

*Leon C. Hirsch, "Unequal Health Care," *New York Times,* July 3, 1985.

After 15 years of skyrocketing health care costs, the Federal Government has lowered the boom on the health care industry. By replacing Medicare's cost-plus reimbursement system with a fixed-payment program, the Government dramatically slowed the cost spiral.

Unfortunately, some patients were hit harder than others when the boom fell. By assuming all patients require the same treatment, the Federal Government forces private hospitals to push aside those with more serious medical problems—typically the elderly and poor—into public hospitals. Without returning to wasteful spending, Congress should stop the unintended incentives that now result in unequal treatment.

The new Medicare payment system groups medical procedures into 468 related groups. After diagnosis, each patient is assigned a group number. Based on this category, the hospital is reimbursed a predetermined fee regardless of the total cost of treatment. In most cases, if costs exceed the reimbursement fee, the hospital takes a loss.

The program is an affront to common sense. Without logic or reason, it presumes that everyone gets sick with equal severity and, further, that elderly people are afflicted with only one illness at a time. The payment system ignores a very significant fact—people are not all medically equal. Pre-admittance physical condition, economic status, ancillary medical problems, hereditary factors and severity of illness all affect the treatment course and, therefore, the hospital's total expense.

Under Medicare's previous cost-plus reimbursement system, there was no incentive for sound business practice. Today, hospitals have no choice but to cut costs drastically. Administrators are eliminating inefficiencies, reducing inventories and introducing money-saving technology.

Signs of progress are clear: The average hospital stay for Medicare patients declined 20 percent in 1984, and occupancy rates are the lowest in more than 20 years.

However, because of the rigid reimbursement system, many hospitals are also forced to reduce necessary tests, discharge patients sooner than physicians prefer and, increasingly, transfer high-cost patients to public hospitals. The payment system may reduce costs, but it creates separate and unequal health care for the nation's poor and elderly.

The urban poor, admitted to public hospitals, often suffer from three or four unrelated and long-neglected diseases, each a separate group classification. Under the current payment system, the hospital is reimbursed for only one of these additional illnesses. For example, a hospital treating a patient with hip degeneration on both sides is reimbursed for only one diseased hip. The hospital can either replace only one hip or lose money.

A study by the New York Health and Hospitals Corporation showed that the indigent are more often seriously ill than their wealthier counterparts. It analyzed 25 common patient disorders at 15 public hospitals in New York City and at 60 private nonprofit hospitals in the city, Westchester and Long Island. In all but five categories, public hospital patients had more serious illness than those in the private group.

Private hospitals are now facing the ugly choice of transferring elderly and poor patients to public hospitals when costs exceed reimbursements. In the two years since the new payment system was adopted, transfers from private hospitals quadrupled at Parkland Memorial Hospital in Dallas and at D.C. General Hospital in Washington; they are up 680 percent over the same period at Cook County Hospital in Chicago.

American enjoy the highest standard of medical care. Medicare can never return to the bankrupting cost-plus reimbursement system, but the Federal Government should develop a new program based on incentive, competition and free enterprise.

Even a group payment system can be made to work if the program is not rigid, recognizes the differences between human beings and is redesigned to promote sound cost control. If the incentives are right, private hospitals will compete for patients, not transfer them. The resulting competition will drive costs down.

6 Income Maintenance and Welfare

Welfare and income maintenance have traditionally been local government functions in Western democracies. National involvement in such functions began at different times in different countries: in Britain by 1911; in France in the 1930s (Ashford, 1986). In the same decade income maintenance and welfare entered the national political agenda in the United States as a result of the Depression. In France early involvement occurred largely on a sector-by-sector basis and, as in the United States, provided minimal monetary appropriations. In the United States involvement was gradual and largely based on direct insurance principles (as in the case of old age benefits) or on the co-payment of welfare benefits administered through state governments. The incremental expansion of the welfare and income maintenance systems the latter usually through social security, reflects the episodic expansion of workman's compensation and similar insurance like programs of federal involvement in the other policy areas we have considered here. Congress expanded insurance and welfare benefits as a way of providing constituency benefits of electoral relevance.

Income-maintenance and welfare programs in the United States can be divided into three categories. The first, self-sufficient programs, include the Old Age and Survivors Insurance and Disability Insurance System (OASDI), popularly known as Social Security and private pension plans. Conceptually these represent different forms of forced and voluntary annuities (self-insurance over time) for the employed (see Reading 6-1). The second category includes workman's compensation, unemployment insurance, and aid for the blind and disabled. Although these are not self-annuities per se, they represent a form of collective insurance, spreading each person's risk of becoming unemployed through no fault of his or her own across a number of employees. Reasons for accidental unemployment include blindness, disability, injury at the workplace, or cutbacks in the labor force. The third category includes welfare programs like (ADC) and food stamps, which are grants to some of the poor regardless of their recent work status.

Although the provision of federally funded social security to individuals and many administrative rules governing the management of private pension funds are nationally uniform, other federal programs reflect the historical primacy of the states as policy-makers and administrators of income maintenance. Further, the administration of workman's compensation, unemployment insurance, ADC, and food stamps varies widely across the states. A number of states (New York, for example) require county or other local contributions to various welfare programs, and the welfare system is administered through county offices. In other states no county contribution to the state's part of federally augmented welfare programs is required. Such programs are locally administered, but through branches of a single state administrative apparatus. Some states (e.g., New York, Massachusetts) have extensive supplementary welfare legislation. In New York all the needy are covered by some program, although once the money runs out in any fiscal year, procedural roadblocks may be placed in front of those requiring assistance. New York, Massachusetts, and similar states fix the state-level requirements that must be met by beneficiaries of any welfare program. At the other extreme, California has historically allowed counties to perform this function, while Arizona allows counties to determine both eligibility requirements and level of benefits.

Unlike France, the United States does not (with the single exception of the railroads) exhibit sectoral distinction in the application of Social Security, workman's compensation, and other employment regulations. France incorporated already existing sectoral income-maintenance plans into the national system while maintaining historical distinctions in levels of benefits among plans. In the United States, in contrast, the only real distinction has been between public- and private-sector employees. Public-sector employees often have their own more generous retirement system. With early retirement, some federal employees and members of the military have obtained benefits under both Social Security and their own specially designed retirement plans. A similar situation is found in Germany. In fact, public employees are almost always involved early in the establishment of national income-maintenance plans and nationwide health and unemployment plans in Western democracies.

Income maintenance, whether it takes the form of welfare or insurance, has countercyclical macroeconomic effects: when employment drops for any reason, much consumer purchasing power can be maintained through income insurance or welfare transfers. Indexing income-insurance benefits also transfers some control over the system to those who administer it as opposed to legislatures, which would otherwise appropriate increases in benefits in response to inflation or the need for electoral support.

Professional involvement in welfare programs is less complete at the national level. Congress periodically changes food stamp eligibility requirements and approves changes in the rules governing receipt of money under ADC. Programs that are more welfare- than income-maintenance-oriented also experience more local-level variation; state and local bureaucracies and locally organized professional groups are more important in determining beneficiaries and amounts. In contrast, state and local legislatures and bureaucracies play no role in determining eligibility for and level of Social Security benefits. Although other insurance programs, like workman's compensation and unemployment, can be varied by state legislatures, local-level professionals have little influence.

Congress has managed to guide state welfare programs through both positive and negative incentives, though not to the same extent that it has influenced state and local educational funding (see Chapter 3). States must have and contribute to programs to take advantage of federal monies in the areas of unemployment, aid for the blind and disabled, and ADC. All citizens must have the same standing before state laws in these areas. This was true of Old Age and Survivors Insurance in the original Social Security Act, which was intended to be administered through the states. Hence, in a positive sense states must have programs in order to take advantage of federal monies; in a negative sense they must administer these programs in a manner compatible with federal law or lose the federal contribution to these matching programs. Tables illustrating the ratio of black income to white income by decile show a ratio close to 1.0 at the lower deciles principally because federal regulation of social security and welfare benefits, both positive and negative, has secured comparable benefits for blacks and whites within each state.

Income maintenance and welfare are now on the national agenda of every industrialized representative democracy. In most countries two factors prompted this national attention. Like the extension of the franchise, the development of a national income-maintenance or health system may extend the notion of citizenship and citizen support for the regime (Bendix, 1963). Additionally, such a system may politically benefit one or more national political parties. Usually the latter condition is relevant only when parties have some degree of national scope and each has a coordinated pattern of voting in the national legislature. Hence, one would expect to find an earlier role for the national legislature in income maintenance and welfare in Britain and Germany than in the United States.

National interest in a system of income maintenance and welfare is also inspired by economic emergencies like the Great Depression of the 1930s. Such an event may get income maintenance on the national agenda, if only to preserve the legitimacy of political and economic institutions among the newly unemployed middle classes. Put in other terms, income maintenance and welfare are added to the national agendas of representative, strong-party democracies because of the political advantage that might accrue to the party system and to a particular party. Common examples are the roles of Disraeli and Bismarck in the development of the welfare systems in Britain and West Germany. On the other hand, if the party system is weak, as in the United States, some dramatic event may be needed to make welfare a matter of national rather than local concern.

Once these issues are on the congressional agenda in the United States, the uneven distribution of wealth between urban and suburban areas and the uneven residence patterns of the elderly will gradually introduce federal aid for the elderly and poor into the floor reciprocity system of Congress (see Chapter 1). In other words, there will evolve sets of locally based politicians who are electorally advantaged by the passage of additional income-maintenance and welfare legislation. This accounts for both the incremental development of the program and the number of organized professional intermediaries involved. Only the direct payment from national government to citizens distinguishes old-age income insurance from the other policy areas we have so far considered.

Context

Without benefit of national legislation, problems of poverty and unemployment were handled at the local level in the United States and France. In the latter country Catholic charity and local welfare systems providing in-kind benefits also maintained moral norms (Piven and

Cloward, 1971) and the viability of agricultural production in times of recession (Kelley, 1981). The United States adopted the English conception of providing for the poor; it was up to local charities and local governments to derive funds in a variety of ways to prevent starvation and death through exposure. County-funded almshouses date from the very earliest years of territory and statehood. State-level concern for income maintenance was first expressed through the provision of workman's compensation. The first permanent law applied only to federal employees (1908). By 1920 all but six states had workman's compensation programs (Myers, 1965, p. 199), passed through federal example, but without federal nudging, and managed through private insurance systems. This is still true today. Workman's compensation is an actuarially sound system of insurance, organized on a state-by-state basis, which provides for payments to workers for medical care and time off pursuant to injuries obtained while working. Employers pay into the plan because they expose employees to the risk of injury.

Whereas the British system of national income maintenance and welfare dates from the 1911 National Insurance Act, the Congress resisted national insurance schemes until the effects of the Depression had been felt for several years. Unlike most of the social programs described in other chapters of this book, the basic outlines of our national welfare system date from the 1930s. Food stamps, for example, could be issued under 1935 agricultural legislation. The Roosevelt administration seriously considered medical insurance as well but dropped the idea because of the opposition of the AMA.

The intent of the Social Security Act of 1935 is clear. Roosevelt wanted a bill that would insure almost all Americans against unwanted or unwarranted loss of ability to work and produce income (see Reading 6-2). The thrust of the legislation was essentially conservative. Many corporate leaders were involved in its development and testified at various hearings prior to its enactment. Yet the Social Security could not be too conservative. It had to provide some help for state welfare programs while phasing in an insurance scheme influenced by the cradle-to-grave protection advocated by the popular Townsend movement. The Social Security Act passed without the involvement of organized labor. The AFL was neutral; although it approved of the premise of some kind of insurance scheme, preferred to keep the government out of marketplace activity and supported instead legislation prompting employers to organize a social security system through the AFL.

The best-known part of the Social Security Act refers to the Old Age and Survivors Insurance and Disability Insurance System (OASDI). Under OASDI, contributions by both employers and employees were to begin in 1937, and the first payments to beneficiaries would occur five years later. Sixty-five was set as the eligibility age for OASDI benefits, unless disability occurred. Initial beneficiaries of the act would receive more funds than they put in; however, under subsequent legislation the system was to be actuarially sound and fully funded by the late 1940s. The system would remain that way until 1965, when either a change in the payment schedules or a resort to general tax revenues would occur. The government also provided matching funds for state welfare programs to aid the elderly and the disabled who were unemployed during the Depression and could not be beneficiaries of the newly established scheme. (The hope was that in the future workers would fall into the disabled category later in their careers and would thus be covered by the self-insurance aspect of the Social Security system.) The welfare aspect of the Social Security Act had the effect of forcing states to develop statewide welfare systems for the aged. Alaska already had such a system in place, and Arizona had tried to set one up upon admission to the Union in 1912; however, the Arizona act had been declared unconstitutional (Myers, 1965, p. 12). The Railroad Retirement Act, passed in 1935, has also been considered a precursor of the Social Security Act. However, the Railroad Act was more circumscribed in its provisions for the elderly and came about as part of a larger effort to maintain railroad activity and avoid rail bankruptcies. Moreover, since the act took effect two weeks after the Social Security Act, for that small period of time even retired railroad workers were covered under the latter.

The part of the Social Security Act dealing with unemployment was passed to encourage states to develop their own programs. A federal unemployment tax was placed on all employers of twenty or more workers. By 1937 all states had developed such programs, although the scope of the programs differ and the generosity of their benefits varied. The federal role was to provide grants for the development and administration of such state programs and eventually to provide matching funds and extra funding for long-term unemployment. In order to be eligible for a 90 percent exemption from the federal tax, state plans had to be administratively neutral and provide equal protection and equal access. Although these requirements were not always observed, this was the beginning of minority entry into the unemployment insurance system with the results noted above: by the 1950s the poorest black were not much poorer than the poorest whites.

The last major recipient groups, children and families with dependent children, had a minor place in income security legislation. Very small amounts of money were initially appropriated for children; no one could have anticipated the growth of this element of the program.

The original intent of federal involvement in income maintenance was to provide a cradle-to-grave insurance scheme for all citizens, though in the short term some older uncovered individuals would have to be covered through a supplementary welfare program shared with the states. The welfare component of the legislation, old age assistance (OAA) was expected to grow progressively smaller as more people were brought into OASDI. Although payment to the elderly through OAA have not declined in absolute terms as a proportion the percentage of all federal assistance represented by OAA has steadily declined (Stein, 1980, p. 222). The social insurance part of the Social Security Act has worked as originally anticipated, partly as a result of the ever broadening coverage in subsequent legislation.

Other elements of the original Social Security Act reflect the principle that the noninsurance aspects of the system, particularly ADC, are to be administered and, to some degree, controlled by states. State and local governments can introduce, through their screening procedures, moral and economic norms as part of the qualifications for receiving welfare aid. In some ways ADC and similar welfare programs is a two-edged sword. It increased the amount of welfare money available for the elderly, children, and their families and prompted states to provide matching funds and thus to increase both financial and administrative participation in providing for the poor. Yet it also allowed states and localities to use these resources to advance local moral or ethical values or the availability of seasonal labor.

Agenda

The principal issues in the establishment of federal Social Security and welfare involvement revolved around who was going to pay for them, who would benefit, what would be done with the money collected for the insurance program, whether the states or the federal government would control the administration of welfare, and, later, what was to be the role of the federal bureaucracy and professional service providers in this system.

The Social Security system passed in 1935 produced a huge accumulation of money that had to be reinvested in the economy or used to fund government expenditures. Social Security income used for the latter purpose will represent a claim by the system on future government revenues. When the government reinvests Social Security income, on the other hand, its allocation may or may not be as economically efficient as private investment. Today we would view this aspect of a fully funded system as a potential tool for managing the economy. But aside from a willingness to use small amounts of Social Security revenues to fund future deficits, Roosevelt appears to have been concerned only with the insurance aspect of the system.

Clearly banks and businesspeople were quite concerned about how the federal government would handle Social Security revenues. These revenues would amount to approximately $50 billion in reserves in the 1950s, offering the government a tremendous opportunity to favor current public-sector consumption by using the funds to cover budget deficits or, alternatively, to become the single largest investor in the private economy and exercise a great influence on industrial development. Either course was unsatisfactory to business, Republicans, and even Democrats.

To prevent this enormous build-up of capital through the contributory parts of social security, the Social Security Amendments of 1939 shattered the connection between taxes and benefits. The insurance aspect was less clear in the 1939 amendments than it was in the 1953 act, which had provided for a pay-as-you-go system with a required reserve (Stein, 1980). The 1939 act also increased the federal contribution for ADC to a 50-50 split with the states.

The 1946 amendments to the Social Security Act were the first to increase both the number of beneficiaries of the welfare and insurance systems and the level of benefits. Later the federal contribution to state welfare programs also increased. These increases and their successors have been so popular that only one piece of legislation extending eligibility or benefit levels has ever been vetoed, and Truman's veto of the 1948 amendments was overwhelmingly reversed by Congress. Throughout the 1940s and 1950s, increases in eligibility amounts for the insurance and welfare systems were added to the benefits Congress passed out to definable constituencies. This process was augmented by the movement of the old to the sunbelt states. Once they were concentrated in a number of congressional districts, their needs could enter the floor reciprocity system described in Chapter 1.

The use of the state as the welfare intermediary also increased the opportunities for Congress to make rules about how states administered such programs. In 1939 a Social Security Board policy decision required public assistance records to be kept confidential and to be used only for purposes of administration. In Illinois and Oklahoma, federal matching funds for welfare were withdrawn because the state programs were inefficiently administered. Funds were withheld from Ohio because they were used unethically—the governor increased welfare benefits and then used welfare records to seek support for his reelection campaign—and the administration success fully resisted a congressional attempt to reimburse Ohio for the funds withheld. This established the principle that states must follow procedural rules to be eligible for matching funds.

The 1950 Social Security Amendments established the basic outline of the present system. The act provided for increasing federal matching for the welfare components of Social Security and for liberalization of Social Security benefits. Liberalization continued throughout the Eisenhower era, and although Eisenhower himself was dissatisfied with several of the amendments, particulary those enacted in 1958, he refrained from vetoing them. These amendments modify the equalization formula for welfare aid, relating federal participation to a state's fiscal capacity. In 1953 the administration proposed and the Congress passed legislation establishing the Department of Health, Education and Welfare. Although Social Security and welfare did not become a cabinet-level department, as Roosevelt had envisioned, they did constitute a major function of the new department. This reorganization did not result in any dramatic policy changes—reorganization never does (see Chapter 2)—but it underscored the importance of welfare in future congressional deliberations.

The Eisenhower administration took few steps to control state actions in administering welfare, even when these clearly violated the law or Constitution. HEW refused to cut off support for the Louisiana welfare system when it withdrew ADC money from mothers who bore a second child illegitimately. The vast majority of affected mothers were black. Only a few days before the beginning of the Kennedy administration, HEW ruled that support for the first child could not be withdrawn, but that child might be removed to a suitable environment for purposes of receiving federally sponsored benefits. This regulation, too, could be used in a punitive manner vis-à-vis blacks.

In contrast to the weak federal role advocated by Eisenhower, the Kennedy administration tried in three ways to establish more uniform conditions of welfare payments over the entire country. First, it proposed aid for the dependent children of temporarily unemployed workers, providing a basis for the federal determination of state qualifications for these funds. Although only twenty-seven states applied for federal matching grants under this program, in some states, like Michigan, HEW was especially strict in enforcing the design of the state programs. Since it is difficult to withhold already existing matching payments to states (negative regulation), particularly when there are attributable benefits to congresspeople from these states, Congress chose to force states into an administrative mold compatible with administration intentions when new programs began.

The Kennedy administration also began the transition from a welfare system that provided mostly cash benefits to one that was dominated by professional intermediaries who delivered services to the poor. The 1962 amendments to the Social Security Act emphasized the elimination of poverty as opposed to the alleviation of the consequences of poverty. Monies were intended to rehabilitate those on relief and prevent poverty before the fact. The 1962 act provided for increased grants for social and rehabilitative services and for the training of social workers, for permanent status for aid to the dependent children of the unemployed, for grants to day-care centers, and for the elimination of state residency requirements (see Reading 6-3). This amendment represents the second and third stages of the administration's attempt to change the national role in welfare. Eliminating residency requirements and instituting new programs increased federal control over the details of state programs. The act also led to the extensive involvement of social workers and other professionals in future federal legislation and appropriations involving welfare. Now the HEW and Social Security bureaucracies had a stake in establishing an autonomous region within which Social Security could expand and outside allies who depended upon federal welfare monies for part of their livelihood and professional activities. Professionals within the Social Security Administration set the terms of discourse for changes in the Social Security system, as professionals outside it became heavily involved in lobbying Congress for the rights and needs of their client groups. Attempts to nationalize welfare and attack poverty through its causes expanded the dependence of government bureaucracies and professionals on legislative activity for their incomes or professional prerogatives. In effect a new electorally relevant constituency entered the policy process.

The Johnson administration continued the thrust of dealing with welfare on an organizational and preventive rather than a remedial basis (for organizational initiatives, see Chapter 2). The early days of the administration saw the successful passage of the Food Stamp Act, after ten years of effort, through the most conspicuous vote trading. In the House, urban votes for price supports for wheat and cotton were exchanged for rural and southern Democratic votes for food stamps (Ripley, 1969).

The basic form of the Social Security system has been the same since 1950, although Congress has incrementally expanded benefits and beneficiaries. What has become less certain is how Social Security benefits are to be paid for. During the 1950s and 1960s, some of the glaring exclusions from the Social Security and income-maintenance system were corrected, beginning with income insurance for the totally disabled aged fifty or over, provided in the 1956 amendments to the Social Security Act. Previously, state-level public assistance was available on a means-test basis, except in five states that had enacted temporary disability insurance (California, Hawaii, New Jersey, New York, and Rhode Island). In 1958 coverage was extended to the dependents of disabled workers, and in 1960 Congress eliminated age restrictions for eligibility.

Government activity in the area of non-work-related disability insurance is a hybrid between social insurance and welfare. A work requirement is attached to disability insurance; the worker must have been covered by Social Security in twenty of the preceding forty quarters. Yet benefits can be totally out of proportion to any contribution to the insurance plan, and cause of disability are irrelevant. Disability legislation in some ways reflects the hybrid character of the entire income-maintenance network. Dn the one hand the original legislation and its continued reauthorization provided for increasingly attractive welfare benefits and income floors for most Americans. The income-insurance aspect of Social Security was expanded to cover more and more individuals and to return larger and larger amounts of money upon retirement or disability. Roosevelt, as noted above, believed that the insurance aspects of Social Security would eventually make its welfare provisions unnecessary. However, with the expansion of these welfare provisions to individuals and groups that could not possibly work, it is clear that the expansion of the insurance plans does not imply the withering away of the public component of welfare. Although the percentage of the old and retired who are on welfare has decreased over the years, the number and percentage of people receiving all kinds of federally funded welfare has increased.

Process

In 1965 amendments to the Social Security Act establishing Medicare and Medicaid provided health and hospital insurance for the aged and later the disabled and payment for health care for the very poor. This represents the first small breakthrough toward the kind of national health system commonly found in advanced industrial democracies. Equally important, however, was the clear signal that the national government was going to determine who was eligible for welfare and would set rules for and be the principal payer of income insurance. How this was to occur was not settled.

The late 1960s and the 1970s saw the maturing of the Social Security and welfare system, thus expanding the importance of federal contributions to both systems, and particularly the latter. In this process and in the evolution of the social insurance program itself, the role of government bureaucrats and professionals became even more prominent. Since the 1960s the objective appeal of Social Security indexing has been strengthened by the insurance metaphor. Indexing ensures that benefits are undiluted by the effects of inflation, over which individuals have no control. Remember that although Social Security benefits are paid out of current payments into Social Security funds, the popular belief is that each individual has invested money in the fund and has it returned upon retirement with a degree of real interest. Inflation can destroy the buying power of these old-age payments. Congress had more than amply provided for the effects of inflation with periodic increases in social security benefits. In fact, in real dollars, 1971 Social Security recipients did far better than those in the immediate post–World War II period. However, the advantages of indexing to the Social Security Administration are considerable. The running of the insurance system becomes totally rule-governed except for the discretion with regard to beneficiaries and the categorization of beneficiaries allowed to the social security professionals. Indexing would increase the autonomy of the Social Security Administration, as they continually tried to place the issue on the political agenda (Derthick, 1979). Moreover Nixon and Republicans in Congress were tired of losing political currency and being the bad guys when they voted against benefit increases that surpassed increases in the cost of living. Once the organized elderly and the Nixon White House had picked up on the idea, opposition to indexing became difficult. Democrats had formed the backbone of congressional support for increases in Social Security benefits because they disproportionately represented districts with many elderly residents; if they opposed indexing they would appear to be opposing the rights of the elderly to have what they earned.

During the Nixon administration, social security benefits were increased in 1969, 1970, and 1972. The 1972 increase was to take place prior to the indexing, although it was part of the same piece of legislation. This increase was the price Nixon had to pay for indexing. Nixon favored a 10 percent increase in both 1969 and 1972 (see Reading 6-4); the Democrats in 1972 proposed a 20 percent increase. The same momentum that would carry indexing through Congress made the 20 percent increase almost impossible to veto, since veto would suggest that Nixon opposed indexing. Ironically, indexing was not the critical issue to the public. Most of the responsible commentary and newspaper articles on the 1972 amendments dealt with the conflict between Congress and the President over the extent to which benefits would be increased before indexing (see Reading 6-5).

The 1972 amendments had the effect of overrewarding future retirees under conditions of moderate to high inflation. This was because the indexing legislation increased the base on which Social Security is calculated by the rate of inflation and also increased the benefits derived from the expanded base by the rate of inflation. Hence, inflation was figured in twice. Once this was recognized by all parties, legislation passed in 1977 undid this doubledipping. Two other major features of social insurance remained untouched. Many public sector employees, particularly members of the military, were the beneficiaries of more than one system of retirement insurance. Since promises of future payment are not part of a current budget in the public sector, commitments were made to military and civil service personnel, as well as some state-level personnel, whose cost would be borne in the future. Many of these individuals can retire on rather handsome insurance-derived benefits and still pursue other jobs for a number of years. Those other jobs provide them with significant social security benefits. It is difficult to attack the organized public sector, since its members, according to their various service and interest orientations, are principal lobbyists before Congress

Congress never decided whether a fair insurance scheme should protect individuals from increases in the cost of living, or merely from receiving lower benefits than their peers who were still working. In the latter case Congress would index social security benefits to increases in wages and not to the consumer price index. This course also has the virtue of being relatively flatter than the former; that is, over a period of ten or fifteen years, divergences between the consumer price index and the rate of increase in wages are not large. Over the last thirty years, however, much greater fluctuation has occurred in the CPI than in wage rates. Using wage rates over the long run would be fair and would make demands on social security funds somewhat more predictable.

Interestingly, it was the Nixon and Ford administrations that really expanded the welfare component of Social Security in the 1970s. The food stamp program, authorized in 1964, bloomed in 1970 and 1971. Between 1969 and 1971 the number of people on the rolls nearly tripled, and the value of the stamps issued increased by a factor of seven. Before this the Johnson administration successfully completed the antipoverty agenda that was hinted at in the early Kennedy administration. It created new government agencies (see Chapter 4) and originated programs like the food stamp program and the Elementary and Secondary Education Act as well as the bilingual education amendments to the act in the middle and late 1960s (see Chapter 3). Yet the great increase in welfare benefits provided by the federal government under Johnson did not alter the fact that both ADC and food stamps were administered through states, and that states differ in the types and amounts of benefits they provide citizens. Only some of this variation is justified by differences in the real costs of living in different parts of the country.

It was during the Nixon era that welfare became truly nationalized. In 1969, in *Shapiro* v. *Thompson,* the Supreme Court stated that movement from state to state was impeded by state residency requirements for welfare recipients and, hence, that such requirements were impermissible. This increased the incentive for northern state legislators and governors to encourage further federal contribution to welfare payments. Northeastern states were among the more generous in providing welfare payments and anticipated continued in-migration by people seeking adequate welfare payments while they looked for jobs. The Nixon administration attempted, or at least supported attempts, to regulate the work norms of welfare recipients. Under these, parents of families receiving AFDC would be asked to register for job-training programs, and welfare recipients to register so that they could be assigned if they became available. These initiatives did not pass a Democratically controlled Congress. In 1969 Nixon proposed a negative income tax, later renamed the Family Assistance Plan (FAP). FAP and revenue sharing were the heart of Nixon's domestic programs.

FAP attempted to provide minimum incomes for citizens—for example, at least $1,600 per year for a woman with three children and no males in the house. Even if the woman or the male in the house worked, not all welfare payments would be lost, so that the level of income into the household would increase. The first $60 a month of income from work was not penalized, and a worker could keep 50 percent of benefits above that level until the grant was wiped out and the family was self-sufficient.

Although some Democrats and a number of Republicans supported FAP, it attracted the opposition of those who particularly benefited from welfare. FAP entitlement, like Social Security entitlement, would be on an individual or family basis, without service intermediaries. As one might suspect, the two principal opponents of FAP were organized professionals providing services to the poor and the National Welfare Rights Organization, and association of welfare recipients based primarily in the Northeast. Northeastern welfare recipients might actually receive less than they did under current state plans (with federal contribution), while much more money would be going to the underreported unemployed and potential welfare recipients in other parts of the country.

Since 1935 organized welfare workers have been proponents the federal government's contribution to welfare programs. However, their support is selective. Traditionally, they have not supported cash benefits programs, favoring government money to be spent on services delivered through professionals. The influence of professionals in the area of welfare probably peaked in the 1962 Public Welfare Amendments to the Social Security Act. In lobbying for the amendments, they successfully pushed for increased program benefits and minimized increases in cash contributions. Their influence extended through the Johnson administration up to the point of which the Vietnam War consumed too much time, energy and money, for changes in the welfare program to be of high priority.

The organization of welfare recipients, largely facilitated by academics and social workers, forced a slight change of tactics and position on those professional, who became supporters of cash benefit increases along with increases in programs. Many of the Kennedy/Johnson program initiatives provided for this change in position by making funds for specific tasks contingent upon local organization for purposes of planning and implementing programs in education, housing, and so on (see Chapters 2 and 3). Such local groups have been known to pursue ends other than those of the individuals or the groups that create them. The case of the social workers and welfare rights activists involved an addition to the social workers' political agenda, not a replacement.

In 1974 Congress passed the Employee Retirement Security Income Act (ERISA). This act attempted to promote sound fiscal practices in private old-age pension plans. The congressional intent was that the pensions of the organized work force should be protected from the mismanagement or miscalculation of their employers. ERISA represented the first systematic intrusion upon private pension arrangements between employers and employees. Before that time, many small and several large companies had defaulted on pension schemes. This happened to the Packard pension plan in 1958 when Packard merged with Studebaker. Many Studebaker employees in turn lost 85 percent of their retirement benefits when the Studebaker factory in Southbend closed in 1963. Private pension plans had tens of billions of dollars by the early 1970s. Some of these retirement schemes were handled by companies themselves; others were handled by major insurance companies and other financial institutions that are institutional investors in the stock and bond market. Many of these plans were on a financially weak footing, particularly when their funds were used to support the activities of the companies themselves (compare the 1935 provision allowing the fully funded Social Security system to buy government bonds).

ERISA was a detailed statute that established participation, investment standards, funding standards, fiduciary responsibilities, and cost and actuarial bases for private insurance plans of various sizes. It also provided an insurance fund that would come into play when retirement plans were threatened with insufficient funding even though they adhered to the requirements of the act—as might happen in declining industries like coal and steel. The intent of the act was widely supported by both business and labor.

Consequences

The 1972 indexing of Social Security and the 1974 federal entry into private retirement plans produced as many problems as they solved, if not more. ERISA was underfunded, and continual legislation was needed to make the program financially viable. The program involved extensive costs to the pension plans themselves (see Reading 6-6). The overall goal of the legislation—to ensure a sound and vested base for private retirement plans—has been met. A few companies have declared bankruptcy or have had their pension funds declared bankrupt in order to have the federally provided insurance pick up the cost in lieu of increasing their own contributions. Many detailed amendments to the legislation of the 1970s attempted to remedy this problem. Even under the best of circumstances, however, the federal government has ended up coordinating an insurance scheme supported by and maintained for private pension funds. This is another long-standing function of legislatures and representative systems—to provide an administrative infrastructure for spreading risk to outsiders. Sometimes the demand comes from a company at risks; at other times from individuals and groups representing voters who will actually bear the cost if marketplace or pension arrangements do not work out.

As early as 1973 it was clear that the way in which Congress had indexed social security and the actuarial assumptions made in setting payment and benefit rates were both deficient. Within a year of the passage of the 1972 amendments, the annual report of the Board of Trustees of the Social Security system indicated that problems would eventually arise. Yet even then the major problem that could throw the system into disarray was not recognized: the 1972 amendment's provision for double indexing under conditions of high inflation for future retirees. This problem was corrected in the amendments of 1977.

The 1977 Social Security amendments detached automatic benefit adjustments for active workers from the consumer price index. Instead, the consumer price index was used only to adjust benefits for already retired individuals. For those who had not yet retired, earlier earnings were adjusted upward in a manner that reflected the average changes in wage levels since the time the money was earned. As a consequence,

Social Security for a retired individual was based on the real wages paid during the work career, rather than the average nominal wages boosted by inflation. Oddly enough, even with change, the system was not countercyclical in its macroeconomic effects. During times of high inflation, it would drastically increase the amount of money automatically paid out in social security benefits, providing a high base for newly retired workers and automatically increasing benefits to already retired workers. This would create further inflation. When the inflation rate is below 2 percent, the system of calculating payments would actually have a retrenching effect; it would not throw larger sums of money out into the economy to counteract the cutback in consumption. The system as it existed from 1977 to 1980 reflected the political needs of Congress and the Social Security Administration in its details; it did not provide the executive or Congress with any kind of macroeconomic tool that would dampen periods of inflation or deflation (see Chapter 7).

Even Congress understood the likely deficiency of the 1977 Social Security Amendments. The same act created a bipartisan National Commision on Social Security that studied and reviewed all aspects of the program and eventually informed Congress that the Old-Age Trust Fund could be insolvent by 1981. To prevent that the Social Security Amendment of 1979 allowed payroll tax receipts to be shifted from the Disability Insurance Trust Fund to the Old-Age and Survivors Trust Fund. Even this would not prevent bankruptcy at some point in 1982. The Old-Age and Survivors trustees reported in 1980 that the long-term actuarial imbalance was 1.52 percent of raxable payroll [under reasonable cost assumptions].

It was in response to this situation that Reagan proposed benefit cutback and privilization (see Reading 6-7). New beneficiaries would receive about 7 or 8 percent less income for a given work career than would old beneficiaries. Those who retired early would be penalized. Reagan, however, had not been sensitive to the public's perception of Social Security as an insurance system. This perception is reflected in a December 1981 *Washington Post* / ABC poll in which 92 percent of all respondents opposed cuts for those already retired, 85 percent rejected cuts for future retirees, and 39 percent opposed raising taxes to strengthen the system (Rothouse, 1983, p. 68). Reagan and the Republicans and Democrats knew that the Social Security system had to be "fixed" again. The Democrats, however, were quite willing to hold resolution of this problem hostage until they had gained the benefits of Reagan's radical position in the 1982 congressional elections. Very soon after those elections, they reached a compromise (see Reading 6-8). The new fix, hailed by politicians as solving the problems of Social Security forever, was a temporary solution for which the reserves might be entirely inadequate under reasonable sets of assumptions concerning future economic growth (Rothouse, 1983, pp. 88–92). Central to making the new funding scheme work at all was the future inclusion of federal workers. This would have the effect of providing lower levels of retirement than benefits to already employed federal workers than they had under an already existing plan: one can expect that they will rally against this proposal. They can do so easily because many are professionals whose organization and communication costs are quite low due to the organization of the executive departments.

Hidden in the provisions of the 1983 Social Security Act are three ways in which general revenue funds would be used for the first time to support the Social Security system. The first involves business-expense tax deductions for the self-employed; the second and third involve the lump-sum payments to the Social Security system from general revenues to compensate for past unnegotiated checks and for the cost of gratuitous military wage credits, which had been borne by the system. A precedent is set here: any time the Social Security system has even a predictable expense that is included in the actuarial basis of the system but does not represent a direct payment to the retired, it can claim general revenue reimbursement. As long as this use of general revenues is indirect—as it is for particular expenses that are not part of the transfer system—greater use can be made of general revenues in the future. To the extent that this occurs, the system will cease to be self-supporting, even as a pay-as-you-go insurance scheme.

An alternative to bringing the Social Security system into the orbit of general revenue programs is the attempt to privatize the retirement system. Since 1981 the Reagan administration has intermittently encouraged studies of a voluntary Social Security system (see Reading 6-8). It is unclear what the consequences of a private income-insurance system would be for those individuals who receive welfare through the social security system. Although privatization of ADC is not under consideration, changing Social Security for the disabled is a possibility. Already the Reagan administration has attempted to cut the amount of money channeled through the program for the disabled. No executive can change the rules of eligibility without the agreement of Congress, but the executive branch can change its interpretation of the rules. By doing so the Reagan administration removed several hundred thousand people from the social security disability rolls between 1981 and 1983, when a series of congressional and judicial acts forced it to stop. The shifting back and forth illustrates three principles of modern policy. The first is that bureaucracies cannot formally change laws, but they can change the beneficiaries of social legislation by changing the interpretations of the laws. Such changes occurred when the disabled first received Social Security and also when the federal rules for ADC changed. Second, legislatures can always resist such changes, but to do so they must take positive action. Finally, an income-security or welfare system is a prime target for attempts to exert fiscal control over public-sector spending. But although governments may achieve in the area of welfare, people in almost all countries view income-insurance schemes as providing benefits to which they are entitled as citizens.

Income maintenance and welfare have always been on the political agenda because the poor are always with us. These issues become part of the national political agenda when catastrophic events reveal that people's needs cannot be effectively and efficiently met by local governments. Massive local redistributions of income or money take benefits away from taxpayers. At the national level, the lack of fiscal equivalence for welfare and income maintenance programs means that they are more readily adopted. Citizens across the country do not notice that a portion of their rule-governed tax payments goes to support ADC as well as defense, highways, and so on. Once on the agenda, the welfare component of income maintenance will become larger as the scope of the government providing welfare benefits become more general.

Throughout the evolution of income-maintenance and welfare systems, a clear distinction has been made between the deserving and undeserving poor. The deserving poor are those who have worked or would work, and they receive money through what is known as an insurance system. Those who are simply poor receive welfare money from the federal or local level. Their level of benefits is not indexed and is at the discretion of legislatures. Yet in spite of our political ambivalence about welfare, it provides benefits to voters. Hence, members of Congress from districts in which the poor are concentrated are concerned with getting an increased scope and increased levels of welfare benefits onto the congressional agenda.

Welfare programs, unlike rule-governed Social Security benefits, are run by states under federal guidelines to ensure nondiscrimination. States have the choice of accepting optional features of a federal program like ADC (compare this with Medicaid; see Chapter 5). It is at the state level that money is translated into programs for the poor. By no coincidence, state-level professional groups who service the poor are most effectively organized in programmatic terms. Congress is best equipped to provide money and eligibility rules, but it is at the state and local levels that the intermediate beneficiaries organize money into programs. (Compare educational programs like ESEA Title I, and School Act described in Chapter 2.) State level variation in social programs like ADC occurs in lieu of the industry or profession based distinctions in some components of health and welfare programs in Western Europe.

Although state welfare programs vary, the income-insurance components of Social Security did not have to absorb a large number of diverse state or industry-wide programs of income insurance as did the nationalized European social security systems.

In the case of Social Security, no phase of negative regulation of state activities was needed, because states were not involved in this aspect of income maintenance. In the area of welfare, a certain degree of negative regulation came from the Congress from the 1970s on. Criteria of nondiscrimination, due process, and equal access were set to ensure that money gets to the groups intended by Congress, not the groups that would most benefit state and local politicians. As a general rule, when Congress provides money to support state and local activity, it engages in negative regulation to direct benefits to specific groups. When public-sector spending is funded directly by the federal level, as in the case of old-age and income insurance, the legislation detailing the administration of such a program through federal departments is what ensures that the intended beneficiaries are the actual beneficiaries. Thus, as we have seen, Congress intervened in 1983 when the regional offices of the Social Security Administration thwarted congressional intent in the distribution of disability payments.

Readings

6-1. THE ORIGINS OF SOCIAL SECURITY*

The most controversial components of the 1935 Social Security Act were the nonvoluntary provisions that required membership in the system and required workers to retire before they received benefits. These drawbacks were balanced by the contractual income security that the deserving poor received from the legislation.

Most men have always been insecure. The stream of goods and services upon which life depends has never flowed with unfailing regularity. During the past century or two, however, the individual has become less secure because capitalist societies have become more complex and more easily put out of balance. Four types of insecurity have now developed into problems of major social importance: insecurity due to old age, insecurity due to unemployment, insecurity due to sickness, and insecurity due to the death of a breadwinner. . . .

The Social Security Act

The Social Security Act has been paseed with the object of lessening this shocking insecurity. It has been hailed as "affording protection against the loss of income due to the unemployment, old age and the death of a breadwinner," and as laying the foundation stone "in a security structure which aims to protect our people against the major hazards of life." If it protects the individual against these four main hazards to his security, it is indeed an achievement deservedly regarded as "a milestone in our progress toward a better ordered society." But does it?

This formidable and confusing Act occupies 32 pages and is divided into 11 involved parts. Sorting out the various sections reveals that some action has been taken in each of the four fields of insecurity. The federal government establishes a fund to provide annuities as a right to certain people when they are over sixty five. It obtains the necessary money by taxing employers on their payrolls and workers on their wages and sal-

---

*Excerpts from Eveline M. Burns, *Toward Social Security* (New York: McGraw-Hill, 1936), pp. 3, 6–8, 19–20.

aries. It encourages the states to provide more adequate assistance in the form of old-age pensions for people to whom its annuity plan does not apply and who can prove that they are in need.

The Act seeks to provide against unemployment by encouraging the states to set up so-called unemployment compensation plans providing cash benefits as a right to unemployed workers.

Money is granted under the Act for general public health purposes while the states are assisted to provide health services for two groups particularly unable to provide against sickness, namely, mothers and children. Persons incapacitated from earning because of blindness may be given more adequate pensions because the federal government offers to share their cost with the states. Those otherwise physically handicapped will obtain more advice and training because the security Act provides additional money for this purpose.

The Act also recognizes the problems of dependent persons who have been deprived of their breadwinner. The federal government is empowered to offer money to states willing to grant cash incomes to those who are caring for needy dependent children. The states are also encouraged to provide various services for dependent children who have no relatives or friends who will provide them with a home.

Finally, the Act sets up a Social Security Board of three persons to administer the whole of this federal program and to study the needs of the country and the ways in which security can best be increased. For the first time a department of the federal government will devote its full time to the problems of insecurity.

Old Age Security as a Right

. . . [T]he Social Security Act guarantees to aged people, in return for the wage taxes paid when they were younger, an income of between $10 and $85 a month for as long as they live. They will obtain this income as a right and not as a charitable gift which can be withheld at any time. No one will inquire how much other income they possess or whether they have any savings. In this respect the payments are quite different from the pensions which in the past have been paid to needy aged people in a number of states. Yet these annuities are not exactly similar to those which people could obtain by paying contributions to a private company; for in order to obtain his annuity at sixty-five a man must give up his job. He loses his right to his annuity for every month that he works.

This condition conflicts with the idea of a contract which, as we saw, was the very essence of this kind of annuity in contrast with the old age assistance hitherto given.

6-2. THE PURPOSE OF SOCIAL SECURITY LEGISLATION IN 1935*

Edwin Witte was staff director of the committee that created the draft of the 1935 Social Security act. The following excerpts give his view of the mandate he had from the President and Congress.

The President, for his part, gave us his ideas in the subject, but without insisting that the committee should necessarily recommend what he deemed desirable. The views which he expressed on this occasion were very much the same as those which he had presented in his message of June 8, 1934. He felt committed to both unemployment insurance and provisions for old age security and also wanted the committee to explore thoroughly the possibilities of a unified (package) social insurance system affording protection against all major personal hazards which lead to poverty and dependency. He expressed decided preferences for state administration of unemployment insurance, but again stressed that the reserve funds must be handled by the federal government; also, that unemployment insurance should be set up to give encouragement to the regularization of employment. He also again stated that all forms of social insurance must be self-supporting, without subsidies from general tax sources, but the conversation developed that he understood that assistance from general tax revenues would have to be given to people already old and without means. He indicated, however, that he still held the view which he expressed when, as governor of New York, he signed the old age pension law of that state, to the effect that the only long-term solution of the problem of old-age security lies in a compulsory old age insurance system. . . .

The President stated that the program which he would recommend to the incoming Congress would include unemployment insurance to be developed as "a cooperative federal-state undertaking," with the administration vested in the states, but with the federal government par-

*Excerpted from Edwin E. Witte, *The Development of the Social Security Act* (Madison: University of Wisconsin Press, 1962), pp. 17–19, 119.

ticipating to encourage the states to enact unemployment insurance laws and holding and investing all unemployment reserve funds, to the end that these funds might serve "the purpose of decreasing rather than increasing unemployment." The President, also, again expressed his concern that unemployment insurance must not be allowed to become a dole through the mingling of insurance and relief: "It is not charity. It must be financed by contributions, not taxes." He also again urged that unemployment insurance should be set up in such a way as to encourage the stabilization of employment.

6-3. THE INCLUSION OF PROFESSIONALS IN FEDERALLY FUNDED WELFARE SYSTEMS*

The Public Welfare Amendments of 1962 (H.R. 10032) provided for the intervention of professionals in the welfare process. The bill responded to the position of organized professionals by enlisting them in the coordination of services, particularly to women and children, provided by the states. The bill also provided funding for professional activities that might help prevent poverty.

A bill to extend and improve the public assistance and child welfare services program of the Social Security Act and for other purposes.

Be it enacted by the Senate and House of Representatives of the United States of America in Congress assembled. That this Act may be cited as the "Public Welfare Amendments of 1962."

Declaration of Purposes

Sec. 2. The purpose of this Act is to amend and improve the Federal-State cooperative public welfare programs through a new, constructive approach which recognizes State responsibility for development of realistic and sound public welfare programs and provides the states with more flexibility in developing such programs in the light of their particular needs and conditions which emphasizes—

(1) Services—services to help families become self-supporting and independent.

*Excerpts from the Public Welfare Amendments of 1962. H.R. 10032 87th Congress, 2nd session. Washington D.C. U.S. Government Printing Office, 1962.

(2) Prevention—prevention of dependency in dealing with the problems causing dependency.

(3) Incentives—incentives to recipients of public assistance to improve their condition so as to make public assistance unnecessary and incentives to States to improve their welfare programs.

(4) Rehabilitation—services to rehabilitate recipients or those likely to become recipients of public assistance.

(5) Independence—useful community work and training programs and other measures to assist recipients to become self-supporting and able to care for themselves.

(6) Training—assistance in the provision of training in order to increase the supply of adequately trained public welfare professionals, this being necessary for achieving the foregoing objectives.

State Plan Provisions of Services

(b)(1) Section 2(a) of such Act is amended by striking out paragraph (10) (C),m by inserting "and" after the semicolon at the end of paragraph (10) (A) by redesignating paragraphs (10) and (11) as paragraphs (11) and (12), respectively, and by inserting after paragraph (9) the following new paragraph:

(10) provide that the State agency shall make available to applicants for or recipients of assistance under the plan at least those services to help them attain or retain capability for self-care which are prescribed by the Secretary; and include a description of the steps taken to assure in the provision of these and any other services which the State agency makes available to individuals under the State plan, maximum utilization of other agencies providing similar or related services;

(2) Section 402(a)(12) of such Act is amended to read as follows:

(12) provide that the State agency shall make available to at least those services to maintain and strengthen family life for children, and to help relatives specified in section 406(a) with whom children (who are applicants for or recipients of aid to families with dependent children) are living to attain or retain capability for self-support or self-care, which are prescribed by the Secretary; and include a description of the steps taken to assure, in the provision of these and any other services which the state agency makes available to individuals under

the State plan, maximum utilization of other agencies providing similar or related services.

Welfare Services for Each Child Under Dependent Children's Program

Sec. 103. Section 402(a) of the Social Security Act is amended by striking out "and" after the seimcolon at the end of clause (11), and by inserting before the period at the end of clause (12) ";" and (13) provide for the development and application of a program for such welfare and related development for each child who receives aid to families with dependent children as may be necessary in the light of particular home conditions and other needs of such child, and provide for coordination of such programs, and any other services provided for children under the state plan, with the child welfare services plan developed as provided in part 3 of title V, with a view toward providing welfare and related services which will best promote the welfare of such child and his family.

6-4. THE INDEXING OF SOCIAL SECURITY*

The following represents the Nixon administration's statement on the indexing of social security benefits. To make the proposal irresistible to a Democratic Congress, it includes an immediate 10 percent benefit hike. The promise that tax rates would not have to be increased proved illusory. Here and in the next reading the proposed maximum social security tax rate is 5.5 percent for both employers and employees. The current tax rate is 7.05 percent for both.

The President has recommended a benefit increase to bring the benefits up to date with increases in the cost of living that have occurred since the last benefit increase, in February 1968.

The increase would apply to all beneficiaries, including those getting the special payment for uninsured people age 72 or older. Under the proposal, effective for March 1970, benefits would be increased for all the 25 million beneficiaries. The total additional benefit outlays for the

*Hearings before the Committee on Ways and Means, U.S. House of Representatives, 91st Congress, 1st sess., 1971.

first calendar year in which the increase is effective would be approximately $3 billion.

Beyond the initial ten percent increase, the President has recommended that the provision be made in the law for social security benefits to be automatically adjusted to take account of future increases in the cost of living. The platforms of both political parties recognize the need to have a way of keeping the social security program automatically up to date. Such an automatic adjustment system would increase the security of the one out of every eight people in the country who now receives monthly social security benefits. The automatic provision would also adjust the benefits for millions of future beneficiaries whose major source of income could well be their social insurance payments under social security. Because of the time lags that have occurred between past cost-of-living adjustments of benefits, the purchasing power of the benefits has been seriously decreased between benefit increases. With automatic adjustments, the changes necessary to restore purchasing power will be on a more current basis.

The administration proposal finances the automatic increases in benefits without increasing social security contribution taxes. This can be done so long as the contribution and the benefit base—the maximum amount of annual earnings counted for social security purposes—is increased from time to time. The legislation we support contains a provision to automatically adjust this base in the future to keep pace with increases in earning levels.

The point that I would like to stress here, Mr. Chairman and members of the committee, is that, although as a generalization it can be said that the Congress in the last 15 years has acted generally to restore the purchasing power of benefits, so that they end up the period with approximately the same purchasing power—nevertheless there have been substantial periods in which people have had to go a long time with benefits reduced in value before action has been taken to restore their values. And I think the most important point about an automatic provision is that it would keep closer to the actual level of the purchasing power of the benefits, rather than having to take the time for legislative action.

Now, to finance this kind of an automatic provision, it is necessary to have another automatic provision in the law. It takes no increase in the contribution rate to have this automatic provision as long as we keep the maximum earnings base up to date. The same percentage rate of contribution will produce enough money to slightly more than keep up, actually, with the cost of living if you can apply that percentage to the constantly increasing payrolls that would certainly accompany any increase in the cost of living.

So the provision for automatic increases in the maximum earnings base is what makes it possible to say that this provision for automatic increase in benefits tied in with the cost of living is soundly financed.

6-5. THE POLITICS OF INDEXING SOCIAL SECURITY*

The following news articles illustrates that the 1972 cost of living adjustments (COLAs) to social security were much less visible than the accompanying 20 percent benefit increases. The COLA was rarely acknowledged; at most, an observer would comment that the 1972 bill had something for everybody and hurts almost nobody. This could not be true, as subsequent legislation would prove. Someone has to pay for income transfers.

Congress voted a 20 per cent increase in Social Security benefits tonight after days of election-year maneuvering.

The pension rise for 27.8 million Americans, which was attached to a debt-ceiling bill earlier in the day by the Senate, was cleared by the House, 302 to 35, and sent to the White House. Earlier, the Senate approved the increase 82 to 4.

By attaching the benefit rise to the debt-ceiling measure, which was designed to avert fiscal paralysis of the Government at midnight tonight, Congress sought to force President Nixon to sign it.

Administration sources said late tonight that the President had not decided whether to sign the bill or veto it.

However, since the Social Security rise won handily in both Senate and House, it appeared that Congress would have the votes to override a veto.

Administration spokesmen sought in recent days to block the 20 per cent pension measure, arguing that it would be inflationary and would swell the budget deficit.

The Republicans sought, instead, to limit the increase to 10 per cent, double the amount that President Nixon had proposed. But the Senate,

*"20% Social Security Rise is Voted In Both Houses; Nixon Approval in Doubt," *New York Times.* July 1, 1972.

by a vote of 66 to 20, rejected the 10 per cent proposal and then approved the 20 per cent increase.

The House, too, by a vote of 253 to 83, rejected a move by Representative John W. Byrnes, Republican of Wisconsin, to hold the increase to 10 per cent.

The benefit increase, the biggest ever, would become effective Sept. 1, with the higher payments first reflected in checks mailed in early October. . . .

The major burden of financing the benefit increase would fall on workers in the middle-income and upper-income brackets, with poorer workers paying even less tax than they would have under an earlier scheduled change in tax rates.

Both the present Social Security tax rate of 5.2 per cent and the $9,000 wage base on which the tax is paid would continue for the rest of this year, for a maximum payment of $468 by both employer and employee.

But starting next January, the tax rate would rise to 5.5 per cent and the wage base to $10,800 with still another increase in the wage base to $12,000 a year. . . .

Beyond 1974, the wage base on which taxes are paid would automatically rise as the general wage level in the economy rises. Thus, the wage base could reach as high as $20,000 in the years ahead, with a possible maximum tax of $1,100 a year.

The automatic upward adjustment of the wage base would be used to finance future increases in benefits. Under the bill passed today, benefits would rise automatically when the consumer price index rises 3 percent or more. These automatic increases in both benefit levels and the wage base represent two of the most significant changes in the Social Security system since its creation 37 years ago.

6-6. SOCIAL SECURITY REFORM AS A POLITICAL FIX*

Within a year after passing the 1972 cost of living amendments and reforms, the trustees of the Social Security system declared that the "fix" did not adequately repair the income-insurance program. This pattern was to be repeated several times over the next decade. A critical

---

* "Social Security News: Good and Bad," *New York Times,* July 3, 1972.

problem was that each fix had to satisfy the short-term electoral needs of Congress and the President, which are often inconsistent with the long-- term requirements of an actuarially sound income-maintenance program. The board of trustees of the Federal Old-Age and Survivors Insurance and Disability Insurance trust funds predicted a 3 percent shortfall in the funding of the system soon after the reforms were passed.

The Social Security bill rushed through Congress and signed by President Nixon last week has major, and not widely known, implications for all employers and for the millions of high salaried working men and women in the country. For employers the bill will mean higher costs next year and thereafter, though perhaps not quite as much increase in costs in later years as would have occurred under the former law.

But most important for the relatively affluent workers—and only for those workers—Social Security taxes will go on rising indefinitely, a little each year. This is because of the little-noticed provision for "escalation" of the Social Security wage base to finance the new cost-of-living escalation of benefits for those who are retired. . . .

The news in the big bill is not all bad, however, for employees and the better-off workers.

First, the bill will for the first time halt the creeping rise in the Social Security tax rate, which at 5.2 per cent this year has become a significant cost for employers. After an increase to 5.5 per cent next year for both employer and employee, the rise will cease, instead of moving toward the 8 percent as was scheduled for later years under the old law. . . .

The system will be more "progressive"—or at least less regressive—than before. The tax on lower-paid workers (already more than the income tax for many of them) will stop going up after next year when it reaches 5.5 per cent. All of the added financing will come from the better-off, thanks to the higher, and rising, wage base—plus, of course, the modest tax increase on any worker as his pay goes up though his earnings are still below the wage base.

Under the former law, the tax rate on all workers—and hence, obviously, the lower paid—would have risen above 5.5 per cent next year and crept upward toward 8 per cent.

The bill is not all pain for the better-off worker, either. The much higher wage base is not all loss because it means much higher benefits for him or her after retirement.

6-7. PRIVATIZING SOCIAL SECURITY*

The Reagan administration has attempted to privatize many govern-ment programs. Its members also believe that program competition with or within the private sector increases efficiency. But Social Security is now regarded as almost a birthright (like the British National Health Service), and suggestions that it be privatized have been poorly received.

Top officials of the Social Security Administration have been studying proposals for changes in the retirement program, including some that would make participation voluntary while encouraging reliance on pri-vate insurance, pensions and savings to a larger degree.

Martha A. McSteen, the Acting Commissioner of Social Security, confirmed that she attended a meeting in June at which agency officials discussed "private alternatives to Social Security." She said that the briefing was part of an "educational process" and that the Administra-tion had no plans to submit any of the proposals to Congress if President Reagan is reelected. . . .

Edwin L. Dale Jr., a spokesman for the Office of Management and Budget, said he knew of "no Administration initiative to change any-thing" in the Social Security program. "There's nothing cooking on Social Security," he said. "There's no reason to have anything cooking. The system is perfectly solvent as far ahead as you can see, even under pessimistic economic assumptions. There will be large surpluses in the Social Security Trust Fund in the 1990s." . . .

Mrs. McSteen said the discussion of private alternatives to Social Security reflected her "inquisitiveness" and her desire to be prepared for possible questions on the subject. At the time of the briefing, Admin-istration officials had not ruled out future changes in Social Security, as several officials, including President Reagan, did this week. . . .

The briefing paper said the support for private alternatives to Social Security was based on these propositions, among others: "Private retire-ment plans would eliminate the adverse effects of Social Security on the economy. Social Security reduces private saving. Private retirement plans would increase saving."

The document said that, according to those who favored private alter-natives to Social Security, "the gains from shifting to a private retire-

* "Voluntary Social Security Plan Studied," *New York Times*, October 14, 1984.

ment system are so large that the transition is both desirable and politically feasible." . . .

Under Federal law, a worker 65 to 69 years old now can earn up to $6,960 with no reduction in Social Security benefits. But the worker loses $1 in benefits for every $2 of earnings over $6,960.

6-8. THE LATEST SOCIAL SECURITY FIX*

The most recent fix of the Social Security system occurred in 1982–83. As before, electoral politics provided the outside boundaries of any possible legislation. Even with the 1983 legislation, a recession in the late 1980s or early 1990s will imbalance (bankrupt?) the system.

Moments after he was sworn in for a second term, Senator Daniel Patrick Moynihan of New York walked across the blue-carpeted Senate floor and tapped Senator Bob Dole of Kansas on the shoulder. "Are we going to let this commission die without giving it one more try?" he asked.

His plea was prompted by an article on Social Security by Mr. Dole that appeared that morning on the Op Ed page of the New York Times. In it, the Kansas Republican had written, "Through a combination of relatively modest steps, the system can be saved."

Until that point, said Mr. Moynihan, a Democrat, the Republicans had talked of grandoise schemes to offset what they called a prospective 1,500 [dollar] billion shortage, "the largest bankruptcy in history."

"They were talking about scrapping the system, making it voluntary or welfare based," Mr. Moynihan recalled. . . .

In the year long negotiations, the Democrats reflected Mr. O'Neill's views and supported closing the fiscal gap by increasing taxes while the Republicans reflected Mr. Reagan's views and spoke of reducing future benefits. Both the President and the Speaker insisted that the negotiators come up with recommendations supported by an overwhelming majority of the participants.

Against this background, hardly anyone expected the negotiations to succeed. In the end, Democrats attributed the negotiators' success to Mr. Reagan's need for a strong victory in the face of a mounting budget deficit and widespread reports that his Administration was in disarray.

*"Social Security: Compromise at Long Last," New York Times, Jan. 20, 1983.

Republicans attributed the success to a new spirit of confidence on the part of Mr. O'Neill, based on last November's election in which Democrats gained 26 House seats.

The 15-member National Commission for Social Security Reform came into being through an executive order of the President of December 16, 1981, and was charged with recommending changes in the Social Security system to assure its continued solvency. . . .

The group's first major crisis occurred last May, when the Senate Budget Committee included a $40 billion reduction in the Social Security deficit in its budget for the fiscal year 1983. Representative Claude Pepper, the Florida Democrat who was then chairman of the Committee on Aging, said the commission's independence had been "compromised."

The second crisis occurred in the election campaign. Mr. Pepper became his party's front man in accusing the Republicans of planning to scuttle Social Security. He campaigned for candidates in more than 40 House districts, and the Democratic slogan, "Save Social Security— vote Democratic" appeared in brochures and on bumper stickers. . . .

After the election, the commission began to show signs of progress at a three day meeting at the Holiday Inn in Alexandria, Virginia. Specifically, the commission agreed on the scope of the problem: $150 billion to $200 billion would be needed to maintain the system's solvency through 1989. Without some infusion of new funds, they concluded, the system would be unable to pay retirement benefits as early as July. . . .

Perhaps more significantly, the Democrats came up with their own proposal, which included coverage of all new Federal employees and a three-month delay of cost-of-living increases (which was finally adopted as a six-month delay). That persuaded the Republicans that the Democrats were as eager as they to find a compromise. . . .

"I expect to support what they come up with." Despite signs of movement, however, the White House was silent, and in the face of such silence, progress appeared stalled. "We can't do anything until we get a sign from the President," Mr. Dole told the negotiators.

The Commission held what it thought would be its final meeting on Dec. 10.

All that changed, however, when Mr. Moynihan tapped Mr. Dole on the shoulder. The next day the two Senators met in Mr. Dole's offices with Robert Ball, the Democratic member of the commission regarded as most knowledgeable on Social Security. The day after that they invited Mr. Greenspan and Mr. Conable to join the group, and the "gang of five" was formed. . . .

The Democrats came up with most of the proposals. It was Mr. Ball, for example, who proposed extending the delay on cost-of-living increases for six months. And it was Mr. Ball who said that the Democrats would never agree to a Republican proposal to reduce benefits for those who retired before the age of 65, one of the President's original proposals. He argued that blue-collar workers, who were more likely to vote Democratic, retired early, while white collar workers waited until 65 or later.

It was Mr. Constable, however, who held out for a premium for those who retired after 65, a proposal that was ultimately accepted. . . .

The first hint of White House approval of a compromise came from Mr. Baker, in a speech in San Francisco, when he said that the President might be willing to accept the acceleration of an increase in Social Security taxes.

7 Economic Planning

The preceding four chapters described both the evolution of federal policy in several areas and the limits on such policymaking in the United States. The evolution of policy and of the groups that benefit from federal spending is remarkably similar across policy areas. The same is true of the evolution of policy tools used in congressional legislation. Legislation must initially respect the federal aspects of the American system in order to be passed in a Congress that is locally nominated and elected. It is only with the expansion of federal funding and the scope of programs that more direct national involvement and control are possible. Congress also exercises greater oversight over fiscal than program components in all four areas. It can appropriate money far better than it can investigate the content or impact of ADC, remedial education, or clean-air regulations around the country. The flow of program funds into congressional districts is a particular focus of congressional interest, since it is through this process that members attempt to direct the constituency benefits that support continued incumbency.

Significant funding allows Congress to influence the ways in which state and local governments fund and administer programs in all four policy areas. This capacity for influence does not depend on whether capital construction or program delivery is involved, or whether there is explicit constitutional support for federal action in the area (e.g., interstate commerce) or not (e.g., education). In fact, the vast expansion of federal funding and subsequent positive and negative federal policy control has revealed the limits of localism in public-sector activity. Federal directives and concomitant bureaucratic pressure for policy homogeneity can be ignored only at the peril of losing massive amounts of federal-level transfers. Since citizens in all local areas pay federal taxes and many of them express organized program preferences, state and local governments can seldom resist federal funding with its positive and, later, negative strings.

Federal pressure, however, does not translate into program coordination or consistency. States still pursue a variety of policies independently of, and sometimes inconsistently with, federal programs. Even the latter are not well coordinated at the local level, in part because of Congress's electoral need for a program-by-program fiscal trail all the way up to the implementing federal bureaucracy in Washington. Federal policy is responsive to a geographically diverse set of interests and able to deal with problems of health, transportation, education, or old age as they affect clustered groups of citizens. Yet this responsiveness is not the consequence of any systematic planning or consistent view of the role of the state. Rather, Congress makes policy in response to problems and pressures, and if the results are somewhat consistent and mutually efficient, fine; if policy consequences are inconsistent or undesirable at some later time, Congress will fix the problem.

This ad hoc approach is illustrated even in the evolution of economic policy, one of the two areas (the other is defense) in which the federal government is given its most explicit grant of legislative power through Article I, Section 8 and 9: the right to mint currency, oversee banking, honor state debts, control bankruptcy, and manage foreign affairs involves economic management. Yet the use of these powers is usually on a case-by-case or policy-by-policy basis. In most cases of congressional action, the beneficiary groups are evident: federal regulation of transportation, for example, benefited meat-packers, railroads, and later small towns. Later partial deregulation of transportation benefited economic activity in urban centers and, more recently, organized consumer advocacy groups.

The historic and current tools of economic policy reflect some of the same distinctively U.S. features found in other policy areas. The federal government facilitates private-sector interests; it does not replace them. Hence, "natural monopolies" (telephone, gas transmission) are regulated but not owned or directly controlled by the public sector. Credit and the availability of capital to either public- or private-sector entities are almost totally privately controlled. Even when economic coordination has been needed in time of war or depression, such coordination has occurred mostly in the private sector in "voluntary" response to the admonitions of the federal executive and legislative initiatives of Congress.

Congress has legislated federal economic policy in at least five areas:

1. The fiscal policies of the federal government. These determine the magnitude of the deficit as well as the areas in which federal monies will be spent. Will the government spend more on housing and highways, which stimulate the economy, or on building missiles, which provides less stimulus?

2. The tax budget. This relates to the overall taxes collected and hence to the deficit or surplus in the federal budget. More importantly, however, tax budget decisions involve the use of differential tax rates to provide particular groups, like farmers or overseas investors, with benefits that others similarly situated do not obtain. Often these benefits or foregone taxes stimulate jobs or growth in some areas of the economy while discouraging growth in others.

3. Trade policies. These include both the tariff policies of the federal government and any implicit subsidies or loan guarantees given by the government to export-oriented industries.

4. Monetary policy. This has been chiefly the province of the Federal Reserve Board. The Federal Reserve Board and the Federal Open Market Committee can affect interest rates and the amount of money banks make available for lending through the board's own discount rate, its reserve requirement, and its activities in buying and selling government securities.

5. Regulation. Both traditional economic regulation and more recent regulation of social and civil rights fall into this category. Almost all regulation imposes costs on some sectors of the economy and provides benefits for others, thus affecting the availability of capital and jobs there. Because Congress passes most regulatory legislation in response to a particular need or a demand from a particular constituency, such legislation tends to be uncoordinated, if not inconsistent, in its effects on the economy.

The same lack of coordination is found across the economic policy areas. The federal budget deficit might encourage expanded consumption at the same time that the Federal Reserve Board is pursuing interest rate policies that tend to the opposite effect. Lack of coordination is a consequence not only of the incremental evolution of economic policy mentioned earlier, but of the deliberate fragmentation of policymaking bodies so that no one group in the Congress or the executive can become too powerful. Ironically, at just the time when federal involvement in the economy may have been sufficient to allow for some planning and coordination, the increasing internationalization of the marketplace began to remove power over economic affairs from domestic hands, public or private.

Context

Originally, the function of the federal government was not to manage the economy but to facilitate commerce. Evidence of this comes from the Constitution itself. Article 1, Section 8, lists those areas in which Congress is to legislate, often to facilitate interstate commerce. It allows for no internal tariffs. "Individuals" can declare bankruptcy only once every ten years, so that they may not repeatedly borrow and avoid their debts. The federal government directed its spending in the first half of the nineteenth century toward the development of interstate transportation. The first federally guaranteed loans made investment in the construction of the first transcontinental railroad more attractive in British and American banks.

By the latter part of the nineteenth century, national government was called upon not only to facilitate commerce, but to deal with the effects of monopoly power on other organized groups in the economy. In pursuing this role, Congress set up regulatory agencies to establish the rules of competition of fairness. The ICC (set up under the Interstate Commerce Act of 1887) established an arena in which, by negotiation, the transporter and supplier could divide value added to buy products (see Chapter 4). Additionally, it removed from railroads the burden of having to comply with many different state laws, some of them populist inspired and intended to limit management prerogatives in the area of pricing (see Dos Passos, 1987, Chaps. 1–2). Congress established the Food and Drug Administration in 1906 partly in response to fraudulent claims about foods and patent medicines.

In 1890 and 1914, the Sherman and Clayton acts controlled price fixing and monopoly profits obtained through bargaining among oligopolists. The acts did not regulate company size per se but did regulate explicit collusion over pricing, market shares, and geographic division of the market (from the late 1930s through the mid 1960s size per se was an antitrust issue; see Kaysen and Turner, 1962). In 1914 Congress established the Federal Trade Commission to implement the Sherman and Clayton acts.

In 1921 the Budget and Accounting Act authorized the President to submit to Congress an annual budget governing revenues and expenditures for the year ending and estimates for the year ahead. To assist in this, the act created the Bureau of the Budget. Not until the Legislative Reorganization Act of 1946 did Congress establish a joint committee on the legislative budget to centralize its own review of the materials presented by the President (see Chapter 2).

Congress legislated the first peacetime income tax in 1894, but the Supreme Court ruled it unconstitutional in 1895. In 1909 President Taft suggested a moderate corporate excise tax and a constitutional amendment to authorize the individual income tax. The necessary thirty-six states ratified the amendment in 1913 for the first thirty-five years of the tax's existence, debates centered on thresholds (initially high) and progressivity.

When the depression suffered by the rest of the industrailized world penetrated the U.S. economy in 1929, the federal government had very little capacity to deal with overall levels of consumption and investment through monetary or fiscal policy. Further, federal regulatory bodies were policy-specific, and their actions were not coordinated with each other or with federal fiscal policies.

As a response to the Depression, the Roosevelt administration proposed the National Industrial Recovery Act. Drawing on the experience of World War I, the National Recovery Administration (NRA) also provided an umbrella for private-sector interests. Unlike the War Industries Board of 1917–19, the NRA had a coercive public-sector component. Each industrial sector created its own code governing pricing, division of market shares, and minimum wages for labor, or the NRA would establish one for them. All of the almost 500 industrial sectors managed to come up with a set of standards in 1933–34.

Advocates of the NIRA included some large businesses, particularly those in industrial sectors characterized by some smaller firms and many large firms. A code of production and competition would prevent smaller firms from attempting to take away the market shares of larger firms as consumption decreased. In effect, the industrial codes prevented individual entrepreneurs from engaging in "free-riding" when "more responsible" larger firms had to maintain prices, wages, and market shares in order to prevent a continuing downward spiral in the economy. The codes represented an instance of nonvoluntary but still private-sector-governed compliance with norms established within the private sector. One might compare the professional codes and rules developed in medicine and law at the state level (see Chapter 5). These codes would have been inconsistent with previous antitrust legislation had Congress not acted.

No government agency could do much about loans and commitments already outstanding at contractually fixed rates in 1933. This and the failure of the Roosevelt administration to legislate lower interest rates and principal payments as consumption spiraled downward represent two of the ironies of New Deal legislation. The continued flow of monies into nonconsumption cul-de-sacs operated against the other provisions of the 1933 NIRA, which was attempting to maintain or increase demand. This inconsistency reflects the very high value placed on contracts involving property and our view of monetary instruments as private property. Congress was most responsive to the needs of those groups that had had access to it the longest: both the NRA and the nonregulation of capital and interest rates benefited industry, banking, and transport most. The same hierarchy of values was reflected in New York State's legislated response to the New York City fiscal crisis of 1976–78.

Although the Supreme Court declared the NIRA unconstitutional in 1934, the federal government enacted many of its provisions in a piecemeal way, sometimes as direct government actions and sometimes as regulatory legislation. Upon the U.S. entry into World War II, Congress gave the executive authority to limit consumer credit, to reduce domestic consumption in materials needed for war, to establish wage and price controls for the economy as a whole, and, in particular, to establish rent controls to prevent the diversion of resources needed for the war into housing. Price controls ended in 1946, and the control of consumer credit ended November 1, 1947. Rent control lasted longer, since almost all professional and consumer groups—except realtors themselves—favored rent control. Moreover, housing was still scarce, and representatives feared that if Congress left rent controls to the states the rural-dominated legislatures would undo it entirely.

During World War II tax rates went up dramatically, and the total percentage of the gross national product represented by all government expenditures reached a level not approached again until recent years. In the 1940s, however, most of this expenditure occurred at the federal level. Congress reduced individual and corporate tax rates in 1945 and 1948, reflecting the government's need for less revenue. Truman vetoed the 1948 bill because he thought that the government should use tax revenues to pay off the national debt. With the advent of the Korean War, tax rates again went up. As before, arguments arose over the extent to which individuals, as opposed to corporations, would bear the increased costs of the war. The resultant tax code of 1952 was a relatively simple document by today's standards. (One commentator [Witte, 1982] has suggested that from the 1920s through the 1940s the tax code was not much longer than the Table of Contents of the tax code in the 1970s and 1980s.) Truman had also recognized that changes in the tax rate could affect the rate of inflation by increasing purchasing power more rapidly than production.

Congress created the Federal Reserve System in 1913. Its decentralized structure again reflects congressional preference for setting up even national banking policy on a regional or state basis. In response to the Depression, the 1933 and 1935 amendments to the Federal Reserve Act pulled the twelve federal reserve regions further under the umbrella of the central bank. Congress designed these and other changes to allow the "Fed" to influence national interest rates and the money supply in at least four ways:

1. By changing requirements for the reserves that member banks must maintain in the Federal Reserve bank against their own deposits;
2. By raising or lowering the discount rate charged to member banks;
3. By buying and selling government securities and other bills of exchange through the Open Market Committee, an activity that can alter interest rates;
4. By specifying the amount of money that must be deposited when securities are bought on credit.

In orthodox economic theory, there has been a trade-off between rates of inflation and unemployment in the economy as a whole. The Federal Reserve System was designed to balance the two by controlling interest rates and the money supply. Until 1954, however, interest rates had always been low, and the Fed had very little peace time experience in exercising control over the money supply. The only serious episode of inflation came immediately after World War II, when neither Congress nor the Fed was particularly alert to the availability of policies that might affect it. In more recent eras concern with both inflation and unemployment and the failure of one to go down when the other goes up has become considerably greater.

The federal government's involvement with labor has revolved around two foci: the creation of jobs either to undercut domestic unrest or to stimulate demand in the economy, and the creation of the context within which labor and employers bargain. For many years the government was conspicuous by its absence in the latter arena. When the federal executive did intervene, it was invariably on the side of employers, either through the use of federalized state militia to thwart labor unrest (as in 1896 Pullman strike) or through injunctions issued under laws that regarded strikes and boycotts as a denial of the property rights of owners of firms.

By 1932 the American Federation of Labor was a large organization that encouraged orderly and peaceful behavior. The potential for massive and organized unrest existed, however. In response to this potential, Congress overwhelmingly passed the Norris-LaGuardia Act, which limited the use of injunctions against unions and made yellow dog contracts unenforceable. In 1933 Section 7a of the NIRA included statements about the rights of workers to join unions and also required industries to set wage minimums. Although the wage minimums failed, particularly in the South (Perna, 1981), the legislation regularized union recognition for the first time.

Ironically, the fact that single unions represent all employees doing the same work within an industrial sector came about through administrative necessity. The National Labor Board's jurisdiction extended beyond unionizing elections into future labor-management relations. The board, set up under Section 7 of the NIRA, did not have the staff to deal with the many contending unions that might represent each plant. It ruled that the winner of a majority or plurality of the workers' votes would represent all the workers in a plant. This clearly strengthened the role of labor in its dealings with management. On the whole, however, business supported some of the labor provisions of the NIRA and subsequent legislation as a way to regularize labor costs.

Federal Legislation of rules governing labor-management relations do not necessarily work to the advantage of labor (McConnell, 1966). This is particularly true when labor is opposed by large corporations, which can bear the costs of prolonged stalemates much more effectively than the individual worker, even aided by a union strike fund. At least in this sense, many sets of labor-management bargaining procedures, particularly when they involve courts, favor management over labor.

In 1945 Truman proposed a bill that embodied a program for postwar expansion and full employment. The Senate version of the bill stated that the federal government was to ensure the existence at all times of sufficient employment opportunities for all able people seeking work. If this goal was not otherwise achievable, the federal government had the responsibility to use investment and expenditures to provide such employment. By 1946 the Senate and particularly the House of Representatives had emasculated the bill. The final product, the Employment Act of 1946, contained no requirement that the government be the direct or indirect provider of employment of last resort. In effect, the act stated that it would be nice to have a healthy economy, and that full employment is part of a healthy economy. This was one of the first declarations of national policy to include systematic benefits to labor, but the declaration was without substance (see Reading 7-1). Further, it is unclear that the federal government could meet the conditions of the original Senate bill even today. Government can transfer money but cannot always make jobs.

Agenda

The principal task of the Eisenhower administration was to get the government out of the economy and business back in. Much of Congress agreed to this as an agenda. In 1953 Congress passed a bill extending general rent control only to July 31, 1953, and control in critical defense housing areas to April 30, 1954. Under Eisenhower federal spending for highways and public housing increased markedly to provide for the national defense, create an infrastructure for commerce, and stimulate both business and consumption (see Chapter 4). Eisenhower also attempted to extend the repayment period of the national debt, claiming that too much of the debt had to be rolled over each year. To do this, the Treasury offered five-year, ten-month bonds with a total increase in interest cost of $136 million. The Federal Reserve Open Market Committee refused to support bond prices at that level by purchasing them when demand seemed to fall. It seems clear that Eisenhower was willing to pursue monetary policy (borrowing) that would allow the government. to plan its cash flow, even at the cost of a higher interest rate and higher profits for lenders than many in Congress would desire.

Congress rewrote the tax code in 1954, for the first time accelerating depreciation rates beyond a straight-line rate. This allowed businesses to claim additional depreciation in the first years after an investment and to use this additional depreciation to offset earnings, producing lower tax liability. Benefited in this way, businesses would invest more, produce more, and, hence, employ more labor, creating a balancing increase in consumption. Management of the economy through changes in the tax code of this kind first benefit those engaged in commerce and agriculture. Whether benefits reach those who might be newly employed is problematic. Leaving aside Roosevelt's concern for the middle-class unemployed in 1933, economic policies that would target benefits for service providers or workers were still a decade away.

In 1954 Eisenhower's first economic report described his view of the role of government in the economy: government can use monetary policy, debt management, federal insurance for private obligations, modification of the tax structure, and the construction of public works as tools for keeping overall economic activity at a steady level—to prevent serious swings in the economy, but not to correct for minor variations. Government meddling will not occur. The goal is to provide a stable economic environment while bringing down the scale of federal activity and public taxation.

However, somewhat against his will, Eisenhower was forced to use fiscal policies in a countercyclical manner. When economic activity slowed down in 1953–54, in 1957–58, and in 1960, federal revenues fell short of budgetary predictions, and Congress would not agree to spend less money on mandated programs creating accidental countercyclical budgets. The only deliberately countercyclical budget during the Eisenhower administration occurred in response to the recession in 1958, when the Democratic Congress passed an emergency housing bill that created a revolving fund of $1 billion for the purchase of FHA and GI mortgages. Additionally, an emergency highway bill infused $600 million into state economies by temporarily suspending the pay-as-you-go provisions of the highway trust fund and permitting payment advance to states for highway construction (see Chapter 4). Congress also expanded the federal component of unemployment compensation benefits, provided that states also carried an additional burden, and made the Small Business Administration a permanent agency, increasing its revolving fund for lending purposes by 65 percent.

Yet the monetary policies of the Federal Reserve Board were consistent with Eisenhower's views. In 1959 congressional representatives from farm states and large cities accused the Fed of creating unnecessarily high rates of interest, which were deflating economic activity and, hence, employment. The source of congressional concern was the steady growth in the base level of unemployment. After the 1947–48 recession, 3 percent was considered the full growth rate of unemployment, the level below which unemployment could not be reduced no matter how vital the economy. After the 1953–54 recession, 4 percent became the norm. Toward the end of the 1957–58 recession, unemployment did not move below 5 percent. This growth served as evidence that the administration's policies, combined with those of the Fed, had produced a stable environment for business growth, but with insufficient demands for goods and services to employ all those who wished to be employed. The "burden" of moderate growth was borne by the blue-collar unemployed, not management. This is no surprise, of course; many federal policies have evolved this way as we have seen in previous chapters.

At the end of the 1960–61 recession, Kennedy and a Democratic Congress found the unemployment rate to be almost 6 percent. Hence, both the President and Congress were more willing to introduce into the 1961 budget items that induced a higher level of demand for goods and services. Congress increased Social Security benefits by $800 million. ADC (also part of the original Social Security net) expanded greatly (see Chapter 6). The federal government was clearly now willing to use the tools Eisenhower had spoken of on a continual, though piecemeal, basis. This willingness extended to measures to increase business investment. In 1962 Congress further liberalized depreciation rules and provided business with several billion dollars of tax relief through investment tax credits.

In 1962–63 the administration and Congress developed the concept of the full-employment budget. The budget presented to Congress in 1963 contained a level of expenditure that would have matched tax income if there had been full employment and a high rate of growth. Since growth was in fact modest, this meant that there would be a modest budgetary deficit that, the administration estimated, would be recaptured through growth by 1967. The administration was clearly using this device as a conscious attempt at countercyclical fiscal management, with benefits to both labor and business.

Kennedy's proposed mix of economic policies hardly constitutes an economic plan. Nevertheless, because it responded to constituency need, it attracted the support of diverse members of Congress who would obtain attributable benefits useful at election time. Social Security increases and ADC likewise benefited definable constituencies.

The investment tax credit was a classic "trickle-down" economic measure. Many of these programs of the early 1960s worked through business incentives first, just like their predecessors.

In January 1962 Kennedy's first economic report introduced a set of wage-price guidelines developed by his Council of Economic Advisors. The administration intended these guidelines to keep wage increases in line with productivity and to keep price modifications dependent upon the productivity of each sector of the economy. In particular, the Kennedy administration successfully pressured the United Steelworkers to agree to a noninflationary wage settlement with the steel industry. However, on April 10, the United States Steel Corporation announced an increase of six dollars per ton in the price of steel. Some other steel companies followed suit. Kennedy asked the Department of Justice and the Federal Trade Commission to investigate the antitrust aspects of the case. The Defense Department ordered its contractors to shift their steel purchases to companies that had cooperated with the administration. The backgrounds of major steel executives were investigated. In the end, the administration secured a rollback on steel prices, although a more modest increase went through a year later without much comment. The significance of the steel crisis was that the executive could bring strong pressure to bear on one industrial sector without congressional approval. Kennedy chose the steel because his involvement in persuading steelworkers to agree to a noninflationary contract had placed the credibility of the administration at stake (see Reading 7-2).

Throughout the Kennedy administration and much of the Johnson administration, the Federal Reserve attempted to maintain interest rates at higher levels than either President wanted. One reason was that the Federal Reserve has always paid more attention to controlling inflation than other economic indicators, including unemployment. The beneficiaries of inflation are unclear. Labor seems to be hurt in the short run but may, particularly if unionized, benefit in the long run (Peretz, 1983). Businesses, on the other hand, may benefit from short-run increases in spending that are used as a hedge against anticipated price increases, but inflation introduces an element of uncertainty into the business environment that management usually prefers to avoid. Most importantly, banks, insurance companies, and other institutions that lend money at fixed rates clearly do not benefit, and members of the Federal Reserve are largely drawn from banking.

In 1964–65 the rate of inflation was 4.5 percent (a large figure for those days), and the Federal Reserve set its policy largely in response to the administration's inability to cut the budget. The Vietnam War and congressionally mandated and targeted social programs were both costly and impossible to cut out of the budget. As a later consequence of demand-led inflation, Johnson had to trim 10 percent of proposed government spending for all domestic programs in 1968 as a condition for Congress's passage of a 10 percent income tax surcharge. Many businesses that still viewed large budget deficits and uncontrolled inflation as factors stimulating an uncertain business environment supported the surcharge.

The Kennedy and Johnson administrations and Congress in the 1960s were much more active than their predecessors in using fiscal and tax policy to regulate overall levels of economic activity. Both Presidents and Congress evidenced increased confidence in and willingness to use government planning in lieu of private-sector decisionmaking for some resource allocation. One ironic consequence of their intervention in the economy and use of media to extend the effect of administration positions was that the blame for the increased inflation that began in the mid-1960s became attached to the government. Government, not business or labor, was seen as responsible for macroeconomic indicators, particularly when they were bad (Peretz, 1983, pp. 111–26). The agenda of getting businss going and getting the government out of business was not rejected in the 1960s. But newly organized groups demanded the government's help in claiming their share of economic prosperity, and Congress for its part attempted to encourage steady growth and the wider distribution of the benefits of such growth.

Process

Once the federal government was held at least partly accountable for the health of the economy, the executive and Congress could no longer merely react to the needs of particular groups. Yet the necessary tools for government management of economic activity do not exist. Consumer credit and investment decisions are totally in private hands. Using monetary policy, regulation, the tax budget, and fiscal policy, a fragmented federal government has at best blunt and unreliable tools for economic management.

In particular the federal government was unable to dampen the effects of overseas-induced inflation or unemployment. Historically, the foreign trade component of the U.S. economy had been small when compared to that of Britain, France, Germany, and, more recently, Japan. This was still true in the late 1960s and early 1970s. Yet the effects of trade were not insignificant in the U.S. economy. The reciprocal tariff building of European countries in the late 1920s had helped bring the United States into the worldwide depression. By the late 1960s the United States was dependent on overseas countries for the raw materials for a number of industrial processes and was using far more oil than it could produce.

In the late 1960s the Nixon administration presented a number of conflicting trends in government involvement in the domestic economy. Price supports for farm commodities remained high. Government made a major loan to a defense contractor, Lockheed, to keep it from going out of business. Both the executive and Congress had to keep providing targeted benefits to groups. Many groups benefited from the extension of support for categorical programs and the detailed, targeted regulatory legislation passed under the Nixon administration in the areas of education (Chapter 3), housing (Chapter 4), health (Chapter 5), and welfare (Chapter 6). At the same time Nixon encouraged fiscal decentralization through federal revenue sharing and the creation of major block grants.

The Comprehensive Employment and Training Act (1973), the Housing and Community Development Act of 1974 (see Chapter 4), and Title XX of the Social Services Act, and the 1974 amendments to the Social Security Act, all consolidated targeted federal programs into block grants. Much greater state and local program discretion was allowed. Consistent with the general thrust toward planning in the early 1970s, however, each of these block grants contained planning requirements; that is, the recipient level of government had to develop a plan for the use of the block grant money over several years.

One of Nixon's first acts as President was to establish an urban affairs council, which developed a national urban policy. It is almost impossible to do this without engaging in some form of national economic planning. Nixon also promoted the establishment of the Domestic Council and the Office of Management and Budget to replace the Bureau of the Budget. Both moves were intended to consolidate the planning of federal domestic programs and the regulation of both the economy and social programs. To pursue these ends, OMB and the White House staff more than doubled in size between 1969 and 1972. Nixon wanted to limit the independence with which the many bureaus in the federal executive could respond to congressional committee and subcommittee funding and oversight (see Chapter 2). This effort at consolidation set the Office of the President and OMB against the perceived self-interest of other parts of the federal executive as it pursued the mandates of Congress without concern for costs to citizens.

Oddly enough, while Nixon was reorganizing the executive to reduce the power of departmentally based bureaucrats and professionals, Congress was establishing a number of other regulatory bodies that would increase costs for business, state and local government, and school districts. The Occupational Safety and Health Administration (OSHA, 1970), the Environmental Protection Agency (EPA, 1970), and the Consumer Product Safety Commission (1972) imposed significant regulatory burdens that only began to be undone in the Carter and Reagan administrations through the intervention of OMB into the regulatory process. Legislation like the Education for All Handicapped Children Act and the increasing activity of the Office of Civil Rights (see Chapter 3) also increased regulatory costs. These costs took two forms: (1) the cost of the administration or regulation itself, and (2) the cost of mandated changes in the way business is done or education provided. A third possible cost, as noted in several chapters, was that of the withdrawal of federal grants.

The agenda of providing a consistent climate for business growth inspired conflicting actions in the late 1960s. Congress targeted appropriations to both business and labor. Off-budget items like guaranteed business loans and loan guarantees increased dramatically. At the same time Congress established environmental and consumer-oriented regulatory bodies in response to newly organized groups. Attempts to coordinate this massive federal activity centered in the executive branch. Nixon, as noted above, wanted to coordinate federal economic and social policies while eliminating the influence of career federal bureaucrats in determining them (see Chapter 2). Yet block grants were often taken over at the state level by the very professionals Nixon detested. These inconsistencies in federal policy are largely a result of the blending of several conceptions of limited government with the electoral imperative. Interest-group-based liberalism or conservatism in Congress, and attempts at fiscal decentralization and centralized policy planning in the executive, do not necessarily produce a coherent economic program.

This lack of coherence might have had little political or economic consequence if it had not been for the 1972–73 Arab oil embargo. Although the relative involvement of the U.S. economy in international trade had been increasing throughout the 1950s and 1960s, trade as a component of the gross national profit was still small compared with its role in most other large, industrialized democracies. However, the United States was highly dependent on some basic commodity products like tin, tungsten, uranium, and particularly oil: in the early 1970s the United States imported about one-half of the oil it used, largely from the Middle East.

When many of the oil-exporting countries collectively raised their prices in 1971, the effect on the U.S. economy was dramatic. Greatly increased energy costs fueled an inflation that was already supported by a failure of negotiated prices (for medical care, steel, etc.) to go down when demand decreased. In the spring and summer of 1972, Nixon used the standby controls of the 1953 Amendments to the Defense Production Act (reauthorized despite Nixon's resistance in 1970) to freeze wages and prices. Congress regularized this freeze three months later, resisting most of the exceptions proposed by organized constituents. It is striking that the freeze occurred in peacetime under a Republican president who said he wanted to disengage the government from the economy. In this case, as in others, Nixon initiated or concurred with legislation that had the opposite effect.

Ford to opposed government involvement in business and much economic and social regulation. He also opposed the habitual distributional responses of Congress and vetoed an extraordinarily large number of spending bills during his short time in office. Additionally, he was the first President actually to use the implicit capacities of OMB to help control the effects of executive branch rules and regulations.

In November 1974 Executive Order 11821 required that an estimate of the inflationary impact of any proposed rule or regulation accompany the proposal itself. The director of OMB listed the following as issues to be considered: (1) increased cost for consumers, business, or state and local governments; (2) effect on productivity; (3) effect on competition; and (4) effect on critical supplies or services. OMB used the Council on Wage and Price Stability to help in its analysis. Unfortunately, the council and OMB reviewed regulations *after* they had passed through the entire bureaucratic process within agencies. This meant that agencies and even agency heads had often developed vested interest in the major outlines of the programs as offered.

Upon election Carter tried (unsuccessfully) to block twenty-four already appropriated water projects benefiting many members of Congress. At the same time he increased the use of OMB for purposes of regulatory review. In 1978 he established the Regulatory Analysis Review Group (RARG), chaired by the head of the Council of Economic Advisers (see Readings 7-3 and 7-4). The Council on Wage and Price Stability again provided staff for RARG analyses of a number of regulations. In March of the same year, Carter signed Executive Order 12044, designed to make regulation less burdensome, clearer, and more cost-effective. Each agency had to publish a semiannual agenda of all regulations and hearings. The order required advanced notices of proposed rule making and extended the period allowed for public comment from thirty to sixty days. Each agency had to review existing regulations to determine their economic impact and their technical necessity. Any regulation that could cost more than one hundred million dollars would be subject to regulatory analysis. A draft regulatory analysis must be available for public review, and a final regulatory analysis must be issued with the regulation. In the regulatory analysis, all of the major alternative ways of dealing with the problem must be considered along with their effects. Of 109 regulatory analyses done by the executive agencies, RARG reviewed only 19 throughout the rest of the Carter administration. Unfortunately, the RARG reviews became a somewhat adversarial process. Instead of working with RARG, the agencies preparing regulations kept their plans secret and usually allowed RARG to see only their final products. These products ranged from proposed rules prohibiting educational discrimination against students who were not proficient in English to national ambient-air-quality standards for carbon monoxide to labeling requirements for prescription drugs. However, the fact that such analyses were done and subject to public scrutiny made agencies involved in both economic and social regulations much more sensitive to alternative means of achieving the same ends and even caused some to question the desirability of the benefits themselves. Of course, this occurred most often in bodies engaged in economic regulation. Agencies engaged in social regulation often effectively bypassed RARG (see Chapter 3). A striking example is the implementation by the Department of Education and the Office of Civil Rights of the Education for All Handicapped Children Act and Title VI of the 1964 Civil Rights Act (see Reading 7-4).

The Carter administration explicitly tried to deregulate three significant areas of the U.S. economy—natural gas, trucking, and airlines. Congress approved because in some cases deregulation could lower costs to identifiable constituents: the southwest in the case of natural gas, urban areas in the case of trucking and airline deregulation. The Airlines Deregulation Act of 1978, after a transitional period, ended restrictions on entry into the industry and fares and provided for the eventual demise of the Civil Aeronautics Board. The Motor Carrier Act of 1980 liberalized to a lesser degree entry into the trucking industry and began to negate trucking firms' antitrust immunity in cases of collective rate setting. The more complex Natural Gas Policy Act of 1978 allowed for gradual increases in the average price of natural gas by maintaining a high degree of transitional regulation on already existing production but largely deregulating pricing on new production. The Holding Company Bill Act of 1936, the Natural Gas Act of 1938, and intrastate regulatory bodies already regulated local service provision and pipeline monopolies.

Tax changes benefiting particular groups continued under Carter, though as a Democrat with a Democratically controlled Congress, he proposed some to benefit labor as well as business. A 1978 provision gave a tax credit to businesses that created new jobs. In practice, of course, the major beneficiaries were firms engaged in the episodic or seasonal employment of large numbers. In these cases new jobs credit would be given for hiring people that the same firm had sent back to the unemployment roles six months earlier. Thus, even though labor was the intended beneficiary, business benefited more.

Although the deregulation of the 1970s was supposed to reduce consumer costs, the late 1970s were characterized by high rates of inflation and unemployment. Economic theory had difficulty explaining this phenomenon, known as "stagflation." One possible explanation was that costs remained artificially high because of government regulations and the power of professionals and other organized groups at the local level.

The many prerogatives of professional groups as legislated at the state and local level remained untouched. Moreover, many sectors of the economy, particularly the production and distribution of goods and services, remained concentrated, and firms were able to pass on any cost increases due to internal inefficiencies to marketers and the consuming public. The federal budget was difficult to control, since the many demands imposed by attempts to maintain congressional incumbency could not be undone. The Federal Reserve's tight money policy—a response to higher rates of inflation—made any investment more costly; in particular the cost of home mortgages increased dramatically, decreasing the demand for new housing and placing a further drag on the economy.

In fact, the late 1970s saw no clear-cut trend toward deregulation.

Although, as we have seen, economic deregulation occurred, state and local spending associated with negative regulation (see Chapters 3, 4, 5) and federal court decisions pursuant to Title VI of the Civil Rights Act and similar measures increased social regulatory costs. The cumulative regulatory activities of the new EPA and OSHA continued to add costs to the economy.

Consequences

Social regulation, economic distributions, and macroeconomic manipulation using monetary and fiscal policy are inconsistent with the principle of small government at the federal level. Recent administrations appear to prefer less government and decentralization of program authority to the state and local levels. Yet, like Congress, each administration has to provide supporters with tangible benefits, whether in the form of business tax credits, defense spending, or the support of moral norms through, for example, prohibiting abortion. These activities are not always consistent with minimal government and decentralization of policy making. Further, the incumbency needs of Congress have not changed. Reducing federal spending in a manner acceptable to both the executive and Congress is therefore very difficult. Even in fiscally austere times, Congresspeople respond to old or new problems by suggesting a new agency (see Reading 7-5).

The Reagan administration continued the deregulatory momentum of the 1970s. On January 22, 1981, Reagan announced his intention to establish a task force on regulatory relief, headed by the Vice-President. Pending its report, all proposed regulations were put on hold and all newly promulgated ones were delayed for sixty days, the maximum extent permitted by law. Review of all regulations was centralized in OMB, which attempted to provide a market-oriented set of guidelines to federal agencies (see Reading 7-6) All major regulations were reviewed by the Office of the President. The EPA pursued other market-oriented mechanisms (see Reading 7-7).

The effects of these procedural changes were less dramatic than envisioned for two reasons. First, traditional economic regulation had always taken a long time—establishing cotton-dust standards, for example, took seven years (1974–81)—principally because of industry's capacity to sustain the cost of appealing every change in regulatory rule making to the entire federal judiciary system. During the period of appeal, the regulations are not in effect. A second limitation is that the new procedures are cumbersome to apply to social regulations. It is difficult to keep minorities or Spanish-speaking populations out of the federal courts when they are denied their civil rights (see Chapter 3), and besides, it is not always clear how OMB guidelines should be translated into areas of social regulations.

An administration or Congress can undo the effects of social regulation. In 1981 the secretary of education withdrew a notice of proposed rule making, a means-oriented document on bilingual education (see Chapter 2). However, the vast majority of school districts had already negotiated compliance with the provisions of that document. Further, they knew that the cost of harassment from the Office of Civil Rights would be minimized if they persisted with compliance. Thus, the withdrawal of the notice did not affect the provision of bilingual education. However, a policy of not filling vacant provisions in the Office of Civil Rights, to the extent that 35 percent of the positions were vacant since 1982, did have an effect on its regulatory capacities. Additionally, the Justice Department often intervened and at least tried to influence the outcome of court cases involving bilingual education, busing, and particularly job quotas (see Reading 7-8).

In addition to deregulating the economy, recent administrations and Congress have attempted to reduce the tax burden on individuals and businesses. Lower taxes were supposed to encourage both consumption and investment. The Economic Recovery and Tax Act lowered personal income taxes 25 percent over a period of two and a half years and provided accelerated cost recovery systems (ACRS) for depreciation. This allowed properties and even race horses and baseball players with useful economic lives of up to fifteen years to be depreciated within three to five years. The policy clearly favors the investment of capital in the hope that there will be a demand for the goods produced. Without this increased demand, ACRS merely provides quicker real-dollar tax benefits for investment decisions that would have been made anyway.

To the extent that tax reduction does not produce sufficient economic activity to produce equivalent tax revenue, deficits increase. This happened throughout the late 1970s and early 1980s, even with a gradual decline in the world price of oil and other basic imported commodities. Further, by 1982 individuals, institutions, and central banks outside the United States held almost 25 percent of the national debt. Continuing a policy of producing such defitics thus implies continually larger interest payments on these debts. The U.S. government must persuade foreign holders of debts to keep refinancing the debt and the interest cost as well. Greater and greater amounts of capital will be taken out of the production of goods and services and used to pay rent on money overseas. This must eventually slow or nullify economic growth.

Congress's need for reelection and bureaucrats' for something to administer do not lessen just because huge federal budget deficits exist. Congress and the administration together agreed to a surreptitious cutting of domestic programs through the nine block grants of 1981. This apparent structural change in financing was, in effect, a budget-cutting device to free money either for further spending on new congressionally originated programs or for reducing the federal deficit. The reduction in domestic spending was small, and when it was combined with the high levels of expenditure in defense industries, which do not particularly stimulate economic growth through the problem of the federal deficit remained.

To further stimulate the economy and lower the administrative costs of taxation, the Reagan administration and Congress have advocated a program of tax simplification. This tax reform is revenue-neutral: that is, the total amount of money collected from all taxes remains the same. It includes lower rates and fewer exemptions, so that for any particular individual or business, the reform will not be neutral. To enact such legislation is difficult because almost all of the beneficiaries of tax exemptions have received those benefits through the activities of Congresspeople representing particular interests located in particular districts. Further, tax simplification can have other policy consequences. Any failure to exempt state and local taxes—property taxes in particular—will almost inevitably result in a lower level of spending on education throughout the United States. This effect will be particularly felt in school districts with low property tax bases. In general, tax reform or any other activity has many spin-offs for other parts of the public sector and the private economy. The uncoordinated activities of any one administration may be contradictory and inconsistent (see Reading 7-9).

There is always an ad hoc quality to economic policy. The Gramm-Rudman-Hollings bill is supposed to force Congress and executive to agree on selectively reduced spending; otherwise all spending will be proportionately cut. Either way reduced deficits will reduce interest rates and stimulate the economy. However, it is unclear whether the longer-term effect of such action will not be simply another round of stagflation (see Reading 7-10). Decentralized electoral politics conducted over a two-year cycle does not promote the passage of legislation that anticipates economic cycles and consequences a decade later. This failure to anticipate longer economic cycles is not a feature of governments alone. Without government intervention farmers seldom plan countercyclically; even with government involvement, domestic companies are not preparing for the anticipated rise in the demand for, price of, and importation of oil in the early 1990s.

Yet we do have an economic policy, even if it is only the sum of relevant programs passed by Congress. It is not a planned policy; it results from disjointed efforts on the part of the executive branch combined with sequences of spending decisions and tax budget changes influenced by the electoral needs of Congresspeople. It involves minimal coordination and planning. For example, Congress has only loosely coordinated these decisions with those made by regulatory bodies, particularly the Federal Reserve Board, and OMB.

Ironically, the initial beneficiaries of uncoordinated regulation and federal involvement in the economy—groups involved with banking, commerce, and manufacturing—are also the principal beneficiaries of deregulation. Even the proposed tax code changes may lower the property and income tax exposure of businesses by penalizing citizens of those states that tax a lot to provide many services. This penalty is as close to negative regulation of state taxing and services levels as federal tax policy can come.

Readings

7-1. THE GOVERNMENT GUARANTEES FULL EMPLOYMENT

Below are the original Senate version (S. 380) and the final House version of the Full Employment Act of 1945 (P.L. 304). A comparison shows that the guarantees given labor in the former remain as only symbolic gestures in the latter.

S. 380

The bill under consideration, S. 380, is as follows:

A bill to establish a national policy and program for assuring continuing full employment in a free competitive economy, through the concerted efforts of industry, agriculture, labor, State and local Governments, and the Federal Government.

Be it enacted by the Senate and House of Representatives of the United States of America in Congress assembled.

Section 1. This Act may be cited as the "Full Employment Act of 1945."

Declaration of Policy

Sec. 2. The Congress hereby declares that—

(a) It is the policy of the United States to foster free competitive enterprise and the investment of private capital in trade and commerce and in the development of the natural resources of the United States;

(b) All Americans able to work and seeking work have the right to useful, remunerative, regular, and full-time employment, and it is the policy of the United States to assure the existence at all times of sufficient employment opportunities to enable all Americans who have finished their schooling and who do not have full-time housekeeping responsibilities freely to exercise this right;

(c) In order to carry out the policies set forth in subsections (a) and (b) of this section, and in order to (1) promote the general welfare of the Nation; (2) foster and protect the American home and the American family as the foundation of the American way of life; (3) raise the standard of living of the American people; (4) provide adequate employment opportunities for returning veterans; (5) contribute to the full utilization of our national resources; (6) develop trade and commerce among the several States and with foreign nations; (7) preserve and strengthen competitive private enterprise, particularly small business enterprise; (8) strengthen the national defense and security; and (9) contribute to the establishment and maintenance of lasting peace among nations, it is essential that continuing full employment be maintained in the United States;

(d) In order to assist industry, agriculture, labor, and State and local governments in achieving continuing full employment, it is the responsibility of the Federal Government to pursue such consistent and openly arrived at economic policies and programs as will stimulate and encourage the highest feasible levels of employment opportunities through private and other non-Federal investment and expenditure;

(e) To the extent that continuing full employment cannot otherwise be achieved, it is the further responsibility of the Federal Government to provide such volume of Federal investment and expenditure as may be needed to assure continuing full employment; and

(f) Such investment and expenditure by the Federal Government shall be designed to contribute to the national wealth and well-being, and to stimulate increased employment opportunities by private enterprise.

Employment Act of 1946, As Amended, and Related Laws and Rules of the Joint Committee

An act to declare a national policy on employment, production, and purchasing power, and for other purposes.

Be it enacted by the Senate and House of Representatives of the United States of America in Congress assembled.

Short Title

Section 1. This Act may be cited as the "Employment Act of 1946."

Declaration of Policy

Sec. 2. The Congress declares that it is the continuing policy and responsibility of the Federal Government to use all practicable means consistent with its needs and obligations and other essential considerations of national policy, with the assistance and cooperation of industry, agriculture, labor, and State and local governments, to coordinate and utilize all its plans, functions, and resources for the purpose of creating and maintaining, in a manner calculated to foster and promote free competitive enterprise and the general welfare, conditions under which there will be afforded useful employment opportunities, including self-employment, for those able, willing, and seeking to work, and to promote maximum employment, production, and purchasing power. (60 Stat. 23)

7-2. THE PRESIDENT VERSUS BIG BUSINESS

United States Steel's announcement of a price increase and Kennedy's response follow. Lost in the turmoil was the question whether United States Steel's production costs had actually increased to the degree the company claimed. If so, the price adjustment was appropriate, given a base year of 1958. However, Kennedy's response was based more on his need for credibility with his labor supporters than on cold economic calculation.

Text of U.S. Steel's Statement on Prices*

Following is the text of a statement of Leslie B. Worthington, president of the United States Steel Corporation. In announcing price increases.

Since our last over-all adjustment in the summer of 1958, the level of steel prices has not been increased but, if anything, has declined somewhat. This situation, in the face of steadily mounting production costs which have included four increases in steel worker wages and benefits prior to the end of last year, has been due to the competitive pressures from domestic producers and from imports of foreign-made steel as well as from other materials which are used as substitutes for steel.

The severity of these competitive pressures has not diminished; and to their influence may be attributed the fact that the partial catch-up adjustment announced today is substantially less than the cost increases which have already occurred since 1958, without taking into consideration the additional costs which will result from the new labor agreements which become effective next July 1.

Nevertheless, taking into account all the negative factors affecting the market for steel, we have reluctantly concluded that a modest price adjustment can no longer be avoided in the light of production cost increases that have made it necessary.

If the products of United States Steel are to compete successfully in the market place, then the plants and facilities which make those products must be as modern and efficient as the low-cost mills which abound abroad and as the plants which must turn out competing products here at home. Only by generating the funds necessary to keep these facilities completely competitive can our company continue to provide its customers with a dependable source of steel, and to provide its employees with dependable jobs. But the profits of the company—squeezed as they have been between rising costs and declining prices—are inadequate today to perform this vital function.

*New York Times, April 11, 1962.

U.S. Steel Raises Price $6 a Ton . . .*

President Kennedy was infuriated by tonight's news that the United States Steel Corporation was raising its prices.

The word from White House intimates was that he regarded the move as an unjustified and deliberate affront to his Administration. There was some feeling here that tonight's unexpected development would have a profound effect on the President's attitude toward the business community and possibly on his economic policies in general.

There was no immediate on-the-record comment from the White House on the increase. However a spokesman for the Department of Justice said:

"Because of past price behavior in the steel industry the Department of Justice will take an immediate and close look at the situation and any future developments."

The reference to "past behavior" was to the usual development of the other steel companies' following the price policy of United States Steel. Senator Estes Kefauver, Democrat of Tennessee, promised an investigation by his Anti-trust and Monopoly subcommittee.

President Kennedy has deliberately leashed some of his liberal instincts in an attempt to create good working relations with business. In the particular case of steel he applied intense pressure on labor to limit its wage demands this year. The breach of the steel price line will embarrass him with his supporters in the labor movement.

The President himself and his principal lieutenants have been working hard for almost a year to get this key industry and its workers to exercise restraint on prices and wages. With last week's signing of a new steel labor contract that the President hailed as "non-inflationary," the Administration throught its mission accomplished.

Roger M. Blough, chairman of United States Steel, went to the White House this evening and told the President of the price increase, after it had been announced in Pittsburgh. . . .

The Administration had staked so much on steel because it believes that the industry's prices and wages are a major factor in price-wage developments throughout the economy. Directly, they contribute to the

---

* "U.S. Steel Raises Price $6 a Ton; Kennedy Angered, Sees Affront; Two Investigations Are Ordered," *New York Times*, April 11, 1962.

cost of the great many things that are made of steel. Indirectly, they set an example for nonsteel industries and labor to follow.

The Administration has been particularly anxious to preserve price stability in the economy in order that this country remain competitive with industry abroad. An added embarrassment in tonight's announcement was the presence in Washington this week of Prof. Walter Hallstein, president of the Administrative Commission of Europe's six-nation Common Market.

There had been some rumors within the Administration in recent days that one of the smaller steel companies was preparing to announce a price increase, but the announcement from "Big Steel"—as United States Steel is known—came as a total surprise. There had been, however, some indication in public statements by the industry that it was indeed thinking of higher prices.

United States Steel announced its increase as three-tenths of one cent per pound and termed it "modest." However, in the tonnage terms that are commonly used, it amounted to $6 a ton, and was about halfway between the biggest and smallest of the ten post–World War II steel price increases.

The company did not blame last week's contract settlement for tonight's action. Rather, it just seemed to justify the increase on the basis of cost developments during the last four years, when there has been no important increase at all. In other words, the company is catching up with the cost increases it has experienced while holding the price line.

The Administration, clearly, does not believe the price increase is justified, either by the new contract or by the last four years' developments.

The Administration started last spring to put pressure on the industry to hold the price line despite a wage increase that was scheduled to take effect in October.

Industry did hold the line, presumably as a result of the public pressure from the Administration, combined with such other factors as foreign competition, slack business and the President's open promise to help the industry resist excessive new wage demands when the union contract came up for renewal this year.

The Administration's attention turned then to the wage negotiations. The President's Council of Economic Advisers published "guideposts" for noninflationary wage and price adjustments in January and the President personally asked the leaders of the industry and the union to sit down and arrange a new contract quickly without a strike.

The new contract was signed last Friday, three months before the old contract expires. The President, in a letter to David McDonald, the union president, called it "forward-looking and responsible."

The new terms—no wage increase at all for one year and new fringe benefits costing about 10 cents an hour—were "obviously noninflationary and should provide a solid base for continued price stability," the President said.

The Administration, and labor authorities here, believed that the settlement was within the general rule set by the council's "guideposts." That is, the increase in labor costs would not exceed the 2½ to 3 percent upward trend of productivity in the industry—the increasing output per man per hour.

In other words, they believed that a price increase would not be justified.

7-3. REGULATORY COST CONTROL*

Executive Order 12044 required government regulations to be highly publicized and to be reviewed by agency and department chiefs. The latter were supposed to consider the costs of regulation and possible alternative methods. Such analysis rarely changes proposed regulations, however, since the same groups proposed and evaluated them.

Improving Government Regulations

As President of the United States of America, I direct each Executive Agency to adopt procedures to improve existing and future regulations.

Section 1.   Policy.   Regulations shall be as simple and clear as possible. They shall achieve legislative goals effectively and efficiently. They shall not impose unnecessary burdens on the economy, on individuals, on public or private organizations, or on State and local governments.

To achieve these objectives, regulations shall be developed through a process which ensures that:

*Federal Register, 43, no. 58, March 24, 1978.

(a) the need for and purposes of the regulation are clearly established;

(b) heads of agencies and policy officials exercise effective oversight;

(c) opportunity exists for early participation and comment by other Federal agencies, State and local governments, businesses, organizations and individual members of the public;

(d) meaningful alternatives are considered and analyzed before the regulation is issued; and

(e) compliance costs, paperwork and other burdens on the public are minimized.

Sec. 2. Reform of the Process for Developing Significant Regulations. Agencies shall review and revise their procedures for developing regulations to be consistent with the policies of this Order and in a manner that minimizes paperwork.

Agencies' procedures should fit their own needs but, at a minimum, these procedures shall include the following:

(a) Semiannual Agenda of Regulations. To give the public adequate notice, agencies shall publish at least semiannually an agenda of significant regulations under development or review. On the first Monday in October, each agency shall publish in the Federal Register a schedule showing the times during the coming fiscal year when the agency's semiannual agenda will be published. Supplements to the agenda may be published at other times during the year if necessary, but the semiannual agendas shall be as complete as possible. The head of each agency shall approve the agenda before it is published.

At a minimum, each published agenda shall describe the regulations being considered by the agency, the need for and the legal basis for the action being taken, and the status of regulations previously listed on the agenda.

Each item on the agenda shall also include the name and telephone number of a knowledgeable agency official and, if possible, state whether or not a regulatory analysis will be required. The agenda shall also include existing regulations scheduled to be reviewed in accordance with Section 4 of this Order.

(b) Agency Head Oversight. Before an agency proceeds to develop significant new regulations, the agency head shall have reviewed the issues to be considered, the alternative approaches to be explored, a tentative plan for obtaining public comment, and target dates for completion of steps in the development of the regulations.

(c) Opportunity for Public Participation. Agencies shall give the public an early and meaningful opportunity to participate in the development of agency regulations. They shall consider a variety of ways to provide this opportunity, including (1) publishing an advance notice of proposed rulemaking; (2) holding open conferences or public hearings; (3) sending notices of proposed regulations to publications likely to be read by those affected; and (4) notifying interested parties directly.

Agencies shall give the public at least 60 days to comment on proposed significant regulations. In the few instances where agencies determine this is not possible, the regulations shall be accompanied by a brief statement of the reasons for a shorter time period.

(d) Approval of Significant Regulations. The head of each agency, or the designated official with statutory responsibility, shall approve significant regulations before they are published for public comment in the Federal Register. At a minimum, this official should determine that:

(1) the proposed regulation is needed;
(2) the direct and indirect effects of the regulation have been adequately considered;
(3) alternative approaches have been considered and the least burdensome of the acceptable alternatives has been chosen;
(4) public comments have been considered and an adequate response has been prepared;
(5) the regulation is written in plain English and is understandable to those who must comply with it;
(6) an estimate has been made of the new reporting burdens or recordkeeping requirements necessary for compliance with the regulation;
(7) the name, address and telephone number of a knowledgeable agency official is included in the publication; and
(8) a plan for evaluating the regulation after its issuance has been developed.

(e) Criteria for Determining Significant Regulations. Agencies shall establish criteria for identifying which regulations are significant. Agencies shall consider among other things: (1) the type and number of individuals, businesses, organization, State and local governments affected; (2) the compliance and reporting requirements likely to be involved; (3)

direct and indirect effects of the regulation including the effect on competition; and (4) the relationship of the regulations to those of other programs and agencies. Regulations that do not meet an agency's criteria for determining significance shall be accompanied by a statement to that effect at the time the regulation is proposed.

Sec. 3.   Regulatory Analysis.   Some of the regulations identified as significant may have major economic consequences for the general economy, for individual industries, geographical regions or levels of government. For these regulations, agencies shall prepare a regulatory analysis. Such an analysis shall involve a careful examination of alternative approaches early in the decisionmaking process.

The following requirements shall govern the preparation of regulatory analyses:

(a) Criteria. Agency heads shall establish criteria for determining which regulations require regulatory analyses. The criteria established shall: (1) ensure that regulatory analyses are performed for all regulations which will result in (a) an annual effect on the economy of $100 million or more, or (b) a major increase in costs or prices for individual industries, levels of government or geographic regions; and (2) provide that in the agency head's direction, regulatory analysis may be completed on any proposed regulation. (b) Procedures. Agency heads shall establish procedures for developing the regulatory analysis and obtaining public comment. (1) Each regulatory analysis shall contain a succinct statement of the problem; a description of the major alternative ways of dealing with the problem that were considered by the agency; an analysis of the economic consequences of each of these alternatives and a detailed explanation of the reasons for choosing one alternative over the others. (2) Agencies shall include in their public notice of proposed rules an explanation of the regulatory approach that has been selected or is favored and a short description of the other alternatives considered. A statement of how the public may obtain a copy of the draft regulatory analysis shall also be included. (3) Agencies shall prepare a final regulatory analysis to be made available when the final regulations are published.

Regulatory analyses shall not be required in rulemaking proceedings pending at the time this Order is issued if an Economic Impact Statement has already been prepared in accordance with Executive Orders 11821 and 11949.

Sec. 4.   Review of Existing Regulations.   Agencies shall periodically review their existing regulations to determine whether they are achieving the policy goals of this Order. This review will follow the same procedural steps outlined for the development of new regulations.

In selecting regulations to be reviewed, agencies shall consider such criteria as: (a) the continued need for the regulation; (b) the type and number of complaints or suggestions received; (c) the burdens imposed on those directly or indirectly affected by the regulations; (d) the need to simplify or clarify language; (e) the need to eliminate overlapping and duplicative regulations; and (f) the length of time since the regulation has been evaluated or the degree to which technology, economic conditions or other factors have changed in the area affected by the regulation. . . .

Sec. 8. Unless extended, this Executive Order expires on June 30, 1980.

The White House
March 23, 1978

7-4. COST CONTROL REVIEW PROCEDURES*

The Regulatory Analysis Review Group (RARG) was to participate in and extend review of executive branch regulations. Unfortunately, departments allowed such review only after the regulatory format was largely fixed and ready to be defended by the department involved. Following are RARG procedures.

Executive Order 12044 (as extended by EO 12221) requires an agency to make available to the public a draft Regulatory Analysis whenever that agency publishes a major regulatory proposal in the *Federal Register.* A limited number of these Regulatory Analyses are reviewed by an interagency Regulatory Analysis Review Group set up early in 1978 by Presidential directive to complement the Executive Order in stimulating improved regulations.

The Regulatory Analysis Review Group is chaired by the Council of Economic Advisers (CEA) and has as members the principal economic and regulatory agencies of the Executive branch. [1] A four-member Exec-

*Council of Economic Advisors, Procedures of the Regulatory Analysis Review Group, Oct. 1980, Washington, D.C.

1. Economic members include Council of Economic Advisers, Office of Management and Budget, and the Departments of Commerce, Labor, and Treasury. Regulatory members include Departments of Agriculture, Education, Energy, Health and Human Services, Housing and Urban Development, Interior, Justice, Transportation and the Environmental Protection Agency. Other participants include the Office of Science and Technology Policy as a member and the Domestic Policy Staff and the Council on Environmental Quality as advisers.

utive Committee (CEA, the Office of Management and Budget, and two rotating members serving six month terms, one an economic and one a regulatory member) is responsible for selecting ten to twenty Regulatory Analyses per year (with no more than four from any one agency) for full Review Group attention. The reasons for selecting a Regulatory Analysis can reflect a variety of considerations, but in general the following criteria seem dominant:

large total cost—relative to other regulations being proposed by that same agency a substantial burden is associated with compliance (including capital outlays, operating and maintenance costs, government expense, etc.) *and* this total cost exceeds $100 million in any one year;

large sectoral impact—overall costs or average prices for some industry, level of government or geographic region would increase by a substantial percentage, perhaps 3 percent or more, as a result of compliance, *and* this percentage is large relative to that associated with other regulations being proposed by that same agency;

deficient Regulatory Analysis—incomplete or inadequate analysis, particularly with respect to alternatives, costs or benefits;

precedential importance—the regulation sets a noteworthy precedent that will influence subsequent rulemakings;

broad policy issues—the regulation raises important methodological or other broad questions encountered in a variety of rulemakings.

Staff support for the Review Group is provided by the Council on Wage and Price Stability (CWPS). CWPS has statutory authority to intervene on its own behalf in regulatory proceedings, and from time to time CWPS on its own initiative elects to comment publicly upon certain proposed regulations. However, for proposals which *are* selected for Review Group action, CWPS has agreed to participate in the proceedings on behalf of the Review Group and not separately on its own behalf.

In order to avoid delaying regulations, Review Group action is completed during the public comment period following publication of a Notice of Proposed Rulemaking. Review Group procedures are outlined below.

After an agency publishes a Notice of Proposed Rulemaking (NPRM) for a major regulation, any member of the Review Group can request that the Executive Committee consider a review of the draft Regulatory Analysis. A decision to conduct a review generally is made within two weeks after publication of the NPRM. If two or more Executive Committee members are in favor, review will be held and notice to this effect will be submitted to the agency's public record for this regulatory proceeding.

Once the Executive Committee votes to review a Regulatory Analysis, CWPS prepares a draft statement of concerns which it submits to the Review Group for approval. After taking into account any agency suggestions, CWPS then submits the Review Group's statement of concerns to the agency's public record for this proceeding.

About two weeks before the rulemaking record closes, CWPS delivers a draft report that focuses on these concerns to the Review Group, which meets to discuss the acceptability of this draft and any needed changes. CWPS has a week to revise this draft, incorporating written and oral comments submitted by Review Group members.

After review by the Review Group chair, the final draft is made available to all Review Group members. Any member may elect to make qualifying or dissenting comments on this final draft; such comments are cited in the text of the final report and/or attached in an appendix. CWPS submits the final Review Group report into the rulemaking record on the last day of the public comment period.

7-5. A DEPARTMENT OF TRADE*

Congresspeople usually solve problems by reorganizing or throwing money at them. To be fair, Congress can do little else; it is poorly equipped to monitor or modify programs at either the local or the international level. In the following case, senators called for dealing with a particular problem—trade policy—through a new cabinet-level department, but ignored the interactions such policy must have with, for example, domestic grain-price supports. Such proposals are often symbolic, much as the creation of the Department of Education was.

Four senators who said America must organize its fragmented trade policies to effectively compete in the world market proposed Wednesday

* "Senators Urge Creation of Department of Trade," *Indianapolis Star*, June 27, 1985.

establishing a Cabinet-level Department of International Trade and Industry.

The department would combine functions of the Office of the U.S. Trade Representative with the various trade duties of the Commerce Department. Similar legislation passed the committee last year but did not clear the Congress.

"Last year, this idea was before its time," Sen. William Rogh, R-Del., one of the sponsors, said. "Events have caught up with us. We're in a crisis situation. . . . It's an idea whose time has come."

The senators said American trade policy is scattered among so many government officials and agencies that the nation does not speak with one strong voice.

The sponsors stressed the importance of provisions in the legislation that would require the department to include an office of competitive analysis to help American industries cope with growing foreign competition.

7-6. REAGAN'S INTERIM REGULATORY GUIDELINES: A RETURN TO THE MARKETPLACE*

OMB has presented guidelines to the executive departments concerning the factors to be considered before any new regulations are issued. Although the following principles may be easily applied to deciding whether the Army Corps of Engineers should build a reservoir, they are less well adapted to social regulation. Just how much is the ability to speak English or to vote worth, and to whom? Guidelines that emphasize costs, benefits, and values in the private sector are not intelligible when one is dealing with many nonmarket activities. However, such regulatory evaluations do provide bureaucracies (and Congress) with an artificially concrete and quantitative rationale for action or inaction.

A regulatory Impact Analysis (RIA) should demonstrate that a proposed regulatory action satisfies the requirements of Section 2 of Executive Order 12291. To do so it should show that: (1) There is adequate information concerning the need for and consequences of the proposed action; (2) The potential benefits to society outweigh the potential costs;

*Office of Management and Budget, Interim Regulatory Impact Analysis Guidance, June 12, 1981.

and (3) Of all the alternative approaches to the given regulatory objective, the proposed action will maximize net benefits to society.

The fundamental test of a satisfactory RIA is whether it enables independent reviewers to make an informed judgment that the objectives of E.O. 12291 are satisfied. An RIA that includes all the elements described below is likely to fulfill this requirement. Although variations consistent with the spirit and intent of the Executive Order may be warranted for some proposed or existing rules, most RIAs are expected to include these elements.

This document is written primarily in terms of proposed regulatory changes. However, it is equally applicable to the review of existing regulations. In the latter case, the impact of the regulation under review should be compared to a baseline case of no regulation and to reasonable alternatives.

Elements of a Regulatory Impact Analysis

Preliminary and final Regulatory Impact Analysis of major rules should contain five elements.

(1) Statement of Need for and Consequences of the Proposal

The statement of the need for and consequences of the proposed regulatory change should address the following questions: (a) What precisely is the problem that needs to be corrected? (That is, what market imperfection(s) give(s) rise to the regulatory proposal? Causes, not just symptoms, should be identified.) (b) How would the regulatory proposal, if promulgated, improve the functioning of the market, or otherwise meet the regulatory objective(s)? Since regulatory failure may be a real possibility, is it clear that the proposed regulation would produce better results than no regulatory change? (Imperfectly functioning markets should not be compared with idealized, perfectly functioning regulatory programs.)

(2) An Examination of Alternative Approaches

The RIA should show that the agency has considered the most important alternative approaches to the problem and must provide the agency's reasoning for selecting the proposed regulatory change over such alternatives. Although only the most promising alternatives need be evaluated at length, the agency should consider: (a) The consequences of having no regulation. (Are there existing or potential market, or judicial, or state or local regulatory, mechanisms that could resolve the problem? For example, RIAs for health and safety regulations should consider the adequacy of tort law or state programs such as workman's compensation.) (b) The major alternatives (if any) that might lie beyond the scope of the specific legislative provision under which the proposed regulation is being promulgated. (This may require a broad comparison across programs, including those within and outside the jurisdiction of the issuing agency.) (c) Alternatives within the scope of the specific legislative provision. These include: (i) Alternative stringency levels; (ii) Alternative effective dates; and (iii) Alternative methods of ensuring compliance. (d) Alternative, market-oriented ways of regulating (whether or not they are explicitly authorized in the agency's legislative mandate), including: (i) Information or labeling (to enable consumers or workers to evaluate hazards themselves); (ii) Performance rather than design standards; and (iii) Economic incentives, such as fees or charges, marketable permits or offsets, changes in insurance provisions, or changes in property rights.

(3) Analysis of Benefits and Costs

(a) Benefit estimates: The RIA should state the beneficial effects of the proposed regulatory change and its principal alternatives. It should include estimates of the present value of all potential real incremental benefits to society. Benefits that can be estimated in monetary terms should be expressed in constant dollars. Other favorable effects should be described in detail and quantified where possible. An annual discount rate of 10 percent should be used; however, where it appears desirable, other discount rates also may be used to test the sensitivity of the results. Assumptions should be stated, and the RIA should identify the data or studies on which the analysis is based.

There should be an explanation of the mechanism by which the proposed action is expected to yield the anticipated benefits. A schedule of benefits should be included that would show the *type* of benefits, to *whom* it would accrue, and *when* it [they] would accrue. The numbers in this table should be expressed in constant dollar terms.

(b) Cost estimates: The analysis should include estimates of the present value of all the real incremental costs of the proposed regulatory change and its principal alternatives (i.e., the costs that would be incurred by society as a result of taking the proposed action or an alternative). All costs that can be estimated in monetary terms should be expressed in constant dollars. Other costs should be described completely and quantified where possible. An annual discount rate of 10 percent should be used; however, where it appears desirable, other discount rates may also be used to test the sensitivity of the results.

To support the present value estimates, a schedule of costs should be included that would identify the *type* of cost (capital, recurring, etc.), *who* should bear that cost, and *when* that cost would be incurred. The numbers in this table should be expressed in constant dollar terms. Assumptions should be stated, and the RIA should identify the date or studies on which the analysis is based.

Where possible, various adverse effects of the regulation—such as those from reductions in competition, innovative activity, or productivity growth—should also be identified.

7-7. REGULATORY INNOVATION AND INDUSTRY OPTIONS*

From the mid-1970s on, various regulatory bodies pursued ways of emphasizing marketplace and private-sector transactions in the regulatory process. If prices can signal citizen preferences, then using market-place transactions regulation should better approximate the degree and kinds of government activity citizens prefer. Overlooked is the very uneven distribution of the resources people use to signal regulatory options. Moreover, to average, say, pollution over a wide area may not be of much benefit to those who live downwind of one particular smokestack.

. . . The bubble was designed to reduce corporate costs while preserving environmental standards. In the present generally antiregulatory mood, such concepts are being examined and put forward with increasing frequency. Under the bubble program, EPA gives up its much-cherished privilege of saying not only what a company must do but also how it must do it. In lieu of requiring pollution reduction at individual smokestacks, boilers, or other industrial processes, the agency treats an entire plant—and sometimes a series of plants—a single polluter and requires a cutback in the aggregate amount of fouled air (as if the plant were contained by a bubble with one outlet). The company's engineers

---

*"EPA and Industry Pursue Regulatory Options," *Science* 211, Feb. 20, 1981, pp. 796–798.

may then decide whether it is cheaper and more efficient to control the pollution from one valve or smokestack instead of another. Armco decided it would cost less to control sources of open dust than it would to install traditional antipollution equipment. Within certain limitations, EPA is obligated to approve such plans as long as a company can establish that the number of particles in the plant's air decline.

The bubble program is now a year old, and most of its notices have been congratulatory. "We are delighted with how it has worked," says Michael Levin, an attorney who heads EPA's burgeoning regulatory return staff. Alvin Fry, a consultant to the Business Roundtable (of the top 100 corporations), says, "The general attitude of the business community is positive." Officers of companies such as Armco have—after initial skepticism—become committed supporters. Although only one company's bubble plan has been officially approved by EPA, several dozen others are near approval, and as many as a hundred more are expected this year under liberalized qualifications for participation.

The program's modest success has prompted EPA to develop additional regulatory innovations, including such ideas as a futures market in pollution rights and salable permits to pollute with asbestos or chlorofluorocarbons. Many of the ideas have been circulating in academic circles for years, languishing on the federal agenda because of official pessimism and bureaucratic inertia. An influx of economists and policy analysts at the EPA in the mid-to-late 1970s, combined with strong industrial reaction to the increasingly tough provisions of the Clean Air Act, set the stage for the programs now coming to fruition. . . .

. . . The program is vulnerable to a number of criticisms despite the smooth operation. Initially, EPA barred the most unusual trade-off— between smokestack or plant emissions and windblown dust. The argument was that industrial processes emit smaller, more concentrated particles that stay in the air longer and lodge more deeply in the lungs. The agency reversed its position under pressure from the steel industry, largely because the existing particulate standard permits insufficient legal distinction between particulates of different size. Because there seems to be a consensus among scientists that small particulates are indeed more harmful, this amounts to a bad policy chasing an inappropriate standard. Environmentalists have expressed concern that under such trade-offs, toxic pollutants might be permitted while benign ones are controlled. Michale Levin, of EPA, notes that pollutants designated as hazardous by the agency cannot be offset by reductions in nonhazardous pollutants, while many others remain unlabeled, and thus are available for potentially unequal trading. These would include substances such as formaldehyde, ethylene dibromide, and various polycyclic aromatic hydrocarbons.

Industry initially had several complaints of its own about the program, although much of its discontent has now evaporated. . . .

7-8. UNDOING AFFIRMATIVE ACTION HIRING QUOTAS*

As part of its effort to get the federal government out of state and local affairs, or perhaps to protect the jobs of its predominantly white working-class constituents, the Reagan administration has tried to undo some public-sector affirmative action programs initiated under federal court jurisdiction. The following article outlines the issues at stake. Recent court decisions have clearly indicated that quotas in hiring are permissible, whereas quotas or minority preferences when the work force is cut are not.

The United States Justice Department is to decide by Aug. 5 whether to appeal a Federal judge's refusal to abolish the City of Buffalo's quota system for hiring in the Police and Fire Departments.

The system is intended to increase the number of blacks and Hispanic people in the departments.

The judge, John T. Curtin of Federal District Court, refused a Justice Department request to abolish the system in a decision last month. The ruling was the first of its kind in the country, according to a Justice Department spokesman, John V. Wilson. He said the deadline for filing an appeal is Aug. 5.

Part of a Campaign

The Justice Department's petition to end hiring quotas in Buffalo is part of a campaign to end similar court-enforced systems throughout the nation. Last spring, the Justice Department sent letters to 56 cities, counties and states asking them to join the Justice Department in urging Federal courts to amend affirmative-action decrees.

In only four cities, however, has the Justice Department filed court

*"U.S. Weighing Appeal of Buffalo Job-Quota Case," *New York Times*, July 21, 1985.

motions to end the decrees. The first such motion was filed in Buffalo, and the ruling, Mr. Wilson said, was the only one to deny in full the Justice Department's request to have quotas abolished. In a case in Washington, the Federal court ruled partly for and partly against the request, he said. In San Diego, the court ruled in favor of the request and, in Indianapolis, he said, the court has not yet ruled.

Court Decision Is Cited

The Justice Department's rationale for its effort is based largely on a June 1984 Supreme Court decision that, according to Attorney General Edwin Meese III, "clearly said that quotas are impermissible."

That decision, Firefighters Union v. Stotts, overturned an affirmative action plan in Memphis, Tenn., that called for laying off white firefighters to protect jobs held by less-senior blacks.

"The Justice Department is attempting to use the Stotts decision as a crowbar to upset a number of court-ordered decrees when that is clearly not warranted," said Paul C. Saunders, a partner with the New York City law firm of Cravath Swaine & Moore. The firm opposed the end of hiring quotas in Buffalo on behalf of the Afro-American Police Association, a local organization representing black police officers. . . .

7-9. AN IMPLICIT FEDERAL ECONOMIC POLICY*

Nothing resembling industrial or economic policy exists in the United States. Taken together, however, the policies advocated by an administration constitute a policy of sorts. Recent policy could be characterized as "interest group conservatism": penalize high-taxing industrialized states; promote high technology and finance; allow unregulated labor markets. But Congress is organized to produce a flow of public-sector benefits that facilitate incumbency even for members from areas out of favor with the Reagan administration.

The 1984 Presidential campaign buried the idea of "industrial policy." Or did it?

Not long ago, several Democratic Presidential aspirants were talking about industrial policy. Although the precise meaning of the term remained elusive, the general idea was that the Government should be

---

* "Reagan's Hidden 'Industrial Policy,' " *New York Times,* Aug. 4, 1985.

more purposeful in easing the transition out of basic industries like steel and textiles into high-tech businesses.

The argument was that without an explicit industrial policy—encouraging our older industries to reduce outmoded capacity and adapt newer technologies, channeling research and development funds to emerging industries and helping workers retrain—the changes would come slower and be more painful, and in the meantime the United States would have lost out to other nations that had made the transition more smoothly (notably, Japan).

The term "industrial policy" has fallen out of fashion, largely because the Democrats lost the election but also because the economic recovery of 1983 and 1984 suggested that there was no problem to begin with. The idea also went against the ideological drift of the times. The thought that Government should take a role in shifting economic resources smacked of central planning, and conjured up all the forbidden "isms." Anyway, how could the Government competently pick winners and losers? Wouldn't the whole program just end up being another trough at which the special interests fed?

It has taken a concerted effort by Ronald Reagan to rehabilitate the idea of industrial policy. To be sure, the term appears nowhere in his oratory. But his major policies are showing that Government can play an active role in transforming the economy from "sunset" industries to "sunrise." His three-step plan is a more ambitious industrial policy than the Democrats ever dreamed of proposing. Consider:

Shrinking Basic Industry

Standardized goods, such as basic steel, autos, textiles, commodity chemicals and others that rest on mass or large-batch production are particularly vulnerable to price competition. Thus, the easiest way to reduce their size is to increase their price in world markets—making it difficult for them to export and making it relatively easy for foreign producers to threaten them at home. And the fastest way to increase their price is to raise the value of the dollar by running huge budget deficits. Presto: the industries are forced to contract.

The Reagan plan to shrink America's basic industries has been enormously successful. Since 1981, when the value of the dollar began climbing to unprecedented levels as the budget deficit ballooned, some 2 million jobs have been lost in old-line manufacturing businesses. Steel, autos and others have been forced to reduce domestic capacity, set up operations abroad (or enter into joint ventures with foreign producers) and diversify into specialized niches.

Finishing Off Basic Industry

Once they have been crippled by international trade, it is a relatively small matter to finish off "sunset" industries altogether. This would be accomplished with the passage of a new tax-simplification plan, which as proposed would eliminate any lingering incentives to invest in America's older industrial base.

The Reagan tax-revision proposal would end the investment tax credit, which has been worth approximately $25 billion a year—particularly to older, capital-intensive industries in need of modernization. The proposal also would reduce the pace at which plant and machinery could be depreciated; the present accelerated schedule has resulted in billions of extra dollars being channeled into basic industries. All told, the Reagan tax plan would rescind more than $200 billion of such tax benefits, which have proved critical to "smokestack" America.

Promoting High Tech

America's emerging industries—advanced computers, lasers, fiberoptics, new materials biotechnologies and so on—will benefit both from the lower rates in the new tax proposal and from its retention of the tax credit for research and development.

But more important to high tech is President Reagan's military buildup. Since 1981, about $400 billion has been channeled into weapons—most depending on advanced technologies. This demand for state-of-the-art products has pulled these emerging industries down the "learning curve" to the point where commercial spinoffs are attainable.

Mr. Reagan would like another $400 billion for advanced weapons between now and 1990. At the same time, well over 60% of all research and development funds for America's high-technology industries is coming directly from the Pentagon. President Reagan's "Star Wars" proposal would channel an additional $26 billion into these future technologies over the next five years.

Viewed as a whole, Mr. Reagan's budget deficit, tax plan and military buildup comprise an extraordinarily ambitious plan for shifting America's industrial base. This is industrial policy with a vengeance. But because Mr. Reagan is who he is—avowed defender of the free market from the depradations of big government—there are no voices to his right, vigorously denouncing Washington's vulgar intrusion into the temple of the marketplace. As only Richard Nixon could open relations with Peking, so only Ronald Reagan can make economic planning respectable.

But the President's industrial policy may be too amibitious. The collapse of America's basic industries is throwing off far more blue-collar workers than can be reabsorbed into other high-paying jobs, even during the recent years of record growth. What happens at the next downturn?

And our limited supply or scientists and engineers is straining high-tech industries' capacity to meet military needs while staying commercially competitive. What's missing from President Reagan's industrial policy is a plan for helping our work force adapt—through retraining, relocation and education and day care for the kids while the two careers adjust.

The plan is also risky. Such a broad leap from older industries to new carries a danger that the new ones will not be able to sustain our standard of living on their own. Even at best, how many good jobs will high tech deliver? And what happens if the bottom falls out of these fashionable technologies, as seems to be happening to personal computers of late?

A more gradual, responsible industrial policy would not force us to move so convulsively from "smokestack" to high tech but would help put high technologies into our older industries—and simultaneously upgrade workers' skills to handle the new manufacturing process—to render the entire industrial base more competitive.

Ronald Reagan's industrial policy is a major experiment in economic planning. Ironically, it may yet prove the wisdom of Mr. Reagan's own rhetoric—that it cannot be done, at least not with such a heavy hand.

7-10. BUDGETING AND SPENDING REFORM: THE GRAMM-
        RUDMAN-HOLLINGS BILL*

Politics is oriented around short-term election cycles. Yet the economic actions of governments have long-term consequences as well. The possible longer-term consequences of the Gramm-Rudman-Hollings bill are presented in the following article.

*Peter L. Bernstein, "The Gramm-Rudman Economy," *Wall Street Journal*, Jan. 14, 1986.

Gramm-Rudman, the budget balancer, is thought to have lighted a fire under the capital markets (at least until last week's dousing). But the path from lower deficits to a healthier economy is not so easy to visualize. As Keynes reminded us 50 years ago, "There may be several slips between the cup and the lip."

The overwhelming majority of experts and commentators seem to agree that the deficit has been the root cause of high real interest rates, which in turn have been the root cause of the strong dollar, which in turn has been the root cause of insufficient business investment and deteriorating markets at home and abroad for U.S.-made goods and services. In short, the deficit has crowded out the most dynamic and productive sectors of the U.S. economy. This process of strangulation has reduced the overall growth rate to a pathetic crawl with no visible means of escape.

A Nasty Prerequisite

All other things being equal, no one can doubt that lower government spending or higher taxes, or both, will reduce interest rates and will probably—but not certainly—lower the dollar. All other things being equal, these steps should lead to higher levels of business investment and an improving trade balance.

But "all other things being equal" is a nasty prerequisite. Life seldom holds all other things equal. On the one hand, the decline in interest rates and the dollar may fail to provide enough stimulus to business investment or the U.S.'s export surplus. Then interest rates and the dollar will fall all right, but economic growth may accompany them downward. On the other hand, interest rates and the dollar may not stay subdued if they lead to booming business involvement and a handsome rate of growth of exports relative to imports.

The whole thing would be easy if the initial consequence of cutting the deficit were not contractionary or caused no pain. The trick is to make sure that the stimuli provided by lower deficits arrive both on time and in appropriate quantity to offset the contractionary effects.

Cuts in the deficit will lead to a sustained improvement in real investment, the trade balance, and the growth rates of output and employment if two conditions can be fulfilled. First, the private-sector areas that benefit from lower interest rates and a lower dollar must do more than just respond positively. They must expand by enough to more than offset the contractionary influence of a lower budget deficit. Second, the revival in private-sector spending must not be inflationary, must not drive interest rates back up again, and must not drive the dollar back again. If these conditions cannot be met, the whole process will collapse of its own weight.

Will the private-sector expansion be sufficient? On balance, the inclination is to say yes. "On balance," however, implies a narrow margin. The negative side deserves examination.

Remember that the main constraint on private-sector growth in the U.S. at this time, aside from the pressure from the dollar, is an excessive level of debt. This is obvious in the case of households. In addition, the business sector has radically increased its financial leverage, even in a period of low inflation and moderate growth. Finally, some of the best former customers for U.S. exports are so up to their ears in debt that they now have to use precious resources to service the debt they owe the U.S. instead of buying goods and services from it.

We must wonder, therefore, how rapidly borrowers will be willing to enlarge their swollen debt burdens, even at lower interest rates.

Nevertheless, all will be well if U.S. exports can expand by enough to make up any shortage in domestic demand. But will the U.S.'s trading partners help it out? Quite aside from the bind in which the debtor countries find themselves, the major industrial countries continue to drag their heels in implementing stimulative policies.

Now, fiscal rectitude and high savings rates are great for any one country—as long as other countries pursue policies of high growth, so that the conservative country's excess output can still find markets to sell in. This country's policies during 1983 and 1984, for example, enabled its major trading partners to reduce their budget deficits significantly and still enjoy impressive rates of real growth. . . .

Conventional wisdom tells us that a revival in private-sector growth would not be inflationary, not drive interest rates back up again, and not drive the dollar back up again. Real interest rates have been high because the deficit has absorbed private savings that otherwise would have been available to make private-sector investment grow. By eliminating the dissaving represented by the budget deficit, therefore, the U.S. should make it possible for interest rates to fall and will also need to borrow less from abroad.

But why should interest rates stay down if the private sector's demand for savings simply replaces the government's demand for savings? The nation's propensity to save is not going to be any larger than it was before, just because the deficit was cut, and it might be lower because deficit-cutting also cuts private-sector cash flows. . . .

The only way for interest rates to stay down is for the private sector to grow less rapidly. But that is just what the U.S. is trying to avoid. How can it enjoy higher rates of growth unless private demand more than offsets the compression of government demand that everyone is so eager to achieve?

Have no fear, conventional wisdom goes on to reassure us. Monetary policy will come to the rescue and will hold interest rates down as the private sector expands. . . .

One might argue that monetizing private-sector debt is less inflationary than monetizing public-sector debt. Those who accept that argument would do well to remember 1977–79, when the budget deficit fell by two-thirds while inflation leaped from about 5% to 9%. Also, they would do well to remember 1960–65, when the Fed aggressively monetized private rather than public-debt expansion and then spent the next five years trying to overcome the inflationary damage.

Will Pieces Fit?

These arguments needn't lead us to conclude that a soft landing is impossible. Perhaps all the pieces will fit together. The point is simply that such an outcome is by no means preordained. The deficit-cutting process runs the risk of being either seriously inflationary in the longer run or seriously contractionary in the shorter run. Consequently, the pieces have coarse edges and are unlikely to fit neatly even if they fit together at all.

A corollary to Murphy's Law is right to the point. It has a messy pedigree, but as cited in a recent issue of the DeVoe Letter, it reads:

"The actions of government seldom produce the consequences intended, and this always comes as a surprise."

8 The Limits of Localism

In the preceding chapter we saw that federal involvement in the economy has vastly increased; yet federal economic policy cannot be considered integrated or coordinated. One reason for this is that many different parts of the federal government are involved in making many different policies. Each branch or agency may be responding to different sets of interests, although programs can often be coordinated on a policy-by-policy basis. We do not have an integrated national health program, an internally consistent federal policy toward education, a clean-air "plan," or one welfare system.

Yet federal policy does seem to muddle through as a result of the case-by-case responsiveness of a locally selected Congress to the articulated needs of groups and citizens. With increased federal involvement the highway system is bigger and better-built, minorities and non-English-speakers receive much greater educational and job opportunities, almost everybody can get health care, most people have retirement income, and most air is cleaner. One reason the United States muddles through so successfully is that it depends upon state and local governments and the private sector as the actual providers of services funded at the national level. Legislation is sometimes written to allow state- and local-level variation as a matter of policy, as in Medicaid (Chapter 5), urban renewal (Chapter 4), ESEA Title I (Chapter 3), and ADC (Chapter 6).

In all the policy areas we have looked at, local-level administration of programs varies in response to citizen need. This variation is made possible in part by members' concern that citizens within their districts be adequately served once Congress votes money for a program. A corollary to this is that congressional committees and subcommittees hold the federal bureaucracy much more accountable for the flow of money to electoral districts than for the details of the programs actually administered there. Those few federal programs that are nationally administered usually involve sending out checks rather than establishing branch offices all over the country to administer the program to citizens; this is certainly true of Social Security. HUD's regional offices are there only to review grant applications from lower-level government and the private sector (Chapter 4). Even the Department of Agriculture, which has branches throughout the country, composes its budget from the bottom up to reflect the needs of locally organized agricultural groups. These needs are also articulated in congressional committee and subcommittee by the elected representatives from these areas. In fact, the Department of Agriculture at both the local and the national level is a classic example of the bureau–interest group–congressional committee tie described in Chapter 1 (McConnell, 1966).

Federal involvement in policies that affect citizens has grown tremendously over the last 150 years. Before the Civil War less than 10 percent of all public-sector expenditure occurred at the national level. That figure is now around 50 percent (depending upon how one counts Social Security and defense spending), and the total amount of money involved at all levels of government is many hundreds of times greater. This increase has occurred through the use of a variety of tools. Initially, Congress appropriated money to provide a clear benefit to an organized group (a canal, a post office, medical care for veterans, etc.). In the twentieth century matching programs evolved. Usually these programs called for considerable state and local contributions when first put in place. Only 50 percent of highway funding, for example, initially came from the federal government. In the case of highways, medical care for the poor, and welfare alike, the federal percentage has gradually escalated. One effect has been to homogenize the way policies affect citizens across the various states. Although welfare recipients in Mississippi do not receive anything like the benefits of welfare recipients in New York, even considering the cost of living in the two states, the difference is much smaller than it was before the 1960s (see Chapter 6). Of course states are not required to accept federal matching grants—the federal government can not compel them to build highways. For many years West Virginia blocked the building of an interstate highway (I-70) because it refused to contribute its 10 percent share of the funds. Similarly, Arizona never accepted Medicaid.

Congress also passed a number of bills establishing regulatory bodies, some of them with quasi-independent status. The latter are responsible for policymaking within defined parameters; their members cannot be removed by the President, and their behavior can be controlled by Congress only through budget allocations. Regulatory powers were given to independent agencies and to executive departments in part because there is no net electoral benefit to congresspeople from dealing with regulatory issues. Regulation always benefits some definable group of citizens at the expense of others. At one point, for example, truckers and railroad workers were to be found in almost every congressional district, yet legislation that benefited one would be likely to hurt the other. Regulatory legislation has been extended to include laws that benefit consumers and attempts to deal with the problem of market asymmetries (companies versus organized citizens breathing polluted air).

The beneficiaries of classical regulation (like that of the ICC) were all those who had access to the regulatory body. Prices to consumers were increased. The beneficiaries of the EPA are those whose air and water are cleaned up; costs are borne by some manufacturers and eventually some of the beneficiaries in their role as consumers. The recent trend toward deregulation has introduced another reassignment of the costs and benefits of public-sector action. The deregulation of transportation, for example, benefits manufacturers in the Northeast and residents of large cities at the expense of, among others, residents of small towns and farmers. Deregulation is possible only when the vast majority of Americans live in metropolitan areas and hence the vast majority of the people in Congress represent such citizens.

In all legislation up through the 1960s, Congress had sequentially responded to the needs of organized and organizing groups, and sometimes enticed states to share the cost. However, a vast area of public policy was still beyond the grasp of national institutions until the advent of negative regulation: threat to withdraw existing funds if state and local governments do not redirect their own spending priorities in the manner that Congress specifies. If one looks across the policy areas we have discussed, it is apparent that a lot of federal money is involved in this threat. Ignoring the federal mandate to establish a fifty-five MPH speed limit or a twenty-one-year drinking age, for example, can cost states altogether hundreds of millions of dollars of federal highway funds. Even in the area of education, where total federal funding amounts to about 7 percent of all monies spent, withdrawl of federal funds would have a devastating effect on school district budgets.

For the first time, then, Congress can exert some direct control over the policy preferences and spending of state and local legislatures and can redirect in a manner that is responsive to interests relevant to congressional incumbency. It is really with the advent of negative regulation that the United States has unequivocally ceased to be a nation of states.

Recent American public policy is an amalgamation of apparently inconsistent practices. Negative regulation attempts to extend national control over both the amount and the type of state spending in a number of policy areas. Yet fiscal controls (e.g., Gramm-Rudman), block grants to states, and deregulation appear to represent an attempt to withdraw the federal government from the policy process as it affects localities. The inconsistency is partly apparent and partly real. Negative regulation and block grants do operate in exactly opposite directions. However, this simply represents the crazy-quilt character of congressional legislation. Given the way Congress is organized, there is no reason to expect the means and ends of public policies to be consistent with each other. Some block grants (e.g., CETA) were established to increase state-level autonomy and control over social training programs. Others, particularly those passed in 1981, were established to provide a blameless way for Congress to reduce funding for federal programs in education, health, and so on. Moreover, negative regulation is used only on a case-by-case basis as Congress needs to respond to the concerns of organized interests in various constituencies. There is an underlying theme to these diverse policy practices: Each is used whenever Congress (and the executive) must respond to the needs of electorally relevant organized interests. That, rather than some abstract political philosophy, is the organizing rubric for the tools Congress has used recently in carrying out public policy.

Deregulation is not really inconsistent with negative regulation. Negative regulation selectively increases congressional control over state and local *public*-sector priorities and budgeting. Deregulation usually frees *private*-sector economic entities from congressional and federal bureaucratic oversight and control. Thus, it provides a benefit to an organized economic entity and is consistent with the penchant of even the most liberal members of Congress for allowing the private sector to deliver legislated benefits.

In following the development of the national government's role in six policy areas, it is easy to concentrate on the evolution of policies in each area and to miss commonalities across areas. However, it is the commonalities that define what is distinctive about Amercian policymaking and what can be compared and contrasted with policymaking in other industrial democracies.

The evolution of federal involvement in education (Chapter 3) and in more capital-intensive areas like housing and transportation (Chapter 4) was remarkably similar. The first beneficiaries of federal activity were people or groups involved in business, commerce, agriculture, and the military (see Chapter 1). This is probably true in all representative democracies, and the reason is clear. None of these groups has historically had overwhelming start-up costs or the problems associated with "free-riders" (i.e., those who benefit without investing time, labor, or capital). Such groups can organize effectively at a local or state level, and their members are often among the early representatives in state and national legislatures.

The next to organize are professionals and then labor. Such organization is initially done on a smaller scale. Although groups of tinsmiths, doctors, and steelworkers do not need the existence of active governments to organize, they need the help of government to organize and persist on a large scale. To avoid individual free-riding on the activities and contributions of others, such groups must either use the coercive powers of the state to require membership or obtain some kind of collective benefit from which nonmembers are excluded. In the United States professional groups are largely organized at the state level; that is, public authority to organize professionally comes principally from state law (see Chapter 5). Activities involving labor organizations, however, are largely national in scope.

In all competitive party systems—the European democracies as well as the United States—these two groups are inevitably the first to successfully petition state or national legislatures to provide them with benefits at public expense or reduce the risk of doing business. The means by which the U.S. government can facilitate their interests are laid out clearly in Article I, Sections 8 and 9, of the Constitution.

The next group to obtain public-sector benefits comprises bureaucrats and professionals in the government itself. By the 1960s and 1970s, government in its bureaucratic form had become the biggest lobbyist of government in its legislative and benefit-dispensing form. The Community Mental Health Centers Act (Chapter 7), the Elementary and Secondary Education Act (Chapter 2), legislation supporting projects of the Army Corps of Engineers (Chapter 3), the indexing of Social Security legislation (Chapter 5), and the existence and the continued funding of the National Institutes of Health (Chapter 7) all reflect successful bureaucratic lobbying.

Bureaucrats are hierarchically organized and in many cases also share professional affiliation and training. (Typically, where professional affiliation is strong, bureaucracies are less hierarchical, as in the case of U.S. Forest Service.) Such groups were important in the generation of policy in Britain from the 1930s on. In the United States, however, they became central to this process sometime between the end of the Eisenhower administration and Johnson's legislative campaign of 1964–65. The preceding chapters document the massive amount of legislation in the early and middle 1960s (although massive funding awaited Nixon) in all of the policy areas we have considered.

The last groups to demand publicly derived benefits are those within which free-riding is easiest. Such groups, often geographically dispersed and difficult to organize, include consumers, members of ecology movements, and welfare recipients. The last have frequently been organized largely at the behest and through the efforts of already organized professionals involved in service delivery. (Professionally organized recipients are, after all, another bulwark supporting continued public-sector funding.) Model Cities advisory councils (Chapter 4) and parent advisory councils for Title I programs (Chapter 3) are examples of such organizations.

There is no necessary connection between the methods or tools of policy formulation used by Congress and the beneficiary groups involved. The first tools used to deliver benefits to business, the military, and professional groups were grants and state-level regulation. Yet ESEA Title I (now Chapter I) is a fully federally funded grant that effectively benefits the poor. Matching grants may benefit commerce (highways) or the poor (medicine). Probably the only clear tie between policy tool and beneficiary groups is that between negative regulation and consumer groups and the poor. Aid for non-English-speaking students, school desegregation, and state enforcement of civil liberties might not have occurred without congressional use of negative regulation. Such acts as Titles IV and VI of the Civil Rights Act of 1964, Title IX of the Education Amendments of 1971, and the Education for All

Handicapped Children Act use such sanctions to compel state and local performance. Recently organized groups of citizens who wanted to conserve energy by imposing a fifty-five MPH speed limit, require seatbelt use, or obtain cleaner air or water also benefited from this tool. Despite this recent association, however, all groups benefit at different times from the use of the various policy tools at the disposal of Congress.

The Policy Consequences of Decentralized Electoral Politics

This apparently haphazard mixing of policy and process is in part a result of the way political parties and national elections are organized in the United States. Compared with most European systems, the American party and electoral system is highly decentralized. The congressional candidates of the major and minor parties are selected within individual districts. (In Britain the selection of candidates from individual constituencies may be influenced by party activists at all levels, including the national level.) In the American system incumbency is a great advantage. Presidential elections are the only nationwide elections in the United States, and their recent coattail effects—if there are any— may be negative. In 1980, for example, many Democrats stayed at home rather than vote again for Carter. Removal of these votes from the congressional total caused the loss of a number of Democratic congressional seats.

Congress has organized itself so that it can pass a large amount of legislation that funds goods and services delivered to identifiable districts. It does this by breaking up into committees and subcommittees based on policy areas. Assignment to committees and subcommittees is based on party groupings within the House and Senate. However, every attempt is made to give members assignments that allow them to bargain over the details of legislation that affects organized groups in their own districts. Once committees agree on the details of legislation, the remainder of the House (especially) or Senate will often occur. After all, members of Congress almost never run against each other for office, even across party lines. Policies and programs that benefit organized constituents in as many districts as possible facilitate the incumbency of all.

It is through identification with such programs at inception, authorization, appropriation, and delivery that congresspeople keep their candidacy in front of the voters. A corollary is that Congress is more concerned with fiscal accountability than with the programmatic details of federally funded programs. The requirements of fiscal tracking or auditing often lead to federal bureaucratic bungling or intrusion into programmatic decisions that are supposed to be made at the state and local level. We have seen examples in Medicaid (Chapter 5) and ESEA Title I (Chapter 3). A second corollary, as we saw in Chapter 2, is that Congress will resist any reorganization of the federal bureaucracy that would disrupt the alignment between government agencies and the congressional subcommittee system.

When fiscal cuts must be made in federal programs, congresspeople attempt to avoid the attribution that they normally seek. Thus, the 1981 Omnibus Budget and Reconciliation Act used block grants to displace decisions about cuts to the state level. After a year or so, state level legislators also chose to avoid responsibility for cutbacks in education, health, and welfare. Hence, decisions about federal funds in these areas wind up being made by middle-level bureaucrats in state executives.

Congress's style of organization does not lend itself to resource or economic planning. In effect, water and energy policies in the United States are the sum of individual small pieces of legilsation passed by the Congress. It would be difficult to produce a master plan to which all congresspeople would agree. Planning and management of the economy in particular are not systematically approached in Congress (Chapter 7). Even though Congress has attempted on several occasions to organize itself to deal with summary budgets taking taxing and spending together (Chapter 2), such efforts are inevitably abandoned. The budget timetable set up in 1974 was actually met only in 1975 (Chapter 7).

The Legacy of Federalism and Constitutionalism

Two other features of policy formation and implementation in the United States distinguish it from other industrialized democracies. The first of these is the continued legacy of federalism. Almost all the program areas we have looked at initially channeled funds through state legislatures or state-run programs rather than providing benefits directly to citizens. States play a significant role in U.S. policy implementation, whether they contribute to the costs of programs or not. Federal highway money goes to states; Title I money goes to states before it goes to school districts; Medicaid and welfare payments are matched at the state level; Medicaid administration occurs at the state level; federal funding for hospitals and health went first to supplement state programs. Only

Social Security emerged as a direct contract between citizens and the government, in part because it was designed and promoted as an insurance policy as contrasted to a typical funded program. In other countries divisions are likewise honored in policy implementation. In France differences between industrial sectors are recreated in the state-run Social Security program (Ashford and Kelley, 1986). In Germany medical insurance schemes distinguish between public- and private-sector employees and between white- and blue-collar workers and in some cases make distinctions among states as well.

The second distinguishing feature of U.S. policy implementation is its extensive use of the private sector. Except for the Army Corps of Engineers, the federal government has no capacity to build houses or highways. Almost all public policies involving the development of capital infrastructure are contracted through the private sector. In part this practice follows from the articulation of the purposes of national government in Article I, Sections 8 and 9, of the Constitution. Like France, the United States places an exceptionally high value on private property, including monetary instruments, whenever the rights of private policy are in conflict with other values (Chapter 7).

In almost all the policy areas (except Social Security), we have found that Congress will engage in negative regulation as a vehicle for providing goods and services to groups at times when Congress does not itself have the capacity to fund such goods and services: Such regulation has occurred in the education of non-English-speaking and handicapped children, in fair housing codes of federal housing programs, in the establishment of the 55 MPH speed limit and the twenty-one-year-old drinking age, in attempts to control Medicaid fraud and error rates, in attempts to control hospital costs, and in attempt to monitor and control eligibility for aid for dependent children. The effect of such regulation is to redirect state and local funding into areas mandated by the Congress for the benefit of the congresspeople and their constituents.

Redirection through negative regulation has occurred for several decades in some other countries. In the United States it really began in the early 1970s. For the first time the federal government has the capacity to exercise policy control over areas of activity traditionally managed and even funded by state and local governments, however fragmented that control might be. Fortunately this control is ad hoc, applied on a case-by-case basis. As a consequence, although federal involvement in policies that affect our lives has dramatically increased, some independent policy initiatives can still occur at all levels of government in the United States.

In both what Congress does and what it delegates or cannot do, it is a responsive and representative body. Congress appropriates funds for public policies, outlines rules governing the use of those funds, and attempts to obtain some fiscal accountability from the recipients of funds through the federal bureaucracy on a program-by-program basis. Hence, policy formation and implementation are highly fragmented and decentralized. Much actual service delivery in the areas of health, social service, and even road building occurs at the local level, either through local government, local not-for-profit providers, or the for-profit private sector. Professional groups involved in service delivery often set the context for those services, as we have seen in areas of education, welfare, and health care. The system *appears* to work for most citizens most of the time.

References

General

Advisory Commission on Intergovernmental Relations. 1978. *The Partnership for Health Act: Lessons from a Pioneering Block Grant.* Washington, D.C.: ACIR.

Ashford, Douglas E. 1981. *Policy and Politics in France: Living with Uncertainty.* Philadelphia: Temple University Press.

Ashford, Douglas E., and E. W. Kelley, eds. 1986. *Nationalizing Social Security: In Europe and America.* Greenwich, Conn.: JAI Press.

Beard, Charles A., and Mary R. Beard. 1930. *The Rise of American Civilization.* New York: Macmillan.

Bensel, Richard. 1979. "Reciprocal Behavior and the Rules of the House of Representatives." Ph.D. dissertation, Cornell University.

Burnham, Walter Dean. 1970. *Critical Elections and the Mainsprings of American Politics.* New York: Norton.

Elazar, Daniel J. 1984. *American Federalism: A View from the States.* New York: Harper and Row.

Green, John. 1983. "Campaign Contributions and Congressional Behavior." Ph.D. dissertation, Cornell University.

Hartz, Louis. 1955. *The Liberal Tradition in America: An Interpretation of American Political Thought Since the Revolution.* New York: Harcourt, Brace.

Hill, Paul T. and Ellen L. Marks. 1982. *Federal Influence Over State and Local Government: The Case of Nondiscrimination in Education.* Santa Monica: Rand.

Kaufman, Herbert. 1960. *The Forest Ranger.* Baltimore: John Hopkins Press.

Kelley, E. W. 1982. "Consequences of Restructuring Governmental Grants in the United States." Institute for the Science of Public Administration, Milan. Published in the proceedings of meeting.

Kelley, E. W. 1982. "Alternative Federal-Local Policy Structures in the United

States" (with Robert Rich), Institute for the Science of Public Administration, Milan. Published in the proceedings of meeting.

Lowi, Theodore, J. 1969. *The End of Liberalism: The Second Republic of the United States.* New York: Norton.

McConnell, Grant. 1966. *Private Power and American Democracy.* New York: Knopf.

Muramatsu, Michio. 1982. "A Lateral Political Competition Model for Japanese Central-Local Relations." Paper prepared for the conference on Local Institutions in National Development, Bellagio.

Pempel, T. J. 1982. *Policy and Politics in Japan: Creative Conservatism.* Philadelphia: Temple University Press.

Sanders, Elizabeth. 1978. "Electorate Expansion and Public Policy: A Decade of Political Change in the South." Ph.D. dissertation, Cornell University.

Government Reorganization

Aberbach, Joel D. 1977. "The Development of Oversight in the United States Congress: Concepts and Analysis." Paper delivered at the annual meeting of the American Political Science Association, Washington, D.C.

Emmerich, Herbert. 1971. *Federal Organization and Administrative Management.* University, Ala.: University of Alabama Press.

Graves, W. Brooke, comp. 1949. *The Reorganization of the Executive Branch of the Government of the United States: A Compilation of Basic Information and Significant Documents, 1912–1948.* Washington, D.C.: Legislative Reference Service.

Redford, Emmettes and Marlin Blissit. 1981. *Organizing the Executive Branch: The Johnson Presidency.* Chicago: University of Chicago Press.

Seidman, Harold. 1976. *Politics, Position and Power: The Dynamics of Federal Reorganization.* 2d ed. New York: Oxford University Press.

Federal Involvement in Education

Advisory Commission on Intergovernmental Relations. 1977. *Categorical Grants: Their Rolls and Design.* Washington, D.C.: ACIR.

Hill, Paul T., and Ellen L. Master. 1982. *Federal Influence Over State and Local Government: The Case of Nondiscrimination in Education.* Santa Monica, Calif.: Rand.

Katz, Michael B. 1971. *Class, Bureaucracy and Schools.* New York: Praeger.

Piven, Frances Fox and Richard Cloward. 1971. *Regulating the Poor: The Functions of Public Welfare.* New York: Random House.

Rabkin, Jeremy. 1980. "Office for Civil Rights." In James Q. Wilson, ed., *The Politics of Regulation.* New York: Basic Books.

Saunders, Elizabeth. 1978. "Electorate Expansion and Public Policy: A Decade of Political Change in the South." Ph.D. dissertation. Cornell University.

Government Policy in Capital-Intensive Services

Anderson, Martin. 1964. *The Federal Bulldozer: A Critical Analysis of Urban Renewal 1949–1962.* Cambridge: MIT Press.
Freedman, Leonard. 1969. *Public Housing.* New York: Holt, Reinhard & Winston.
Friedman, Bernard J., and Marshall Kaplan. 1975. *The Politics of Neglect: Urban Aid from Model Cities to Revenue Sharing.* Cambridge: MIT Press.
Rose, Mark H. 1979. *Interstate: Express Highway Politics 1941–1956.* Lawrence: Regents Press of Kansas.
Saunders, Richard. 1978. *The Railroad Mergers and the Coming of Conrail.* Westport, Conn.: Greenwood Press.
U.S. Commission on Civil Rights. 1979. *The Federal, Fair Housing Enforcement Effort: A Report of the U.S. Commission on Civil Rights.* Washington, D.C.: Government Printing Office.
United States v. Certain Land in the City of Louisville, Jefferson County, Kentucky. January 4, 1935. 9 Fed. Supp. 137.

Health Policy

American Commission on Intergovernmental Relations. 1977. *The Partnership for Health Act: Lessons from a Pioneering Block Grant.* Washington, D.C.: ACIR.
Bonner, Thomas Nevel. 1959. *The Kansas Doctor.* Lawrence: University of Kansas Press.
Rich, Robert F., and E. Wood Kelley. "Bypassing State Government to Meet National Needs, Assessing Federal Initiatives of the 1960s through the Lenses of the 1980s." Article submitted to *Journal of Politics.*
Schlenker, Robert. 1974. *HMOs in 1973: A National Survey.* Minneapolis: Interstudy.

Income Maintenance and Welfare

Ashford, Douglas E. 1985. "The British and French Social Security Systems: Welfare States by Intent and by Default" in Douglas E. Ashford and E. W. Kelley, eds., *Nationalizing Social Security: In Europe and America.* Greenwich, Conn.: JAI Press.
Bendix, Richard. 1964. *Nation Building and Citizenship: Studies of Our Changing Social Order.* New York: Wiley.
Derthick, Martha. 1979. Policymaking for Social Security: Washington: The Brookings Institution.
Kelley, E. W. 1981. "Social Security in Industrialized Societies: Comparisons on a Theme." Paper presented at the conference on Post-Keynesian Economics, "Rethinking the Welfare State," Cornell University.

Myers, Robert J. 1965. *Social Insurance and Allied Government Programs.* Homewood, Ill.: Richard D. Erwin.

Piven, Francis Fox and Richard Cloward. 1971. *Regulating the Poor: The Functions of Public Welfare.* New York: Random House.

Ripley, Randall. 1969. *Power in the Senate.* New York: St. Martins Press.

Rothouse, Neil. 1983. "Social Security's Financing Crisis: The Subordination of Economic Interest to Political Principles." B.A. thesis, Cornell University.

Stein, Bruno, 1980. *Social Security and Pensions in Transition: Understanding the American Retirement System.* New York: Free Press.

Economic Planning

Dos Passos, John R. 1887. *The Interstate Commerce Act.* New York: G. P. Putnam's Sons.

Kaysen, Carl, and Donald F. Turner. 1959. *Antitrust Policy.* Cambridge: Harvard University Press.

McConnell, Grant. 1966. *Private Power and American Democracy.* New York: Knopf.

Peretz, Paul. 1983. *The Political Economy of Inflation in the United States.* Chicago: University of Chicago Press.

Perna, Frank. 1981. "The National Recovery Administration: The Interest Group Approach to Economic Planning." Ph.D. dissertation, Cornell University.

Witte, John F. 1982. "Incremental Theory and Income Tax Policy." Paper presented at the annual meeting of the American Political Science Association, Denver.

Index